Autolexical Syntax

Studies in Contemporary Linguistics

AUTOLEXICAL SYNTAX
A Theory of Parallel
Grammatical Representations

Jerrold M. Sadock

The University of Chicago Press

Chicago & London

Jerrold M. Sadock is the Glen A. Lloyd Distinguished Service Professor of Linguistics and chairman of the Department of Linguistics at the University of Chicago. He is the author of *Toward a Linguistic Theory of Speech Acts* and co-editor of *Syntax and Semantics,* vol. 8: *Grammatical Relations.*

The University of Chicago Press, Chicago 60637
The University of Chicago Press, Ltd., London
© 1991 by The University of Chicago
All rights reserved. Published in 1991
Printed in the United States of America

00 99 98 97 96 95 94 93 92 91   5 4 3 2 1

Library of Congress Cataloging-in-Publication Data

Sadock, Jerrold M.
    Autolexical syntax : a theory of parallel grammatical
representations / Jerrold M. Sadock.
        p.   cm. — (Studies in contemporary linguistics)
    Includes bibliographical references (p.   ) and index.
    ISBN 0-226-73344-0 (cl. : alk. paper). — ISBN 0-226-73345-9
(pbk. : alk. paper)
        1. Grammar, Comparative and general—Syntax.   2. Hierarchy
(Linguistics) I. Title. II. Series.
P291.S23   1991
415—dc20   90-11058

Contents

Preface

Morris Halle is reportedly fond of saying that autobiography is not science. But since people have asked me how I came upon the idea that underlies this book, and since they will not find the answer in the "scientific" chapters that follow, I will make use of the opportunity that this preface affords to outline the history of the idea as I remember it. Doing so also provides a natural way for me to thank all of those who have helped me to clarify my ideas either by encouragement or by constructive challenge.

In 1982 I was a just barely reconstructed generative semanticist. I still believed firmly that West Greenlandic noun incorporation had to be treated by means of a postsyntactic transformation that removed a noun from its noun phrase and adjoined it to a verb. Every syntactic, semantic, and pragmatic feature of the phenomenon pointed to this. However, since 1979, I had become increasingly convinced of the grammatical centrality of surface syntax, as emphasized by Gerald Gazdar in his budding theory of generalized phrase structure grammar (GPSG). Gazdar had already astonished me once with his tremendously original and successful treatment of presuppositions (Gazdar 1979), so I could not help but pay attention to what otherwise, at the time, might have seemed like a crazy idea—that of eliminating transformations from syntax. A generative semantics–style postlexical transformation of the kind I hinted at in my 1980 article in *Language* (Sadock 1980) could capture the syntactic reality of the pieces of a West Greenlandic word, but only at the expense of surface structure, since any transformation is, after all, disrespectful of surface structure, requiring some notion of conspiracy, or structure preservation, or surface filter to be appended to the theory to give integrity to superficial form.

Another intellectual contradiction I faced around this time was how to reconcile the obvious role that pragmatic reasoning plays in the interpretation of indirect speech acts with the clear indications of conventionality that I had uncovered in a dozen years of research on the topic. I finally became convinced that there was actually no contradiction here at all: these were two independent features of our language ability that reinforced each other, providing robustness to the language through the sometimes redundant prediction of the same range of facts. It occurred to me that this sort of multiple representation might well characterize other subsystems of grammar, a prospect in which I actually came to see virtues rather than paradoxes.

In the summer of 1982, I went to the University of Maryland to teach at the LSA Institute with these rather vague and somewhat unsettling thoughts in the back of my mind. There I found myself in the company of Ewan Klein and Ivan Sag, whose course on GPSG I audited, and with whom I shared a sweltering sorority house. Another housemate was John Goldsmith, whom I did not know well at the time, since he had not yet come to the University of Chicago. I did not know much about his theory of Autosegmental Phonology either, except for how analyses in it looked on paper: various autonomous aspects of the phonological makeup of an expression were displayed on separate tiers and simultaneously associated with a linear string of consonants and vowels.

Sitting at a small table with Sag and Goldsmith in the dining room of the sorority house, I wrote out a Greenlandic sentence, partially separated into its component morphemes:

> Puisip neqi tor punga.
> 'Seal's meat eat I.'

Above the string of morphemes I drew a syntactic tree such as a generative semanticist might have assumed for the deep structure of the sentence. This tree also represented the obvious surface structure of the nearly synonymous sentence *Puisip neqaanik nerivunga*, with an independent verb *neri-* in place of the affixal verb *-tor-*. Below the string, on a separate tier, as in Autosegmental Phonology, I drew a second tree representing the constituent structure of the word *neqitorpunga*; *neqi-* is a stem, *-tor-* is a derivational suffix, and *-punga* inflection. All sorts of words of West Greenlandic have just this morphological makeup, whether incorporative or not.

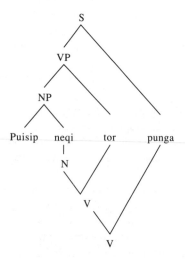

The basic idea of autolexical syntax was there at this time: the apparent complexity of a difficult construction evaporated when viewed as resulting from the simultaneous demands of two individually simple systems of grammar. But there were lots of problems. What about the inflections on the noun in the independent sentence? What about those examples where the syntax and morphology required different orders of elements, resulting in illegally crossing association lines? These difficulties seemed so serious at the time that I put the idea of simultaneous, potentially discrepant representations out of my mind for two years. In the meantime, I devoted a lot of thought to the notion of redundancy in grammar, the results of which are contained in my CLS papers of 1983 and 1984. While these highly methodological pieces were received with apparent interest by a number of people (I recall that Jerry Morgan was especially intrigued, if somewhat disturbed by them), it quickly became clear to me that if these ideas were on the right track, there would have to be some analytical payback.

Sometime in the spring of 1984, I remembered the diagram I had made at the sorority house in College Park. This seemed like the obvious way to demonstrate the analytical advantages of redundant, simultaneous subsystems of grammar. To my great good fortune, I was about to go off to the Center for Advanced Studies in the Behavioral Sciences at Stanford, and were it not for this timely sabbatical, and the opportunity to spend it in the most stimulating and facilitating research environment I have ever known, Autolexical Syntax would still be just a discarded diagram.

At the Center, I not only had the time and support I needed to write the paper that I published in 1985, but I had a wealth of outstanding colleagues to bounce ideas off. David Dowty, Gerald Gazdar, and I conducted a regular workshop on the position of morphology in formal grammar. These sessions were of enormous value in formulating, refining, and discarding ideas about how a grammar of the sort I was examining should work. Bill Poser, Anthony Borgida, and Grev Corbett gave stimulating presentations at these workshops, all of which have found their way into the present work. The Stanford linguists, especially Ivan Sag, Tom Wasow, Joan Bresnan, and Paul Kiparsky gave me much-needed encouragement, or useful trouble, or both. It was a wonderful year.

From the beginning, the factual underpinning for the view presented in this book has been the workings of Eskimo languages. I have been privileged over the years to have received grants from the Inland Steel Foundation (1970), the National Endowment for the Humanities (1980 and 1986), the American Philosophical Society Philips Fund (1981), the Government of Canada (1986), and the American Council of Learned Societies (1988) that allowed me to pursue my research in Greenland and the Northwest Territories.

These trips brought me into contact with a people whose kindness, patience, and friendship I will value forever. I am especially grateful to Simon and Ar-

najaraq Olsen of Sisimiut, and Aakka and Mitti Jeramiassen of Itilleq, Greenland, and to Sally Wa'a of Eskimo Point, and the Kabvitok family of Rankin
Inlet, N.W.T., for opening their homes and hearts to me. I owe an inestimable
debt to my friend, teacher, host, and colleague, Inooraq Olsen of Sisimiut, as
well as to Puju, now of Nuuk, who first got me interested in the challenging
language of the Issittormiut. To all of them: Qujanarujorujorujussuaq!

So many people have influenced me in developing this work that it would be
impossible to acknowledge them all, but a few people have been so important
to the effort that they deserve special recognition. Steve Lapointe has, from
the publication of my 1985 paper right up through the present, consistently
and effectively probed the foundations of the theory and made me think much
more than I otherwise would have about assumptions that I cherished but were
wrong. His infectious enthusiasm kept me going at times when I might otherwise have given up. Likewise John Goldsmith, my esteemed colleague next
door, an early believer in the possibilities of highly autonomous grammar, has
been of enormous help both to my thinking and my feeling about this enter-
prise. I must mention also those colleagues here at the University of Chicago
and elsewhere who have helped me with sections of the book and in other
ways, without, of course, holding them responsible for errors of fact or fancy
that it might contain: Knut Bergsland, Sandy Caskey, Shobhana Chelliah,
Willem de Reuse, Jan Terje Faarlund, Donka Farkas, Don Frantz, Victor
Friedman, Roy Hagman, Eric Hamp, Geoff Huck, Alexis Manaster-Ramer,
Jerry Morgan, Almerindo Ojeda, Geoff Pullum, Greg Stump, Tony Woodbury, and Arnold Zwicky.

I am fortunate to teach at the University of Chicago, where I have had a
continuous stream of excellent students to stimulate and try me. Among
these, a number have flattered me by choosing to work within a novel and
developing framework, including Bill Eilfort, Steve Gordon, Randolph
Graczyk, Zixin Jiang, Carolyn Jenkins, Paul Kroeber, Jeff Leer, Ligang Li,
Robin Schneider, Elisa Steinberg, and Caroline Wiltshire. To Eric Schiller,
who has made some notable contributions, and who has organized and pros-
elytized both here and abroad on behalf of autonomous modular grammar, I
owe an especially deep debt of gratitude.

I am grateful to Iretha Philips, secretary of the Department of Linguistics,
for holding down the fort. Much of this book was written during my stint as
chairman, and I could not have done it without her. Finally, I wish to thank
my long-suffering family: my wife Gail and my son and companion on my
last trip to Greenland, Ben. Without a murmur, they gave me support when I
needed it, and space when I needed that.

Chicago
November 30, 1989

1

Introduction

This book explores the hypothesis that natural-language expressions are organized along a number of simultaneous informational dimensions, in each of which the allowable structural patterns form a system that can be specified by a set of explicit rules. Each of these rule systems, which we may call a component, or module, is an autonomous grammar of a single informational dimension, and therefore, the organization of an expression in one module need not correspond to its organization in another, though there will be definite limits on the degree to which the various autonomous descriptions of a single natural-language expression can diverge from one another.

I will attempt to show that the required components are individually quite simple in nature, and that furthermore, the limits on discrepancies between autonomous modular representations are of a very natural sort. Certain complexities of natural languages will turn out on this view to be by-products of the intersecting demands of individually simple, autonomous modules as constrained by natural principles of correspondence between the structures that they characterize.

A wide range of grammatical phenomena that are perplexing in other views of grammar receive straightforward, in some cases almost disarmingly simple accounts in the present one. Clitics, for example, have to be relegated to a unique, postsyntactic component in traditional Transformational Grammar. But the properties of clitics can be captured directly in an autolexical framework by making them affixes in the autonomous morphology and formatives that combine with phrases in the autonomous syntax, thus modeling the insight that clitics are "phrasal affixes" (Anderson 1987). I will frequently illustrate two simultaneous, and often discrepant, analyses that an expression receives from two modules by means of dual trees, such as that in (1), which gives the bimodular analysis of an English expression containing an auxiliary clitic. (See chapter 3 for details.)

(1)

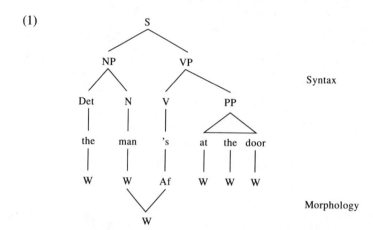

Syntax

Morphology

The core of the analysis is just that the morpheme *'s* happens to be an affix of a certain kind in the morphology, and a verb of a certain kind in the syntax. There is no movement, no reanalysis, no special semantic interpretation—just these two statements.

Since all components in the autolexical model are taken to be essentially autonomous, elements can be bracketed differently in any pair of components, not just syntax and morphology. Structural discrepancy between semantic and syntactic organization, for example, can handle the syntactosemantic characteristics of negation in English in a manner quite analogous to the way clitics are treated in morphosyntactic representations. English *not* (see chapter 7) can be taken to be a propositional operator in semantic structure (should this be the preferred treatment), and a syntactic function from nonfinite VPs to nonfinite VPs (see Gazdar et al. 1985), as in (2). Once again, there is no need for movement or special mechanisms of semantic interpretation.

(2)

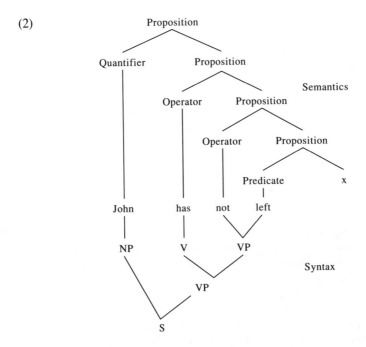

In both of the cases above, modular mismatches occur because of the conflicting properties of an individual lexeme in two components. It can also be that the compositional rules of different components will sometimes produce noncoincident structures, regardless of the lexical material the expression contains. If, for example, discourse-functional notions such as topic and comment are to be located in a rather simple structural component distinct from syntax and semantics, as I suggest in chapter 7, then "topicalization" can be seen as a mismatch between the positional privileges of the topic in the discourse-functional dimension and the syntactic positioning of the topic element. If topics precede comments in discourse-functional representation, and direct objects follow their governing verbs in syntax, then a sentence with an initial topic phrase, like Mary, John loves, would receive an analysis along the lines of (3), where Mary is topic in one autonomous dimension, and direct object in another. Here again, neither movement nor ad hoc rules of construal seem to be needed.

(3)

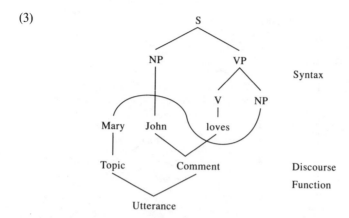

Another important feature of the autolexical model that gives rise to discrepancies between representations in different dimensions is the possibility that a lexeme that is represented in one component is simply not represented at all in another, giving the effect of deletion or insertion without the need for specific rules that actually delete or insert. The empty subject of "extraposition" sentences, for example, can be treated simply as an element with a representation in syntax, but none whatsoever in semantics. The element is neither deleted, as in Rosenbaum 1967, nor inserted, as in Chomsky 1981; it is simply present in one dimension of representation and not in another. (See chapter 2 for a more thorough treatment.)

(4)

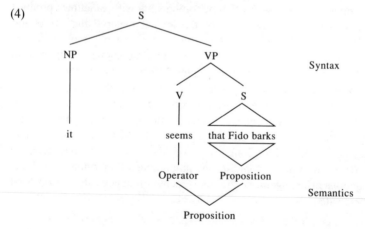

The autonomous view of the status of components sheds light on a variety of problems in linguistic theory from the status of agreement to the treatment of portmanteau morphemes, but it is not a theory of everything. Any number of important grammatical phenomena are properly treated by reference to a single grammatical component, and not as examples of mismatches between autonomous representations in two or more components. Some might find it striking that I offer no treatment of active-passive alternations in this book, but the reason I do not is that I find no positive evidence that such alternations are to be taken as involving discrepancies of structure. Passive verb phrases and passive participles may just as well be given meanings such that combining them as one does to form a passive sentence, the desired meaning naturally results. Thus the meaning of passive sentences would appear to be organized in much the same way as the syntactic constituent structure is organized, and mechanisms other than the autonomous representation of expressions in more than one module would seem to be appropriate to the treatment of active-passive alternations of the ordinary kind.

The idea that grammar consists of parallel organizational principles is really quite a traditional point of view. This orientation resembles, in broad outlook, the sort of view that underlies descriptive grammars of the last century, where one finds the discussion divided into more or less independent sections called something like "phonology," "flexion," "word building," and "syntax." I shall take as a starting point the more modern division of grammar into phonology, morphology, syntax, and semantics. Also in keeping with modern practice, I will assume that the informational patterns of each dimension can be exactly characterized by a generative grammar in the broad sense, that is, a grammar that is explicit and formal and that makes clear and testable predictions. The principles interconstraining the several autonomous representations can also be made precise, giving the entire scheme the same empirical quality as any explicit grammatical theory.

1.1 The Tradition of Hierarchiality in American Grammar

A grammar that separates components in this way departs in a fundamental way from the mainstream American tradition of linguistics,[1] which, for fifty years and more, has taken the organizational dimensions of language to be "levels," obtainable from one another in a certain fixed order, thus depriving them of any genuine autonomy. It is this hierarchical view of grammar that I challenge here. The specific features of the model I will present, the formal and substantive claims about each of the components I assume, are all secondary to the main point, the demonstration that insightful grammatical descriptions of complex linguistic facts can be obtained by dividing the burden of description among several autonomous components.

The assembly-line metaphor of grammatical description, according to which representations are passed from higher-level components to lower level components that modify them and pass the resulting representations on to other components, is a direct descendant of the structuralist tradition that reached its flowering in the work of Zellig Harris. For the American structuralists, it was simply unscientific to think of grammar in any other way. Science for them had to be based directly upon observation, and in linguistics the observable was the phonetic signal, upon which all scientific description of language therefore had to rest. One began by describing and classifying the sounds themselves, whereupon one could proceed to the discovery of regularities in the distribution of sounds, which one could then capture in terms of a phonemic description. Then, and only then, was it allowable to seek generalizations covering the distribution of phonemes, then morphophonemes, morphemes, phrases, and sentences. At each stage, a rigorous method was required such that the relationship between elements of the lower level and that of the next higher level was unique and unambiguous (Harris 1951).

For the structuralists, it was not merely a practical consideration that analysis proceed in a strictly hierarchical fashion, making use at each stage only of the results of the preceding stage, it was a matter of scientific honor. As Hockett (1942, 107) put it: "There must be no circularity; phonological analysis is assumed for grammatical analysis, and so must not assume any part of the latter." To behave in a way not constrained by such a methodological dictum was for the structuralists to be guilty of mentalism, a synonym for metaphysical, unscientific thinking.

Both the methodology and the philosophy of science that underpinned this abhorrence for "mixing levels" and required a strictly hierarchical arrangement of components, were entirely overthrown in the generative revolution. Indeed, the rejection of this methodology could be equated with the generative revolution (Newmeyer 1980, 20). In his famous review of *Syntactic Structures* (Chomsky 1957), Lees persuasively argued that such a methodology is not characteristic of any other science and should therefore not characterize the empirical study of language either. By rejecting the quest for a discovery procedure in favor of a hypothetical grammar which, while not motivated directly by observed data, could be tested against linguistic fact, American grammarians made vastly more progress in a few years toward understanding the syntax of natural languages than their structuralist predecessors had made in decades, thus vindicating the rejection of the Method in the most convincing way. But with the abandonment of the top-down methodology of structuralist philosophy, there did not come a rethinking of the hierarchical view of grammar that it necessitated. The system of levels in *Syntactic Structures* was more or less the same as that of the structuralists, now turned upside down to reflect the generative style of the new grammar.

The most important technical innovation of the early Chomskyan model was the addition of the transformational level of analysis. The transformational component was sandwiched between the base component (a phrase-structure grammar including a lexicon of morphemes) and the "morphophonemic" rules that specified how sequences of morphemes were realized phonologically. The following diagram, adapted from Chomsky 1957 (p. 46), illustrates the orgainization of an early transformational grammar.

Figure 1.1

These components were related to one another in a strictly hierarchical fashion: the output of one component served as the input to the next; no component had more than one input; and there was only one base component, in which all of the generative power actually resided.

The abandonment of the structuralist ethic also legitimized the open and explicit discussion of meaning and its relation to grammatical structure. Here there was an apparent deviation from strict hierarchiality, for Chomsky argued in *Syntactic Structures* that some aspects of semantics were to be connected to surface form, while others were best associated with deep structure. Thus it would appear that the complete model deviated from strict hierarchiality in that one component, the semantics, had two inputs. Strictly speaking, though, this was not the case, for Chomsky took the output of the transformational component to be not the surface structure, but the whole sequence of trees reflecting the entire transformational history of the sentence, an object he called the Transformation Marker, or T-Marker. Since one of these trees (the first) is deep structure, and one of them (the last) is surface structure, the model was still strictly hierarchical in that the semantics received only one input, the T-marker.

1.2 The Arrangement of Components

In the thirty years since the advent of transformational grammar, an amazing variety of component arrangements has been advocated. Restricting our attention to the phrase-structure component, the transformational component, the lexicon, semantics, and word-formation (or morphological) components, some dozen or so different hierarchizations can be found in the literature. None of the later organizations, however, is as strictly hierarchical as the one found in *Syntactic Structures*.

In *Aspects of the Theory of Syntax* (Chomsky 1965), the next landmark of syntactic theory, two significant changes were made. First, a lexical component was added, operating on the output of the base component and providing the input to the transformational component; and second, the semantic component was made to act on the same lexicalized deep structures, before any transformations applied.

Figure 1.2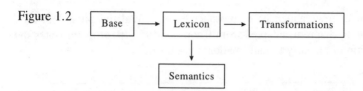

A slight modification of this view was made by the generative semanticists, who argued that if the base component provided everything necessary for semantic interpretation, there was no real need for a separate semantic component: the output of the base component could be taken as both syntactic deep structure and semantic representation. For this to be so, however, it had to be the case that the deepest level of representation did not contain actual lexical items, but semantic primitives; lexicalization had to take place later. In one popular view (e.g., McCawley 1968a), lexicalization was left to the end of the transformational cycle on the root node, as in figure 1.3, but in others (cf. Lakoff 1971, 233) it occurred nonhierarchically, as in figure 1.4, along with the stepwise transformational modification of deep structure.

Figure 1.3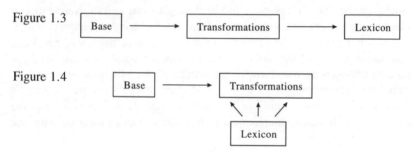

Figure 1.4

In its most developed form, the generative semantic model also included a set of Global Derivational Constraints (Lakoff 1971) capable of relating any two (or even more) transformational strata, an innovation that seriously weakened the autonomy of the transformational component.

Figure 1.5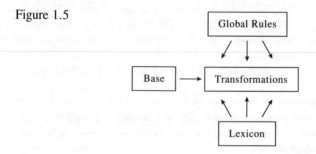

Besides generative semantics, the other significant branch of development from the aspects model was that leading to the *Government and Binding* (Chomsky 1981) and *Barriers* (Chomsky 1986) models, theories in which semantic interpretation takes place after transformations apply, not before. Since much of what had been taken to be transformational syntax in earlier views clearly obscures semantics (e.g., deletions and local movements) these operations were lumped with phonology on a separate, postsurface-structure branch, yielding the famous forked-stick diagram below,[2] which is adapted from Chomsky 1981.

Figure 1.6

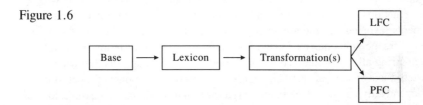

Represented schematically in this way, the theory of Chomsky 1981 gives the appearance of strict hierarchiality, but this hierarchiality is greatly compromised by Chomsky's coupling it with the apparently independent methodological assumption known as the Projection Principle. This principle requires that subcategorization requirements of lexical items be observed at every level of representation (except PF). Lexical insertion could just as well take place after the transformational adjustments, or even after the rules of the LF component have applied, since all the requisite information is present at all of the relevant levels of representation. The placement of the lexicon between the base component and the transformations was decided on "largely as a matter of execution" (Chomsky 1981, 93).

Along the way from *Syntactic Structures* to the present day, numerous other arrangements have been suggested. Figure 1.7, for example, is adapted from Fiengo 1980, and figure 1.8, from Borer 1988.

Figure 1.7

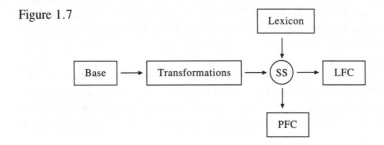

Figure 1.8

Word	*Lexical Insertion*	
formation	⟶ D-structure	⎱ Syntax
component	⟶ S-structure	⎰
	⟶ Phonology (PF)	

Drawing flow charts proposing alternative hierarchizations of grammar seems to have been one of the major preoccupations of generative linguists during the past thirty years. The result has been a striking diversity of opinion with regard to which component feeds which component, which is interpretive, and which generative hints that the hierarchical view itself is wrong. Interactions of various sorts can be demonstrated—and have been—as arguments favoring one hierarchization over another. So while each of the different arrangements has its merits, no single hierarchical ordering is capable of capturing all of the interactions of components. This suggests that what is required is a system of parallel, highly autonomous components, operating independently to specify the several organization dimensions that expressions of natural languages clearly manifest. It is this sort of system that I shall sketch in the succeeding chapters.

1.3 Modularity

Autolexical grammar is clearly modular in that it recognizes the existence of various components. But this sort of modularity does not distinguish it from other current theories of language structure (or perhaps from any that have ever been seriously entertained). The kind of modularity to be found here, however, is different from what is found in mainstream generative linguistics. In the present model, the modules are individual grammars of various dimensions of representation, including syntactic form, morphological form, and semantic form. The existence of these independent levels, each of which is characterized by an autonomous grammar, contrasts strikingly with the modularity of a theory such as GB, where the modules (government theory, binding theory, bounding theory, Move-Alpha, etc.) are systems of principles, constraints, or rules that cross-cut the several levels of representation. In the various recensions of GB theory, there do not seem to be independent well-formedness conditions on the various syntactic levels (D-structure, S-structure, and LF) other than those that shared among them all in virtue of the Projection Principle.

The components in the view proposed here are also modular in that the units with which they deal are distinct. The units of the morphology are stems, affixes, inflections, and so on, namely units that are appropriate to word construction; the units of the syntax are words, phrases, clauses, and so on, that is, units appropriate to sentence structure; and the units of the semantics are predicates, arguments, variables, and the like, that is, meaningful units. The components of an autonomous, modular grammar of this kind are thus "informationally encapsulated," in the terminology of Fodor (1983), whereas the modular building blocks of a GB style grammar, such as the rule Move-Alpha, have access to all representational dimensions, and are therefore not informationally encapsulated.

Hallowed linguistic terminology, which I am in no position to alter, can unfortunately obscure the fact that units in the several dimensions that I have assumed are actually distinct. Thus the word "noun," for example, is used to refer both to a morphological entity and to a syntactic entity. In syntax "noun" means something like "potential head of $\bar{N}$," whereas in morphology it means (variously) "word inflected for case and number," or "stem that is susceptible to certain derivational, and compositional processes." There is also some terminological confusion between semantics and syntax, where such terms as "predicate" and "argument" are used in quite different senses. A predicate in the semantics is a function from one or more entity expressions to propositions. In syntax, "predicate" is often used to designate either the XP complement of the copular verb, or the VP immediately dominated by S. A semantic argument is an entity expression that a predicate combines with, whereas a syntactic argument is a nonoblique noun phrase whose position is subcategorized for by a verb, clearly a very different usage.

A second caveat is in order here. There are default associations between the category to which a sign belongs in one component and the category to which it belongs in another. For instance, it is overwhelmingly the case that a word which is a syntactic noun, in the sense explained above, will count as the sort of thing called a noun in the morphology, and vice versa. This is, in fact, the reason that the same terminology tends to be used in both spheres. But, *pace* Selkirk 1982, morphological and syntactic characterizations do not always pick out the same set of lexemes. To take a simple example, consider a language, more or less like English, that manifests a clear syntactic distinction between prepositions and complementizers, but has no particular morphological operations that affect either class. For such a language it seems unnecessary, indeed otiose, to set up separate morphological categories of prepositions and complementizers just on the basis of the existence of such contrasts in the syntax. The difference in their behavior is entirely syntactic, so from the point of view of morphology, such "indeclinables" constitute a single, undifferentiated group, which we might comfortably call particles (see Zwicky 1985).

Since grammatical modules conceived of in this way are "domain specific computational mechanisms" (to borrow another felicitous term of Fodor's (1983)), their modularity does not depend upon their being specified by for-

mally distinct computational principles. In a hierarchical model, on the other
hand, where the organizational independence of the levels is diminished, or
vanishes entirely, formal distinctness of the combinatoric principles would
seem to be the sine qua non of the existence of separate levels, for if the formal principles relating strictly hierarchical levels are the same, then there is
no sense in which the levels belong to separate systems. This was clearly observed in Harris's (1951) very strict construction structuralism. Harris rea-
soned that if the same technique, the method of substitution, was to be
employed at all levels of analysis, there was no principled distinction to be
drawn between its application at earlier and at later stages of the process. Harris's system at this time was, in other words, hierarchical, but nonmodular. To
quote Wells ([1947] 1957, 197):

> One of the points implied by Harris's article From Morpheme to Ut-
> terance is that in describing what occurs in that language, the distinc-
> tion between morphology and syntax may be dispensed with. . . . In
> doing one part of the task of grammar, namely describing the utter-
> ances of the language in question, the division into a morphological
> phase and a syntactic phase of this description may be given up.

In fact, I will assume that the basic formal nature of each of the modules is
the same: each is to be a phrase-structure grammar constrained by X-bar principles of the general kind suggested originally by Chomsky (1970), and extended (in a different fashion) to word structure by Selkirk (1982). Though
there are some differences in detail, the formal distinctness of the various
modules that will be fleshed out in succeeding chapters of this book is quite
slight. The modular nature of the components of an autolexical grammar resides in their autonomous ability to define distinct sets of structures, not in any
profound difference in their formal nature.

1.4 Redundancy in Grammar

Some years ago, Jerry Morgan (1972) studied the details of subject-verb
agreement in English and ended up with a picture of the phenomenon that was
disturbingly complex when compared with the ideal that would seem to be
available to speakers of the language. One obvious principle operating in determining subject-verb agreement is something like the following:

1. Inherent grammatical features of the syntactic subject of a clause are
   replicated on the main verb of that clause.

This principle refers to syntactic notions and is the sort of generalization that
delights grammarians. But even a fairly superficial study of almost any language with subject-verb agreement will reveal a number of deviations from

this principle. (See Corbett 1983 for a sampling of the kind of complexities that arise in actual agreement systems.) Among others, the following are important competing principles that Morgan uncovered in English:

2. Inherent grammatical features of the nearest NP that is morphologically a possible subject of a clause are replicated on the main verb of that clause.
3. Singular verb phrases indicate properties of individuals, plurals indicate properties of sets of individuals. Singular noun phrases designate individuals; plurals designate sets of individuals. The semantics of the syntactic subject of a clause must be appropriate to the semantics of the verb phrase of that clause.

In this description of German, Whitney (1870, 145) described the competition among these three competing principles elegantly:

> A verb having for its subject more than one singular noun is put in the plural. . . . To this rule there are frequent exceptions, either as the several subjects are regarded as combined into a single idea; or as, when preceding or following an enumeration of single subjects, the verb, by familiar license of speech, is suffered to agree with the one nearest it alone.

Sometimes the existence of alternative principles covering roughly the same range of phenomena allows a free choice of form, but at times conflicts among competing principles like 1–3 make problems for speakers of the language. Morgan found cases where nearly everyone was so unsure of the principle governing agreement that many preferred to switch to another mode of expression rather than attempt to resolve the dilemma. Examples such as (5), in which there is a tension among the competing principles, seem to puzzle almost everyone, so speakers sometimes steer clear of such constructions altogether.

(5)   He is one of those linguists who is/are unable to speak a foreign language.

From a syntactician's point of view, the language appears to be more complex than it needs to be. Why is a straightforward grammatical generalization such as we find in 1 rarely, if ever, the whole story concerning subject-verb agreement in a natural language? Why should subject-verb agreement be so complex as to actually interfere with the comfortable expression of meaning in certain cases? Why, to paraphrase Sapir ([1921], 1949), do all agreement systems leak?

In Sadock 1983 and 1984 I suggested that the answer to these questions was to be found in the fact that the existence of overlapping but distinct modular structures results in beneficial redundancies. Note that the three principles above refer to radically different kinds of linguistic abilities. Principle 1 is syntactic; 2 involves a processing strategy (Bever 1975, and the references there); and 3 is semantic, relying on our ability to deal with the meanings that linguistic expressions convey. In the simplest cases, e.g., in sentences like "Seymour is slicing the bagels," or "The cats are on the mat," the three principles converge on the same result. Thus in the case of the most central examples, this multifaceted phenomenon is robust in a way that it would not be if it were accounted for in only one module. In the core of the language, the part learned earliest and used most, three different strategies, making use of different kinds of knowledge, are individually sufficient to predict the correct agreement pattern.

Though redundant descriptions of linguistic facts are often frowned upon as methodologically undesirable, the fact is that there are functional reasons for actual linguistic systems to be redundant.[3] A multimodular specification of a linguistic phenomenon would be of service both to speakers, in allowing them separate strategies for conveying what they wish to convey, and to hearers, in providing alternative analyses of what is being said. Not least of all, redundancy is crucial to language learners who, presented with data that could be accounted for in one of several ways, would not be forced to choose among them. Initially, any and all hypotheses that fit the facts could be included in the child's emerging model of the language.[4]

Returning to our case study of redundancy, we may note that while the several principles governing verb agreement do coincide in the core cases, there are less central examples where the parallel analyses do not give the same answer. In fact, if they always coincided, there would be no evidence available to speakers (or grammarians) that independent principles were at work. You might employ a semantically-based strategy, and I might employ a grammatically-based one, but since our outputs would be identical, we would have no evidence whatsoever that we were in fact behaving differently. The conflicted cases are thus not mere glitches in a redundantly specified system, but in fact serve to demonstrate the independence of the principles and provide the impetus for the setting up of largely overlapping but quite distinct grammatical subsystems, i.e., for modular grammar.

I suppose that part of what is felt to be objectionable about the double or triple specification of the same set of linguistic facts is that it seems unparsimonious. Even if this were true on the descriptive level, it might, as I argued in Sadock 1984, still be the case that for functional, evolutionary, or purely accidental reasons, the language faculty of our species really is characterized by redundancy. But in fact, when looked at from the point of view of a grammar containing highly autonomous, overlapping components, the complexity of the description itself might turn out to be something of a chimera. The simplest description of the language, that is, the description in which the coverage of the facts in EACH of the several modules is optimal, might well turn out to be one that overlaps to a large extent in the central cases, produces conflicting statements in some peripheral cases, and yields no statements at all in others.

It seems to me that the sort of manifold redundancy that is apparent in verb agreement is widespread in natural language grammar, characterizing some of the most basic constructs that describers of language have seen fit to employ. To take just one example, consider the crucial notion of subject in natural languages. In an important paper, Keenan (1976) provided a long list of the sorts of properties that typify subjects. But as pointed out by Schachter (1977), Keenan's list conflates two radically different constellations of properties that need not characterize the same NP in a sentence, and do not in fact do so in Philippine languages, namely properties that relate to discourse topics and properties that have to do with the semantic notion of actor. I would suggest that there are actually two other subsets of subject-like properties on Keenan's list: properties that regard morphology and properties that regard syntax per se. In the former category is the fact observed by Keenan that subjects tend to occur in the least-marked morphological case, and in the latter category, the fact that subjects tend to precede objects. Note that each of these classes of properties can reasonably be seen as relating to a distinct dimension of representation: discourse-functional organization (see chapter 7), semantics, morphology, and syntax. The fact that it is easy enough to find examples where the various properties that are typical of subjects are not associated with a single NP finds easy expression in a grammatical theory such as the one to be developed below, where the essential autonomy of each of these representational schemes is accentuated.

There is of course a strong tendency for the unrelated properties that Keenan mentioned to cluster around a single NP, which may be simultaneously topic, actor, morphologically least marked, and sentence initial. A subject with all of these characteristics is thus redundantly characterized, a rather mundane state of affairs in natural-language systems.

1.5 Linguistics as Anatomy

One line of thought that has led to the idea of formally distinct, nonredundant, hierarchically interacting linguistic modules is an anatomical analogy, which Chomsky has frequently invoked, as when he speaks of "mental organs" in *Language and Responsibility* (Chomsky 1977, 83):

> [T]he mind is a complex of interacting faculties, which do not develop by means of uniform principles of "general intelligence"; it is constituted of "mental organs" just as specialized and differentiated as those of the body.

This is more than just analogy, since we, and all our abilities, are the result of one and the same evolutionary pressure. It seems to me that we should therefore take this analogy very seriously, and when we do, we are lead to quite a different picture of the organization of grammatical ability from the hierarchical one that is our legacy from structuralist days. The uneven course of biological evolution has produced intricate, redundant, yet cunning structures that deviate from preconceived notions of optimality; we should not be surprised to find that pretheoretical, Platonic notions of simplicity fail to characterize the part of our biological inheritance we call grammar, for indeed, biology yields any number of examples where an engineer could easily provide "simpler" solutions than the ones that nature has, for whatever reasons, chanced upon. In this connection, R. L. Gregory (1963, 315) writes,

> [T]he retina . . . is inside out. The light has to pass through layers of blood vessels, ganglia, and supporting cells before it reaches the receptors. This optically shocking arrangement appears to be dictated by embryological, or perhaps by basically developmental, considerations. Considerations of this kind make use of the criterion of simplicity difficult and dangerous to apply.

Philosophers of biology, such as my colleague William Wimsatt, have done a good deal of thinking about the kind of complexity that characterizes actual organic systems. At the risk of trivializing what they have learned, I think it is worthwhile to give a very brief sketch of one sort of complexity of structure that biological systems display, because, as I shall attempt to show, the analogy between REAL biological systems and what we can infer about the structure of the language system is both striking and suggestive of a view of the modularity of language that is not characterized by absolute hierarchiality. Consider the notion of descriptive complexity described by Wimsatt (1974). Suppose we use two different criteria for mapping the different areas of a physical system, say, chemical makeup and thermal conductivity. In the case of a simple system, such as a piece of granite, it is clear that we will get easily reconcilable maps from the application of either criterion. Anything that is a component on one of these criteria would be a component on the other. If we add other criteria, such as electrical conductivity or density, we will, in the case of a simple system, continue to get entirely consistent views of the internal structure of our object of study. Any pair of points that belongs to a single part according to one of the tests, belongs to a single part according to the others.

But biological systems are not, in general, descriptively simple. Quoting Wimsatt (1974):

> By contrast, decomposition of a differentiated multi-cellular organism into parts or systems along criteria of being parts of the same

anatomical, physiological, biochemical, or evolutionary functional system, into cells having common developmental fates or potentialities, or into phenotypic features determined by common genes will, almost part by part and decomposition by decomposition, result in mappings which are not 1–1—which are not even isomorphic, much less coincident. This surely involves substantial "descriptive complexity."

Natural biological organisms are not completely hierarchically arranged, either in terms of structure, or in terms of function. The very same substructures are often shared by heterogeneous organs or tissues. The major systems of nerves, blood vessels, and musculature pervade the body and by their distribution help to define individual organs. Nuclear matter is present within every cell of the body, and in every cell in the body its function is reproductive. For the most part this is limited to reproduction of cells of the original type, but in the case of nerve cells, this potential is not invoked, and in the case of sexual cells, it is the reproduction of the entire organism that the mechanism is charged with.

But none of this is to deny the basic fact of modular structure itself. The recognition that the eye is part muscle, part blood vessel, and part nerve, and that one cannot say with complete precision where the eye leaves off and the optic nerve begins is not to deny the existence of the eye. The model of grammar that I will develop consists of modules that decompose expressions in much the same way as the various decompositions of organic systems in Wimsatt's dicussion. As with other biological systems, the dimensions of analysis do not always produce congruent or even compatible results.

1.6 Plan of the Book

In the succeeding chapters I will be developing and motivating one possible implementation of a grammar consisting of autonomous modules. Chapter 2 contains a sketch of a grammar with three modules, each a context-free phrase-structure grammar. In addition to providing fragments of each of these components, the chapter presents a view of what the all-important interface that connects independent representations from the sundry autonomous modules might look like. A crucial feature of this interface is the commonplace idea that lexical entries are not monolithic, but contain information regarding the value of a lexeme with respect to individual components.

Chapter 3 deals with cliticization, a natural-language phenomenon where a simultaneous, noncoincident analysis in terms of syntactic and morphological representation seems especially apt. I discuss the basic facts of cliticization and show how they motivate an autolexical theory in which an elegant and intuitively plausible set of constraints on the interface between syntax and morphology accounts for the basic features of cliticization that have been demonstrated in recent work on the subject.

After a brief historical interlude on the notion of incorporation, I argue in chapter 4 that some of the attested examples of this phenomenon are also amenable to treatment as morphosyntactic mismatches. The principles developed in chapter 3 to cover cliticization are generalized in chapter 4 to include incorporative phenomena.

Chapter 5 is a lengthy survey of morphosyntactic mismatches from a wide array of languages. Some of these fit quite nicely under the theory of cliticization developed in chapter 3, while others pattern in the fashion of incorporation as formalized in chapter 4. Several intermediate examples with characteristics of both cliticization and incorporation are also discussed in chapter 5. The importance of these examples is that they demonstrate the essential commonality of the two kinds of cases, supporting the argument that they should be treated in a similar manner, namely as morphosyntactic mismatches.

The last two chapters are more speculative than the preceding ones. In chapter 6 I explore the idea that autonomous semantic representation creates mismatches with both syntactic structure and morphological structure. I hypothesize that analogs to cliticization and incorporation are found at the semantic interfaces as well. It is suggested here that some of the best-known phenomena that have been traditionally handled by means of movement transformations receive a straightforward interpretation in the present theory as mismatches between syntax and semantics.

Chapter 7 briefly takes up a few extensions of the system that suggest themselves naturally. First, there is the idea that lexemes are nonatomic and are specified not only for their external combinatorics in the several autonomous modules but also with respect to their internal structure in each. The complex internal structure of certain lexical items can generate mismatches in just the same way that productive combinatoric processes can. Next I consider the possibility that lexemes may belong to categories that are usually the result of combinatoric processes in the several modules, rather than always belonging to the least complex category of each component. This idea is then applied to the problem of the inflectional indication of pronominal categories in natural languages. Finally, I consider the advisability of adding other autonomous dimensions of representation to the system, and conclude that having a level of discourse-functional organization, where notions such as topic and comment are represented, is likely to be of value.

2

A Sketch of Autolexical Syntax

2.1 Autonomous Components

Suppose we take a grammar to be a set of subgrammars called modules. Suppose further that each of these modules is a grammar of an independent level of linguistic representation (i.e., the "tactics" of that level in the terminology of stratificational grammar (Lamb 1966; Lockwood 1972). The number and nature of the modules needed for the accurate description of natural languages is a complex, partly empirical, and partly theoretical issue, but for illustrative purposes in this chapter, I will assume the existence of three modules: syntax, semantics, and morphology. The lexicon, a list of the particularities of the language, also specifies a set of structures, but plays a special, transmodular role in the theory I will develop.

The syntax specifies the phrasal constituent structures that the language allows, the semantics gives us the set of well-formed meaning structures in the language, and the morphology the set of well-formed morphological entities, less formally, words. I take it as a virtue of this system of grammar that there is only one autonomous set of semantic principles and one autonomous set of morphological principles, a virtue absent in many theories where both semantics and morphology are split into two or more quite separate components.

Finally let us suppose that, unlike what is assumed in stratificational grammar or transformational grammar, these modules are not hierarchically related to one another. Conceived of as a grammar of a certain dimension of representation, a module need not wait for the output of another to do its work, but has the power to generate (or equivalently, analyze) an infinite set of representations quite independently of what is going on in any of the other components. Each component is a self-contained system, with its own independent set of rules, principles, and basic vocabulary.

On this conception of grammar, an expression must satisfy the independent requirements of each of the modules in order to count as fully well formed. Each module, in other words, acts as a filter on all of the others. An expression that is syntactically well formed may fail to qualify as a sentence because it does not have a well-formed semantic parsing, or because there is no morphologically correct clustering of morphemes corresponding to it, or for both reasons. Similarly, an expression that is generable in the semantics may not be parsed by the syntax or may not be expressible in terms of words allowed by the morphology, or both.

Even if an expression is well formed with respect to its projection in each dimension, it may still not qualify as grammatical, for there must also be principles relating representations in two or more modules. There is, in other words, an overarching control center, an interface protocol that checks to see whether the members of a set of parsings from the individual components fit one another and count as parsings of the same total expression. An investigation of the principles governing the compatibility of autonomous representations from different modules will be the subject of much of the rest of this book.

Schematically, then, the nonhierarchical grammar I will be investigating has the following form: [1]

Figure 2.1

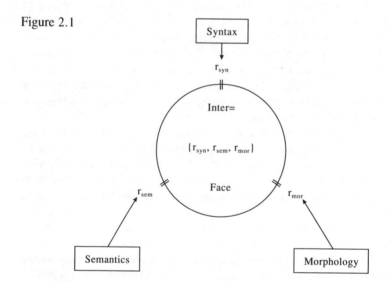

As indicated in the diagram above, an output of such a grammar is a set of triples $\{r_{syn}, r_{sem}, r_{mor}\}$. Each such triple corresponds to a full-fledged expression of the language to which the grammar ascribes the syntactic, semantic, and morphological parsings, r_{syn}, r_{sem}, and r_{mor}, respectively. In any triple, each element must of course be an output of the appropriate component, but in addition, the separate elements must pass certain congruity requirements imposed by the interface. The nature and content of these interface rules will be taken up in subsequent chapters.

To lend some concreteness to this discussion, let me provide some rough approximations of what might be found in the three modules for English. I wish to emphasize that I do not vouch for all aspects of the form and content of the rule systems sketched here. Though in some cases the rule systems I present give excellent results in interaction with one another, it is obvious that they are incomplete and open to criticism on both conceptual and empirical grounds. These modular sketches are provided at this point to illustrate how a grammar of autonomous modules functions, and are not intended as immutable choices that flow in some way from the core idea of autonomous modularity.

There are several methodological strategies that I have tried to keep in mind in fleshing out the components that I shall describe below: First, I have endeavored to keep each component "pure" and give it the power to deal only with what is demonstrably in its own purview. Second, I have tried to endow each component with what seems to me to be the least amount of descriptive and formal power that might have a chance of succeeding. And third, I have felt free to borrow from the work of others whenever it seemed that existing formalisms had properties appropriate to a system such as this. Only in the case of morphology have I suggested anything significantly different from a theory that can be taken off the linguistic shelf, for here there simply did not exist a well-worked out system that was adequate to the task.

2.1.1 Syntax

One of the main thrusts of the present work is the demonstration that various vexing linguistic facts of the kind to be discussed in the remainder of this work are treatable in an intuitively satisfying way within a very restrictive theory of syntax, indeed one which provides only one syntactic level of representation. Many of these phenomena have been taken as providing certain proof of the need for derivational theories of syntax, but as I shall show, the adoption of strictly autonomous subcomponents of syntax, semantics, and morphology defuses many of these arguments. I will assume that a context-free phrase-structure grammar is a sufficient formalism for each of the modules, including the syntactic component.

It is not clear that all of the notational richness of generalized phrase structure grammar will turn out to be needed when morphology and semantics are radically separated from the syntax, but some of the mechanisms turn out to be useful in capturing generalizations in all of the components, and will therefore be adopted here. I will, for example, employ the technique used in Gazdar et al. 1985 of stating categorical and hierarchical facts in terms of immediate dominance (ID) rules and ordering facts in terms of linear precedence (LP) rules.

An ID rule will have the general form (1), where C_0 represents the mother category and each C_j a category that C_0 may immediately dominate. The commas are used to distinguish such a rule orthographically from a standard phrase-structure rule, which includes ordering information as well. The order of the elements on the right-hand side of any ID rule is irrelevant. Such ID statements are to be interpreted as node admissibility conditions as in McCawley 1968b, the distinction between this interpretation and the interpretation of phrase-structure rules as rewrite rules being of some formal consequence.

(1) $C_0 \rightarrow C_1, C_2, \ldots, C_n$

LP rules have the form (2), where $<$ means 'precedes'.

(2) $C_1 < C_2 < \ldots C_n$

As in GPSG, categories will be taken to be bundles of features. Two categories are distinct if they differ in the coefficient of at least one of the features that define them. An incompletely specified matrix is an archicategory standing for the set of all its nondistinct categories.

Subcategorization properties of lexical items are encoded in GPSG as features that in essence reference the ID rule that introduces the lexical item. For example, a rule introducing verbs that take infinitive complements might be written as SF6, where only verbs that have this subcategorization property (e.g., *tend*, *want*, *try*) are listed in the lexicon as bearing the rule feature [SF6].

(SF6)   VP → V[SF6], VP[to]

In this work I will often find it necessary to give a full lexical entry for a lexeme in some language or another. It would be extremely unhandy for the reader to have to refer continually forward or backward to locate the rule referenced by a rule feature, so in much of the work, I will not make use of the formalism of rule features, but instead, will list the lexeme's full combinatoric properties.

(3)   tend: [$_{VP}$ ____ VP[to]]

This practice is obviously redundant with respect to the set of ID rules. Since my concern is to concentrate on the interactions of the various modules rather than to develop adequate versions of each, I will not consider whether this redundancy is tolerable or should be eliminated either in the manner of GPSG or by eliminating the ID rules themselves.

Categories differ fundamentally from one another in two basic respects, first in the nature of the lexical item that constitutes their lexical head, and second in their degree of complementation. Thus lexical nouns, common-noun phrases, and determined noun phrases are alike in that they have lexical nouns as ultimate heads; and lexical common nouns, adjectives, and verbs are all alike in being uncomplemented, basic expressions of the language. I will employ the familiar four-way distinction provided by the two binary features, [+/−N] and [+/−V] as a means of representing the first kind of distinction among categories. A feature [BAR], that takes small positive integers as co-efficients, will be used to represent the degree of complementation. Where no confusion results, I will suppress the feature name. Thus the notation "N[2]" will stand for the traditional class of NPs.

The Head Feature Convention (HFC) will be borrowed from GPSG to cap-ture the basic insight of X-bar syntax, namely that most phrases of natural languages consist of a unique head category and one or more adjuncts. It states that unless other factors override, the mother node and the head are specified identically. In the ID rule for an endocentric phrase, it is thus unnec-essary to spell out the features of both the head and the mother node to the extent that these are implied by the HFC to be found on the one if they are found on the other. For the sake of clarity, however, I will often include re-dundant features in the statement of a rule.

I will close this discussion with a brief list of rules that will figure in the illustrative sketch to follow. In the rules below, the morphosyntactic feature BSE is found on uninflected verb phrases, FIN on finite verb phrases, INDIC on indicative complement clauses, and [to] on verb phrases headed by the in-finitive marker *to*.

(SF1)	$S \rightarrow N[2]\ V[1]$
(SF2)	$N[2] \rightarrow Det\ N[1]$
(SF3)	$V[1] \rightarrow V[0,SF3]$
(SF4)	$V[1] \rightarrow V[0,SF4]\ N[2]$
(SF5)	$V[1] \rightarrow V[0,SF5]\ V[1,[to]]$
(SF6)	$V[1] \rightarrow V[0,SF6]\ V[1,BSE]$
(SF7)	$V[1] \rightarrow V[0,SF7]\ S[1,INDIC]$
(SF8)	$S[1,INDIC] \rightarrow Comp[SF8]\ S[FIN]$

2.1.2 Semantics

The semantic component should provide representations of natural language expressions in terms of the logical relations that obtain among the meanings of the formal elements that make up the expressions. This is not semantics in the philosopher's sense, where the term is understood as specifying the connec-tion between signs and the world, but in the grammarian's sense, where, as always, signs stand in a relationship to one another. It would be appropriate to call this level of representation "logical syntax," but I will continue to use the term "semantics" in the way that is traditional in linguistics.

The most important logical relations that a semantic component of this kind should be responsible for making explicit (and the only ones I shall deal with here) are function-argument relations and variable-binder relations. Such pat-terning can be represented in the tree form, as emphasized by McCawley (1967), so I will once again adopt a context-free phrase-structure grammar as the formal device for specifying this level of representation. I will assume that the rules of the semantic component do not impose a specific ordering on the elements that they connect; in the ID-LP format, this means that no LP statements apply to the semantic trees and every ordering of sister elements is allowable. The operator introduced by LF4 below, for example, may either precede or follow the formula that serves as its argument.

The semantic module might contain rules like the following, which closely follow McCawley 1981 in spirit, and are also compatible with work in generalized quantifier theory (Barwise and Cooper 1981; Gardenfors 1987) in assuming that only restricted quantification is appropriate for natural language semantics. I have adopted a notation for purposes of exposition[2] that owes much to suggestions of Eric Schiller's, to whom I am grateful.

The category names I employ are mnemonic: "F" may be read as "formula" and stands for a predicate combined with the full number of arguments it takes. Negative exponents will be used to indicate the number of arguments a predicate can take, in which case "F" can be read as "function." Thus "F^{-1}" is the class of functions of one variable, or singly unsaturated propositions; "F^{-2}" is the class of two-argument functions, or doubly unsaturated propositions, and "F^{-3}" is the class of three-argument functions, or trebly unsaturated propositions. It is not clear that any other types of predicates of variables are needed in the description of natural-language semantics, but if they are the system can obviously be extended.

I have opted to treat the various classes of predicates technically as functions of one variable to functions of the next lower category. Thus:

$$
\begin{array}{lll}
\text{(LF1)} & F & = F^{-1}(x) \\
\text{(LF2)} & F^{-1} & = F^{-2}(x) \\
\text{(LF3)} & F^{-2} & = F^{-3}(x)
\end{array}
$$

The motivation for this choice is threefold: (1) It makes the semantics maximally distinct from the syntax and morphology, where "flat" structures clearly exist; (2) it allows for logical argument distinctions (e.g., logical subject vs. logical object) to be expressed in terms of hierarchical realtions rather than linear order (Dowty 1982); and (3) the logical constituent structure that is implied seems to characterize even languages that lack corresponding structures (such as VP) in syntax. Thus Anderson and Chung (1977) argue that there is a constituent consisting of transitive verb and object even in VSO languages where, according to ordinary thinking, there is no VP. Anderson and Chung cautiously suggest that it is in semantic structure that this constituent is to be located, a suggestion that I will adopt here.

The lexicon will specify the semantic category to which lexical items belong. Intransitive verbs like *disappear*, nonrelational nouns like *dog*, and property adjectives like *red* will all be specified as F^{-1}. Transitive verbs like *find*, relational nouns like *bride* and *side*, transitive adjectives like *fond*, as well as most prepositions will be F^{-2}s, and so on.

I will assume that sentential operators (O) are categorically distinct from predicates, though the assumption is merely a matter of expedience. These will be introduced by the following rules:

$$
\begin{aligned}
&\text{(LF4)} && F\phantom{^{-1}} = O^{-1}(F) \\
&\text{(LF5)} && F^{-1} = O^{-2}(F) \\
&\text{(LF6)} && F^{-2} = O^{-3}(F)
\end{aligned}
$$

Rule LF4 combines an intransitive operator (like *seem*) with a formula to make a formula; rule LF5 combines a transitive operator (like *think*) with a formula to create an intransitive predicate; and LF6 combines an operator like *tell* with a formula to form a transitive predicate.

For each of the semantic types suggested above, I will also assume the existence of a modificational type that applies to arguments of type X and returns functions of the same type. I will symbolize these as MX, where X is the type of function the modifier takes as argument and returns as value. Thus MF corresponds to the class of sentential adverbs, MF^{-1}, the class of VP adverbs, etc. They are all introduced as special cases of the following rule schema:

$$
\text{(LF7)} \qquad X = MX(X)
$$

Lower case letters will be used to represent basic entity expressions, of which there is an infinite supply in the logical language. They do not correspond directly to any expressions in the object language, but are variables which must be bound by the meanings of real expressions in the language. A description of the interpretation for a language similar to this can be found in Cresswell 1973.

I will designate the semantic phrases that accomplish variable binding as Q, and quantifiers themselves as Q^{-1}. I will take quantifier phrases as restricted quantification, as argued for by McCawley (1981, sec. 4.5).

$$
\begin{aligned}
&\text{(LF8)} && Q = Q^{-1}(F) \\
&\text{(LF9)} && F = Q(F)
\end{aligned}
$$

F is the category of both well-formed formulas (WFF) and formulas with unbound variables. Rule LF1, for example, combines a one-place predicate such as *bark* with a variable to form an open formula, e.g., *bark*(x). To constitute a WFF, this open F must be combined with a Q, whose constituent F contains an instance of the the variable to be bound. Thus the expression $[_Q every(dog(x))]$ can be combined with $[_F bark(x)]$ by LF9 to form a WFF.

The syntactic rules of this logical language do not ensure the proper binding of variables. Unbound variables, doubly bound variables, and vacuous binding expressions are all allowed by the semantic syntax itself. The rules of interpretation, (i.e., the actual semantics, in the terminology employed by logicians) will, however, not be able to assign truth values to expressions in which variables are improperly bound. Thus the expression "*every*(dog(x)) [*bark*(y)]" is grammatically well formed vis-à-vis the semantic component of the grammar, but is uninterpretable.

This treatment of semantics departs radically from what is done in GPSG (Gazdar et al. 1985), which takes its cue from Montague (1970), who argued that an adequate representation of syntactic structure could be taken as a representation of semantic structure. In Gazdar et al. (1985) this nondistinctness of levels is achieved by producing semantic representations (of a kind not dissimilar in spirit from what I have suggested here) along with the syntactic structure. Gazdar et al assume that a semantic rule and a syntactic rule are tied in a predictable way, while I am assuming that the systems are quite separate.

This sketch is obviously imcomplete in a number of ways,[3] but it should serve as a means of illustrating some of the basic properties of logical representations, so that some of the features of the interface of the semantic component with other components can be studied in at least a preliminary way.

2.1.3 Morphology

The function of a morphological component is to make explicit the structure of all and only the grammatical word-forms in the language. The morphological component that I shall develop below treats all processes that are involved in the formation of word-sized entities in one block, not distinguishing, as in most other theories, between pre- and post-syntactic operations, or operations that take place within the syntax.

I will adopt essentially the system of morphology presented in Sadock (1985a). Though there are differences in detail, the basic plan of the morphological component closely parallels the plan of the syntactic component, and in this respect borrows an insight of Dowty's (1979) (cf. also Yoon 1986, Borer 1988, Shibatani and Kageyama 1988). In particular, the morphological component will be a context-free phrase-structure grammar (Selkirk 1982, Spencer 1984), which could in principle have any of the features of the syntax presented above.

The adoption of a phrase-structure grammar of stems and affixes implies that at this level of representation, all morphology is concatenative. I assume that nonlinear morphological phenomena (internal change, infixation, reduplication, etc.) are to be handled morphophonologically by means of autosegmental representations and associations of the kind employed by Goldsmith (1976) and McCarthy (1981). Research connecting the autonomous components dealt with here and an autosegmental phonological component is just being undertaken.

2.1.3.1 The ID-LP Format in Morphology

The ordering of elements in syntax is by and large freer than the ordering of elements in morphology. This might suggest that the separation of categorial-hierarchical information from linear-order information as is done in the syntax through the separate statement of ID and LP principles would not be appropriate in the morphology. Other considerations, however, argue for adopting the ID-LP format in the morphology as well. For one thing, the ID-LP format is indispensable for stating regularities of morpheme ordering across rules in a language, just as it is in syntax. There are languages that fairly consistently order the syntactic head of a phrase before the complement and others that typically do things the other way round. Similarly, there are languages that are preferentially prefixing, and others that are preferentially suffixing. Eskimo is an excellent example of the latter type, a language which, with one non-productive exception, has only suffixes regardless of all other morphological details. This regularity can be neatly captured in an ID-LP morphology by stating a single rule that orders all affixes after any morphological sister.

2.1.3.2 Headship in Morphology

Though there are many vexing questions (Zwicky 1984), it is clear that most complex morphological structures consist of a head and one or more nonhead elements, the head being that daughter whose featural composition is related to that of the mother node by the HFC, in the same way as in the syntax. This is particularly clear in those cases of derivational morphology and compounding where there is a part-of-speech discrepancy between the mother node and one of the daughters. In *Americanize*, *redness*, and *readable*, only the affix can be considered the head since the stem is of a different category from the word that it is an immediate constituent of, and similarly, in the case of compounds like *baby-sit*, *high chair*, and *sky blue*, the right-hand member of the compound must be the head, for it uniquely agrees with the mother in category features (Williams 1981).

2.1.3.3 Bar-Level in Morphology

Morphological structures differ in degree of complementation in much the same way as syntactic structures do. In syntax we take the lexical level to be indicated by the 0-bar feature, the next level by the 1-bar feature, and so on. It will be notationally convenient to look at the bar levels in morphological structure as also starting at the 0-bar level so that a basic lexical form (an uninflectable particle, for example) will have the same representation in both components. I will adopt the convention of indicating bar levels in morphology with negative superscripts, as a means of avoiding confusion with the formally identical system of levels and overlapping system of major categories in the syntax.

The decision to consistently relate degree of complementation in both syntax and morphology to bar level seems a natural one, but it departs from the practice in two other well worked out systems of phrase-structure morphology. Both Selkirk (1982) and Spencer (1984) choose to represent degrees of complementation in terms of features such as "affix" and "stem," which for Selkirk are partly outside the X-bar system and for Spencer are entirely so. At the end of her monograph, Selkirk reconstructs the notions "stem" and "root" in terms of the X-bar hierarchy as representatives of the X^0 and X^{-1} levels, respectively, with affixes falling outside the system. Spencer employs the bar-level system as a means of indicating the number of recursions at a single level. I reject both practices in terms of a consistent reconstruction of all such notions as root, stem, affix, and word in terms of the bar-level hierarchy and other primitives of the system.

The most fundamental distinction in level of morphological complexity is between bases from which full-fledged, potentially independent words can be formed and those words themselves. Following traditional terminological practice, I shall call members of the former class "stems," and those of the latter class "words." Among the class of stems, we may further distinguish between morphologically primitive stems, traditionally called roots, and derived stems. I know of no compelling evidence that suggests that exactly this difference is relevant to the operation of morphological rules and will therefore treat both primitive and derived stems as instances of the $X[-0]$ bar level of the morphology.

I will assume, with Selkirk, but in contrast to Williams (1981), that the stem is the head of an inflected word. The universal schema for deriving fully-formed words is therefore as in MF1, where X^{-0} is the stem, and Y the inflectional morpheme.

$$\text{(MF1)} \qquad X^{-1} \rightarrow X^{-0}, Y$$

Roughly speaking, morphemes that combine with stems to form stems are derivational, while those whose presence is obligatory in the formation of an independent word are inflectional. On the simplifying assumption that there is no level distinction among stems, a derivational morpheme will combine with a morphological category of the 0-bar level to form a category of the 0-bar level, and will thus be introduced by a rule conforming to the scheme in MF2, where Y^0 is a stem and X the derivational morpheme.

$$\text{(MF2)} \qquad X^{-0} \rightarrow Y^{-0}, X$$

The class of clitics is partially defined by the fact that such elements form categories of greater derivational complexity than full words; they will be introduced by rules comforming to MF3.

$$(MF3) \qquad W^{-2} \to X^{-n}, Y$$

Here Y is the clitic, and X^{-n} is the host, usually a full word ($n=1$), or a word itself containing a clitic ($n=2$), such as English *couldn't've*. In some cases the host is the head of the complex morphological expression ($W=X$), and in some cases there is no head, so the complex expression belongs to no ordinary morphological class. I will use the symbol W to indicate acategorial word-forms such as English *I'll* or French *du*.

The last major morphological structure I will talk about is the joining of two stems to form a compound stem. Usually, one of these is clearly the head, as indicated in the following rule:

$$(MF4) \qquad X^{-0} \to X^{-0}, Y^{-0}$$

The head may be on the right, as in English, or the left, as in Hebrew, or there may be no head in the technical sense, as in Romance noun compounds like the Spanish *limpia botas* (Varela 1986). There are several other variations as well. Often either the head or the nonhead member of a compound must occur in a particular form. (See chapter 6 for further discussion of this construction.)

A few other rule types might be required for the description of other languages. A language with "template morphology" (see Yip 1988 and the references cited there) might require a rather specific rule that introduces several categories as sisters in a particular order. Thus the structure of a finite verb in a Bantu language might look something like the following:

(4) $V[-1, FIN] \to Cl[SUBJ] + Tns + Cl[OBJ] + V[-0] + Asp$

Eskimo languages contain a minor rule that makes a stem out of an inflected word. The affix X in a rule like (5) is clitic-like on the inside, since it applies to words, and derivation-like on the outside, since it creates stems.

(5) $X^{-0} \to Y^{-1}, X$

2.2 Lexicon

In the present theory, as in lexical functional grammar (see for example Bresnan 1982) and head driven phrase-structure grammar (Sag and Pollard 1987), the lexicon plays a central role. Here it forms the axis around which the several autonomous modules pivot. The lexicon contains the basic vocabulary for each of the modules and information as to the structural properties of each lexical item with respect to the several autonomous components. Much of this vocabulary is shared, the typical lexeme having semantic, morphological, and syntactic value.[4] As I shall argue, though, there are lexemes in natural languages that lack one or another category of information and hence serve no function whatsoever in one or another component.

Let us take the English lexeme *dog* as a typical example of a lexeme with a role to play in all three components. Its lexical content makes it a noun in the syntax, a noun stem in the morphology, and an intransitive predicate in the semantics:

$$
\begin{array}{ll}
\text{(L1)} & \textit{dog:} \\
& \text{syntax} = \text{N[0]} \\
& \text{semantics} = \text{F}^{-1} \\
& \text{morphology} = \text{N[}-0\text{]}
\end{array}
$$

The syntactic statement in the lexical entry *dog* indicates that the lexeme may be found in structures like (6) because of the existence of the rule of English syntax SF2.

(6)

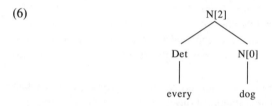

The semantic statement sanctions semantic structures like (7) on the basis of the semantic rules LF1 and LF8, and the morphological part of the entry allows the lexeme to be found in morphological trees such as (8) because the morphological module of English contains rule MF1.

(7)

(8)

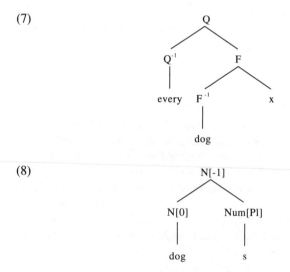

A proper noun such as *Fido* would have a different representation from *dog* in each of the three components. It would count as an NP for syntax, as a full word[5] for the morphology, and as a quantifier expression (including a nonlexical definite quantifier) in the semantics:

(L2)   *Fido*:
        syntax $= N[2]$
        semantics $= [_Q[_{Q[-1]}DEF]\ [_F[_{F[-1]}\underline{\quad\quad}]\ x]]$
        morphology $= N[-1]$

This lexical entry permits *Fido* to be found in syntactic structures like (9), semantic structures like (10), and morphological structures like (11).

(9)

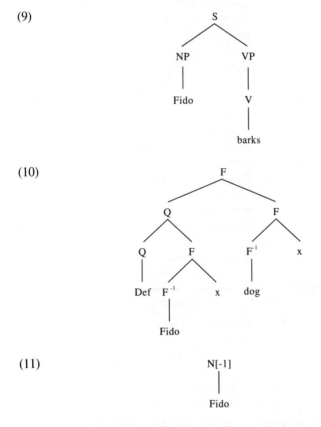

(10)

(11)   N[-1]
                                                 |
                                                Fido

L3–L10 present a sampling of possible lexical entries for other lexemes of English relative to the grammar fragment given above. The symbols in the syntactic and semantic parts of each of these entries refer to the syntactic and semantic combinatoric rules given above. Since none of these entries behaves morphologically as an affix, what we find under morphology in these particular cases never mentions a morphological rule. As members of distinct morphological categories (verbs, particles,[6] prepositions, and so on), the following items can only occur as whole words or as morphological stems.

(L3)   *bark*:
     syntax = [SF3]
     semantics = F^{-1}
     morphology = V[−0]

(L4)   *every*:
     syntax = Det
     semantics = Q^{-1}
     morphology = W[−1]

(L5)   *bite*:
     syntax = [SF4]
     semantics = F^{-2}
     morphology = V[−0]

(L6)   *seem*:
     syntax = [SF5] or [SF7]
     semantics = O^{-1}
     morphology = V[−0]

(L7)   *want*:
     syntax = [SF5]
     semantics = O^{-2}
     morphology = V[−0]

(L8)   *it* (expletive):
     syntax = N[2]
     semantics = nil
     morphology = N[−1]

(L9)   *to* (infinitive marker):
     syntax = [SF6, to[7]]
     semantics = nil
     morphology = W[−1][8]

(L10)   *that* (complementizer):
     syntax = [SF8]
     semantics = nil
     morphology = W[−1]

I am now in a position to illustrate the filtering effect attained when lexemes are taken to have independent reality in more than one autonomous module.

Consider the fact that *Fido dog* is not a sentence of English. From the semantic point of view, this expression is flawless, having a semantic representation like (12).

(12)

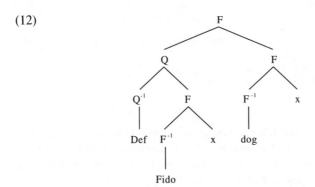

The ill-formed expression *Fido dog* predicates the dogginess of Fido, at least as far as the semantic value of its lexemes goes, and for that reason is quite comprehensible, though quite ungrammatical. What is wrong with this expression is that English (as opposed to numerous other languages) contains no syntactic rule expanding S as NP + Pred. Russian is a language that does have such a rule, and in Russian one can say the equivalent of *Fido sick*, *Fido in Moscow*, and of course also *Fido dog* with exactly the meaning given by (12). In this case, then, the syntax of English filters out a semantically unexceptionable construction.

As an illustration of the mutual filtering effect that the independent representation of lexemes in separate components achieves, consider the following much-discussed paradigm:

(13)   Fido seems to bark.

(14)   It seems that Fido barks.

(15)   *Every dog seems that Fido barks.

(16)   *That Fido barks seems.

Examples (13) and (14) are both syntactically and semantically well formed, each having appropriate structures at both levels of representation. They have exactly the same semantic representation,[9] a fact that is captured here in virtue of the semantic emptiness of the words *to*, *it*, and *that* given in lexical entries L8–L10 above.

(17)

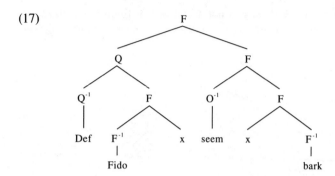

The two sentences do differ in syntax, of course, (13) having a structure like (18), and (14) having the structure of (19). Differing syntactic structures are permitted because *seem* can be inserted into two different subcategorization frames, as indicated in its lexical entry L6.[10]

(18)

(19)

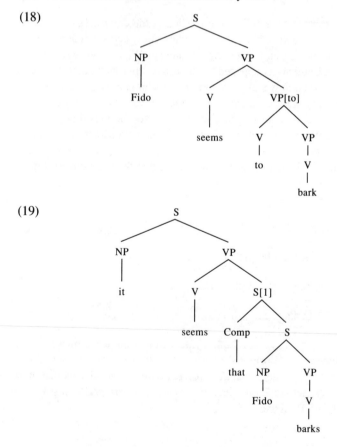

Example (15) comes out as fully well formed in the syntax, having essentially the same structure as that represented in (19) except for the fact that the first NP is *every dog* rather than *it*. Its problem is in the semantics: the lexeme *seem* is an intransitive operator in the semantics and thus may only combine with a proposition. The only two candidates here are "barks (Fido)" or "barks (x)" (see note 9). If *seem* combines with the former, there is no variable left for the quantifier "every [dog (x)]" to bind. If it combines with the latter, it may bind the variable "x," but then there is no variable for the quantifier "Def [Fido (x)]" to bind. In either case, we have an ill-formed semantic representation.[11]

Example (16) is bad for exactly the opposite reason. It is semantically faultless but has no well-formed syntactic structure. The syntactic part of the lexical entry for *seem* demands that it take an S[1] or VP complement, but in (16) it has neither. Thus the syntax acts as a filter on the semantics in some cases and in others the semantics acts as a filter on the syntax.

To close this illustrative sketch of the interaction of autonomous, parallel components, I will give one example of a case where the morphological requirements of a language make a construction that is well formed in the syntax and the semantics ungrammatical. I return to Russian, a language that allows sentences to consist of a noun phrase and a nonverbal predicate phrase. As in many such languages, these verbless sentences exist only in some unmarked form such as the present tense. In more marked parts of the verbal paradigm, the past tense or future tense, for example, a copular verb obligatorily appears. *Fido sabaka* means only 'Fido is a dog'. To express the equivalent of 'Fido was a dog' an additional word is required: *Fido byl sabaka*.

The account of the sudden appearance on the scene of a copular verb is quite straightforward in the system being explicated here. The past tense in Russian is expressed in terms of an inflectional suffix *-l* on verbs. This lexeme is obligatorily a suffix, which we may specify by assigning it a lexical representation along the lines of L11.

(L11)   *-l* (Russian):
         syntax = nil
         semantics = O^{-1}
         morphology = $[_{V[-1]} \text{V}[-0]$ _____] (cf. MF1)

The morphological part of this lexical entry stipulates that the past tense is realized as an inflectional affix to verbs. Forms like **Fido + l sabaka*, or **Fido sabaka + l* though syntactically and semantically well formed, will be ungrammatical because the morphological requirements of the past-tense lexeme are not met. In other words, any completely well-formed expression containing this morpheme will have to have a verb to support it. But since the

verb is unnecessary in the semantics, it will have to be some semantically neutral verb like *byt'*, which in its copular use might have a lexical entry such as
(L12).

$$\text{(L12)} \qquad \textit{by(t')} \text{ (Russian):}$$
$$\text{syntax} = [_{V[1]} \underline{\hspace{1cm}} \text{X}[2]]$$
$$\text{semantics} = \text{nil}$$
$$\text{morphology} = \text{V}[-0]$$

2.3 The Interface

The grammar depicted in figure 2.1 above includes a subsystem called the interface that is charged with the task of coordinating the several representations
produced by the autonomous modules. Thus the interface has direct access to
all varieties of grammatical information. It is not "informationally encapsulated" and is therefore not a module in the sense of Fodor 1983.

2.3.1 The Lexicon as Part of the Interface

The examples discussed in section 2.2 above illustrate the central role the lexicon plays in associating representations from different modules. The lexicon
is therefore a part of the interface in this system of grammar, rather than a
free-standing module. However, the mechanism whereby the lexicon helps in
coordinating distinct levels of representation was left quite vague in the discussion above, so I will partly correct that defect by offering an informal discussion of some of the details of the process of lexicalization.

Natural language expressions are never thoroughly well formed unless they
are completely and correctly lexicalized. A full-fledged expression must be
cast in the actual stuff of language, its lexical substance. This is quite a commonplace idea for the syntax, and is embodied, for example, in the lexicalization scheme of Chomsky 1965, whereby a lexical item is allowed to be
substituted for a complex symbol of a base tree provided its lexical features
are not incompatible with those of the complex symbol. It is further assumed
in that work that unlexicalized complex symbols in surface structure mark an
expression as ungrammatical. I propose simply to extend this basic idea to the
other components as well: each component's representation in a triple structure must be fully and correctly lexicalizable, by means of the same set of
lexical items, for the triple to count as the total representation of an expression
of the language.

As an example, consider the syntactic, semantic, and morphological representations in (20a), (20b), and (20c), which are correct outputs of the grammars SF1–SF8, LF1–LF9, and MF1–MF4 above.[12]

(20) a.

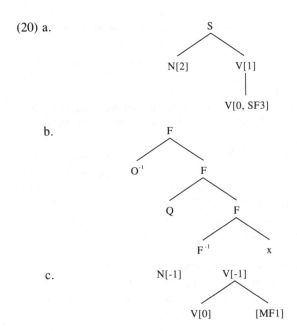

b.

c.

Let us assume the lexical entry in L13 for the English verbal inflection *-s*. Then we can see that the three lexemes *Fido*, *bark*, and *-s* can lexicalize all three trees, allowing this triple to be the representation of the English sentence *Fido barks*.

(L13)   *-s*:
             syntax = nil
             semantics = O^{-1}
             morphology = [$_{V[-1]}$ V[-0] ____] (cf. MF1)

The process of lexicalization breaks down into three similar, parallel problems: (1) Can the lexemes *Fido*, *bark*, and *-s*, as elements of the syntax, lexicalize the syntactic tree; (2) can they lexicalize the semantic tree, when taken as elements of the semantic language; and (3) can they lexicalize the morphological tree, when taken as morphological entities? Even though these three problems are essentially similar, I will go through them all for the sake of clarity.

From the lexical entry for *Fido*, we find that it counts as N[2] in the syntax. It may therefore be associated with the terminal N[2] node in (20a). *Bark* is lexically specified as [SF3], a specification that is compatible with the features of the terminal node V[0, SF3], for which it may therefore substitute. The inflectional affix *-s* has no syntactic value as indicated by its "nil" lexical specification. It is compatible with any syntactic tree, since it does not need to be, and in fact cannot be, associated with any syntactic node.

As for the semantics, *Fido* counts as a Q, and may therefore be associated with that node in (20b). It is a complex binder, however, and its association with (20b) adds the entire semantic substructure given in L2 to the tree. As a semantic F^{-1}, the lexeme *bark* associates with the similar node in (20b), and as a semantic O^{-1}, the verbal affix *-s* can lexicalize the O^{-1} at the top of the tree.[13]

The lexicalization of the morphological string proceeds similarly. *Fido* is an $N[-1]$, and *bark* is a $V[0]$, so these two lexemes may be associated with the corresponding nodes in the morphological string. The suffix *-s* is a morphological category bearing the rule feature MF1, and it occurs in the environment stipulated in the morphological field of its lexical entry. It is an inflectional affix on verbs and may therefore associate with the last terminal node in the morphological string.

What we have seen, then, is that the three lexemes *Fido*, *bark*, and *-s*, completely lexicalize all three structures in (20), and that all of the lexical requirements of each of these lexical entries are met on the appropriate planes of representation.

2.3.2 Paradigmatic Constraints

Though the modular subgrammars and the corresponding multipart lexical entries are radically separated in the present scheme, there are important correspondences operating across modules that need to be captured. Such regularities are easily stated in the present framework.

One important, and much discussed variety of intermodular correspondence is the existence of some interpredictability between semantics and syntax, morphology and syntax, and semantics and morphology. Well-known examples of this include the fact that semantic relations tend to be realized as transitive verbs in the syntax, while semantic property expressions tend to emerge as intransitive verbs; that elements inflected for tense strongly tend to function as syntactic verbs (i.e., as bearers of features such as [SF3], [SF4], and so on); that affixes tend not to be represented as formatives in the syntax, and that semantically empty lexemes tend not to be morphological stems.

A very general set of such correspondences concerns the inflection class of a stem in the morphology and the syntactic behavior of that inflected word. It seems almost tautological to say that items inflected as nouns are heads of noun phrases in the syntax, items inflected as verbs are heads of verb phrases in the syntax, and so forth, but in fact, substantive claims about universal, cross-modular correspondences lie behind such innocent-sounding statements. There is really a pun here, since the idea that a lexeme is a noun from the morphological vantage point is logically quite independent of the idea that a lexeme is a noun from the point of view of the syntax. Morphologically, nouns are lexemes that are inflected for case and inherent number, undergo certain derivational processes only, and enter into compounds in specific ways in certain languages. Syntactically, a noun is a lexeme that heads noun phrases, where NPs are understood as subjects of clauses or objects of verbs or prepositions; the head of a NP controls agreement of its modifiers and will be at the end of the phrase in a head-final language, and so on.

It is often the case, in fact, that features that belong primarily to one module are needed by another. Agreement features, for example, are essentially morphological, for without a morphological marker of the process, we would have no reason to posit agreement in the first place. There could be languages with morphological features for number, gender, and the like, that control the form of nouns, but no agreement in terms of these features. There could not, however, be languages with gender agreement, let us say, that do not indicate gender in any overt morphological terms.

But agreement is essentially a syntactic process in that features that originate in one syntactic position are predictably found in another as well. Thus the agreement features in a particular language must be found in the morphological entries of certain lexemes (say the agreement affixes themselves), but must be available to the syntax as well.

Such examples by no means exhaust the cases where features that, by their nature, belong to one module are made use of in another. I will therefore assume that in general, features spread freely across modular interfaces. The following convention says that in the absence of incompatible feature specifications, features that are found on an element in one module are also found on an associated element of another.[14]

(21) $[\alpha X]$ $[\alpha X, \beta Y]$ Module$_1$
            .   .

            . $\rightarrow$.

            .   .

          $[\beta Y]$ $[\alpha X, \beta Y]$ Module$_2$

Let us consider a simple case of agreement where the passage of features between automodular representations is important. (The discussion that follows is somewhat simplified and the reader is referred to Sadock 1988 for a more detailed but essentially similar treatment.) In a Spanish phrase like *manzana roja* 'red apple', the stem *manzan-* is lexically listed with the feminine agreement feature in its morphological field, but the adjective stem *roj-* has no inherent agreement feature. Both adjectives and nouns (i.e., the class picked out by the feature [+N] consist morphologically of a stem and an inflectional suffix, as in the schema of MF1 above, but for Spanish the instantiation of this rule is more specific, making the inflection a suffix that shares gender features with the stem.

(22) $X[+N, -1] \rightarrow X[+N, -0, \alpha GEND] + Infl[\alpha GEND]$

As for the syntax, I will assume (for the sake of simplicity) that gender features are distributed analogously by the rule that expands N̄s:

(23) $\bar{N}[\alpha GEND] \rightarrow N[\alpha GEND] \, A[\alpha GEND]$

Thus a bimodular structure for this phrase would be as in (24), where only the lexical values of features are indicated, and the gender morphemes have been left out.

(24)

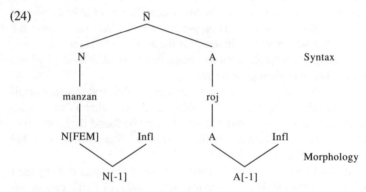

But according to the principles established so far, and in particular (21), the well-formed dual structure would have to be as in (25), where the feature [FEM] is found on every node.

(25)

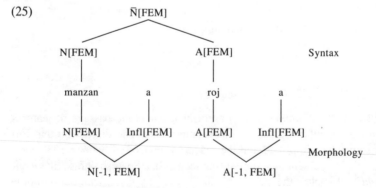

This comes about as follows: The lexical feature [FEM] is a lexical feature of the morphological specification of the stem *manzan-*. This feature will also characterize the N node in the syntax by (21). The syntactic rule (23) insures that the same gender features are found on head nouns, their modifying adjectives, and the N̄ node dominating such a string, so the A and N̄ nodes in the syntax also bear the feature [FEM]. Now since the syntactic adjective node is associated with the morphological adjective node, they will share features according to (21) again, implying that both must be [FEM] as well. Finally, by (22) the inflectional endings of Spanish nouns and adjectives must be the same as those of the stems to which they are attached, so they are both [FEM], the feature born lexically by the suffix -a.

This method of handling intermodular redundancies leaves open the possibility that there will be deviant lexical items that do not display the matching feature specifications of the paradigm case, and this is entirely as it should be, since such cases are plentiful. Consider, for example a Spanish noun like *poeta* 'poet', which requires masculine agreement on modifying adjectives, but which appears to have a feminine suffix. This could be handled by supplying it with the feature [FEM] in the morphological field of its lexical entry, and the feature [MASC] in its syntactic field. Then for morphological purposes, *poeta* will behave like a feminine, forming the diminutive with an -a suffix (*poetita*), but will remain masculine in the syntax (*el poetita*), which is correct.

As another example of the disagreement of otherwise predictable features in the morphology and syntax, consider the lexeme *near* in English, which inflects like an adjective (*nearer, nearest*) but is notorious for taking a plain NP object, rather than a prepositional phrase complement such as all other adjectives take. Its unusual properties can be accommodated in the present system by giving it a more complex lexical entry than typical morphological adjectives, which are adjectives in the syntax also by (21).

(L14)   *near*:
         syntax = [$_{P[1]}$ —— N[2]]
         morphology = [+N, +V]

Another, but more systematic example is the use of adjectives as nouns in German, and similar cases in other languages. In a sentence like *Der Alte sitzt im Wohnzimmer*, where there is no syntactic or discourse context to support the deletion of a head noun in the NP *der Alte*, we may simply give the stem *alt* a lexical entry that includes unexpected morphological and syntactic specifications.[15] In particular, the meaning of the adjective in this use would be complex, including its ordinary meaning and that of an abstract predicate that is true of all human beings:

(L15)   *alt* (German):
         syntax = N[0]
         semantics = [$_{F-1}$ —— [$_{F-1}$ HUMAN]]
         morphology = A[−0]

A lexical item whose features relative to the various modules match in the expected way may be simplified by removing the redundant specifications, but the specification of a lexeme whose meaning, syntax, and morphology deviate from the norm must be more complex and require fuller specification. The entry for English *dog*, for example, need not mention both the syntactic and morphological specifications given in L1, since one can be predicted from the other by means of (21). A simple lexical item like *dog* would be easier to learn than one whose values in the autonomous modules had to be learned separately and would be more stable over time than one whose values could not be refreshed by the application of general principles.

2.3.3 Syntagmatic Constraints

The English person-number-tense morpheme was treated in L13 as having the semantics of an operator and the morphology of a verbal affix. That is, it is capable of occurring as the lexicalization of the circled nodes in simultaneous semantic and morphological representations such as the following (cf. (20b) and (20c) above), where the boxed nodes are lexicalized by the same verbal lexeme:

(26)

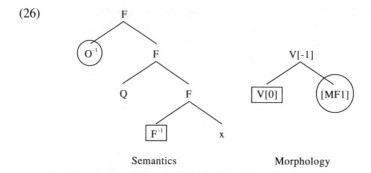

Semantics   Morphology

The existence of such discrepancies between the structural position of a lexeme in two components provides the most persuasive evidence for the autonomy of the representations. For that reason, much of the remainder of this book, especially chapters 3, 4, and 5, will be devoted to the presentation and analysis of facts from a wide range of languages that seem to demand automodular representations that are not congruent.

But the degree of allowable mismatch between the simultaneous positions of a lexeme in representations from two modules is by no means unlimited. There are very powerful principles operating to constrain such mismatches, the elucidation of which will also occupy much of what is to follow. At this point I will simply mention the two most important syntagmatic principles, both of which will be made much more precise in later chapters.

1. The Incorporation Principle (IP): A lexeme that combines with a phrase at some level may combine with the head of that phrase at some other level.

Thus the English tense morpheme is a semantic operator that combines with a proposition but morphologically shows up as an inflection on the main verb of the clause, i.e., the lexical head of the clause.

2. Cliticization Principle (CP): A lexeme that combines with a phrase at some level may combine at another level with a unit immediately to its right or left.

The English auxiliary clitic *'s* combines with predicate phrases in the syntax, but combines with the word immediately to its left, as in *Who do you think's coming?* (For a number of restrictions on this, see Kaisse 1985.)

2.4 Formal Power

What is the descriptive power of a grammar of the kind outlined here? Because the output of an autolexical grammar is not a set of strings or structures, but a set of n-tuples of structures, the question is not an easy one to answer. There is no relevant formal work that I am aware of that speaks directly to the issue of the power of such a grammar.

However, in view of the filtering effect that the interaction of components produces, the question can be cast somewhat differently. We may ask, for example, what the descriptive power of the syntax as filtered by the other components is, and expect a reasonable answer. Here there are some interesting formal results, particularly those of Borgida (1983) who investigated the interaction of two autonomous grammars with an eye toward determining the formal properties of stratificational grammar. The principal result that Borgida demonstrated was that a two-level grammar could have considerably more power than either of the component grammars, a result that extends directly to the framework of autolexical syntax.

I offer here a simplified demonstration of this, making use of a grammar that is a special case of the kind being developed in this work.

Consider a grammar, G, with two autonomous components, C_1 and C_2, defined as follows:

$$C_1: \quad S \rightarrow a\ X$$
$$X \rightarrow b\ (S)$$
$$C_2: \quad S \rightarrow (a')^*\ X$$
$$X \rightarrow (b')^*$$

Component C_1 is a finite-state grammar that generates the regular language $L_1 = \{(ab)^*\}$. Component C_2 generates the language $L_2 = \{(a')^*(b')^*\}$, which is also a regular language, though the grammar used to generate it is only weakly equivalent to a finite-state grammar, since it makes use of the Kleene star.

Suppose that the language L defined by G is that subset of all pairs $\langle S_i S_j \rangle$ (where S_i is in L_1 and S_j is in L_2) such that the terminal elements of S_i can be associated with the terminal symbols of S_j by the interface. Let us assume that what the interface does is match terminal symbols of S_1 to terminal symbols of S_2, one to one, starting with the leftmost symbol of S_1, by associating these symbols with compatible lexical items, as described informally in the preceding section.

The lexicon will be a list of phonological forms, each containing two fields, one for each component of this two-component grammar. A lexical entry will look like (27).

(27) PF_n:
        $C_1 = x$
        $C_2 = y$

This notation is to be interpreted as saying that PF_n counts as an x in the language described by C_1 and as a y in the language described by C_2.

The interface operates to attach lexical entries to the two structures given by C_1 and C_2 in the following manner: The first terminal symbol in S_1 is matched to a lexical item whose C_1 subentry is compatible, if there is one in the lexicon. The C_2 subentry of this lexical item is then matched to the first unassociated, compatible terminal in S_2, if there is one. This procedure is repeated until either all terminal nodes of S_1 and S_2 have been associated with lexical items or the lexicon is exhausted. In the former case, the pair $\langle S_i, S_j \rangle$ is a part of L provided that all lexical fields of all the lexemes used in the association are satisfied; otherwise, $\langle S_i, S_j \rangle$ is not in L.

Suppose the lexicon contains only the two lexical items (28) and (29).

(28)   A:
        $C_1 = a$
        $C_2 = a'$

(29)   B:
        $C_1 = b$
        $C_2 = b'$

Let S_1 and S_2 be the structures associated with abab and $a'a'b'b'$, generable according to C_1 and C_2, respectively. This pair of structures can be fully lexicalized in the following sequence of steps:

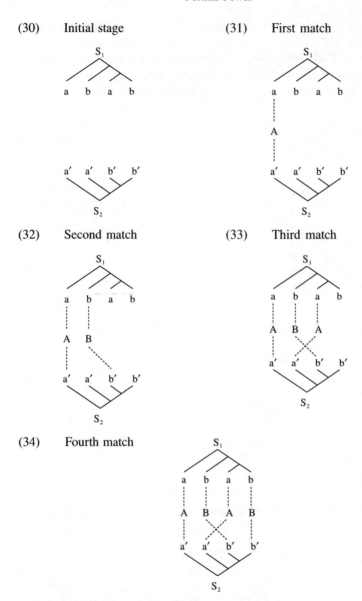

(30) Initial stage

(31) First match

(32) Second match

(33) Third match

(34) Fourth match

The language generated by C_2 by itself is the regular language $a^n b^m$. C_1 by itself generates the regular language $(ab)^n$. But when C_1 acts as a filter on C_2 through an interface such as the one described above,[16] and including a lexicon like (28)–(29), the only outputs of C_1 that are found in the pairs that describe the language are of the form $a^n b^n$—a necessarily context-free language lying at the interface between these two regular languages.

Even more relevant linguistically is the fact that the simple system described above models the notorious cross-serial dependencies of Dutch and Swiss German (Culy 1985; Shieber 1985; Manaster-Ramer 1987) as a glance at the final stage of lexicalization in (34) should suggest.

Suppose the lexicon included the following entries instead of those in (28) and (29).

(35)   Jan: $C_1 = a$
                       $C_2 = a'$
          Piet: $C_1 = a$
                       $C_2 = a'$
          Marie: $C_1 = a$
                       $C_2 = a'$
          laat-: $C_1 = b$
                       $C_2 = b'$
          help-: $C_1 = b$
                       $C_2 = b'$
          zie-: $C_1 = b$
                       $C_2 = b'$

C_1 produces the structure in (36) and C_2 produces the structure in (37).

(36)

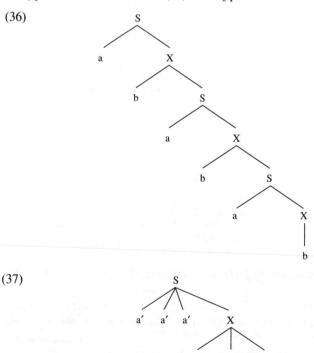

(37)

The pair of representations ⟨(36),(37)⟩ will count as part of the language L since the terminal symbols of (36) can be matched one to one with those of (37). Various lexical items meet the descriptions of the two matched symbols, so the lexicalization procedure described above can have various outcomes, one of which is the lexicalization of the two trees found in (38) and (39):

(38)

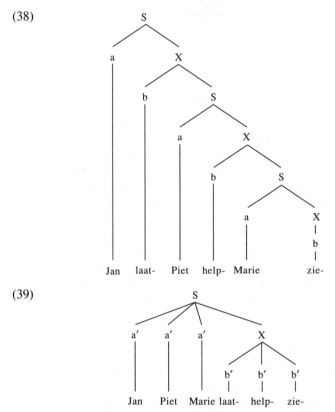

(39)

If we identify the S's and X's in (38) with logical formulas, and the a's and b's with referential expressions and predicates, respectively, (38) is a pretty fair representation of the meaning of the Dutch subordinate clause *dat Jaan Piet Marie laat helpen zien*. Furthermore, (39) is a reasonable representation of the surface structure of that phrase.[17] A grammar with two autonomous sub-components connected by an interface can thus characterize the properties of Dutch and Swiss German that have been the source of so much anguish in other theories without having to deal with the process at any single level. The cross serial dependencies are problematic when attributed to a single level of structure, but not when they reside at the interface between two.

3

Cliticization

3.1 Background

Paramount among the phenomena that supply evidence for the autonomy of modular representations is surely cliticization, an aspect of morphosyntax that has become the subject of much recent study (cf. Borer 1986 and the references there) just because it does not seem to fit well into the smoothly hierarchical view of the relationship between phrase building and word building that current theories provide. Those items called clitics generally display the behavior of bound affixes, but appear clearly to be distributed according to syntactic rules.

Consider, for example, the English third person singular auxiliary clitic *'s*. It attaches more or less promiscuously to the last word of the subject phrase that immediately precedes it, (Kaisse 1983; Klavans 1980; Zwicky 1977; S. Anderson 1987; Marantz 1988) as in (1), and sometimes to something which is not even part of the subject phrase, as in (2) (Schachter 1984).

(1)   The salesman I warned you about's at the door.

(2)   She is the one I think's going to win.

According to one very influential version of the linear theory of component interaction, all morphology is created before any syntax, and word-sized units are thus the smallest units that can be dealt with by the syntax. Now it is clearly the case that *about's* and *think's* in these examples are words, at least in some sense. The clitic auxiliary has precisely the same allomorphy as the third person singular present tense verbal inflection and the regular plural nominal inflection (see Bloomfield 1933; Lakoff 1972), a generalization that seems to demand that we treat it in the ordinary morphological component along with inflectional affixes. Yet it would be absurd to imagine that English syntax is organized in terms of such forms as *about's* and *think's*, for this would engender serious but entirely avoidable complications.

The point probably does not need to be belabored, but let us consider just a few of the most obvious complications that would ensue if we were to assume that words containing auxiliary clitics were syntactic atoms. Let us suppose that in example (3), *man's* is a syntactic atom.

(3)   The man's at the door.

Now presumably, the correct bracketing for this sentence is (4), not (5).

(4)   [the man's] [at the door]

(5)   [the] [man's at the door]

No matter which it is, we will require a new rule of English phrase structure, but if (4) is the correct structure, we at least have something that is attested in structurally similar languages like Russian. The required rule joins an NP and a nonverbal predicate to form a clause. Not just any NP enters into this construction, since the following sorts of things are all quite ungrammatical as clauses.

(6)   *The man at the door.

(7)   *The man'll at the door.

(8)   *That Fred left at the door.

If we call the feature that distinguishes those NPs that can combine directly with predicatives to form clauses [+RUS], the required rule is:

(9)   S → NP[+RUS] Pred

where Pred is the phrase type that the copular verb *be* (coincidentally enough) takes as a complement. NP[+RUS] will have to be allowed in a few other contexts as well. It will have to be allowed with passive VPs, as in (10), and in such cases it will have to be interpreted by some special mechanism as a passive.

(10)   This book's frequently read by high school students.

The special category NP[+RUS] will have to be allowed to occur with modal infinitives, which are otherwise sanctioned (coincidentally) only by FINITE forms of *be*. This would force another special rule upon us.

(11)   Bill's to open the meeting tomorrow.

(12)   *Bill had been/will be/is being to open the meeting tomorrow.

The complement of the putative category NP[+RUS] has unusual conjoining properties that will need to be taken care of. It can conjoin with other Pred's, as expected, (example (13)), but it can also conjoin with FINITE VPs, as in (14).

(13)   Bill's a rake and a scoundrel.

(14)   Bill's lazy and won't amount to anything.

Apparently, we would need an otherwise unattested rule type allowing this special sort of phrase only after NP[+RUS], since other environments that license Pred and conjunctions of Pred's do not license these:

(15)   I remember him as a rake and a scoundrel.

(16)   *I remember him as a rake and won't amount to anything.

Problems also arise in trying to specify which NPs bear the feature [+RUS]. The generalization is clear: an NP is [+RUS] if and only if the last word of the NP contains the clitic. Now Nevis (1985) and Zwicky and Nevis (1986) actually have suggested a feature-passing mechanism that allows a phrase to inherit a feature from any peripheral word. So far as I know, though, this mechanism is only of use in dealing with clitics, and could otherwise be dispensed with.

This is by no means the end of the complications that will arise if a word including clitic 's is taken to be unanalyzed by the syntax, but it should serve to make such an analysis extremely unpalatable. Every one of these problems can be avoided simultaneously by recognizing a level of structure in which the bracketing of (3) is neither (4) nor (5) but (17):

(17)   [the man] ['s at the door]

This analysis is directly formulable in the present theory by assigning this clitic a lexical morphological specification that makes it a suffix, and a lexical syntactic specification that makes it a verb that takes XP complements, thus allowing it to occur in morphological structures such as (18), and simultaneously in syntactic structures such as (19).[1]

(18)

(19)

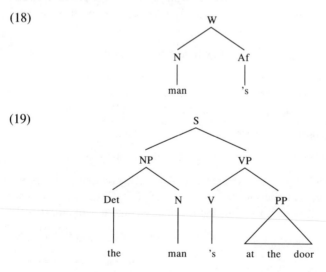

Exactly this sort of analysis is clearly foreshadowed in the work of the American structuralists. Wells (1947), for example, noted clearly the problems that the English possessive clitic 's posed for immediate constituent analysis, and particularly for the principle that "every word should be a constituent" (p. 196). After a cogent discussion of this and similar facts from other languages, he concluded:

> Instead of proclaiming, therefore, that every word in every language must be a constituent of any sequence in which it occurs as a part, the most we may say is that every word should be so regarded unless it engenders a conflict or complication in the description of the language. (P. 198)

In a similar vein, Nida (1976) provided the following discussion of the promiscuous Chanca Quechua clitic *-na*:

> An investigation of the structures in which this *-na* occurs reveals that it is an immediate constituent with entire phrases and not necessarily with the word immediately preceding. The very fact that it is postposed to all types of words leads us to suspect that it has the same sort of positional freedom as syntactic items have. In the inventory of morpheme classes we must list these simple types of clitic structures, but their distribution is described in the syntax, since they form immediate constituents with phrases. (P. 97)

But the simultaneous treatment of clitics foreshadowed in these earlier works is precluded in a hierarchical model of grammar, where the output of one component is modified by the next component downstream. Therefore the standard method of capturing the morphosyntactic duality of clitics within generative grammar is to supply a postsyntactic rule of cliticization that takes the syntactic auxiliary, which subcategorizes an XP complement, and attaches it leftward to the end of whatever word precedes it (see Bissantz 1983).

Figure 3.1

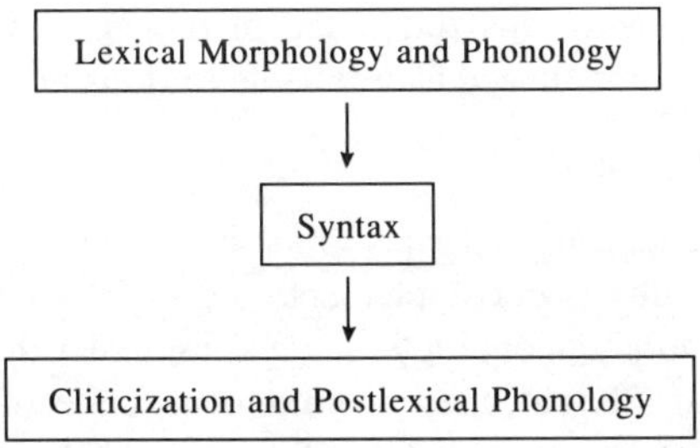

In effect, then, the standard treatment recognizes two kinds of words: those that are outputs of the ordinary morphology and are therefore present as such throughout the derivation of a sentence, and those that exist only after syntactic processing is complete. The task of structuring words is thus split between at least two components: the morphology proper and a postsyntactic cliticization component such as is explicitly recognized in recent work by Zwicky (1982) and Bissantz (1983), among others, and almost explicitly recognized in work by Kiparsky (1982a) and Pranka (1983).

3.2 The Multimodular Nature of Clitics

The elements we call clitics are often characterized by a constellation of properties from diverse grammatical realms. Among the most commonly mentioned of these are the following:

   I. Morphology
      a. Clitics are bound morphemes.
      b. They attach outside inflection.
      c. They block further morphology.
      d. They attach without regard to the morphological class of the host.
      e. They are completely productive.
  II. Syntax
      a. Clitics are independent elements of syntax.
      b. They are syntactically adjacent to their morphological host.
 III. Semantics
      a. Clitics are semantic functions.
      b. They take the meaning of a phrase as argument.
 IV. Phonology
      a. Clitics are phonologically dependent.
      b. They are agglutinative.
      c. They are stressless.
      d. They are subject to automatic phonological rules only.
  V. Lexicon
      a. Host plus clitic forms are not lexicalized.
      b. Clitics alternate with free words.

An example displaying this full range of properties is the English contracted auxiliary *'d*, pronounced as a syllable [əd], as in (20).

(20)   Pat'd have done it.

Starting with the lexical properties at the bottom of the above list, we see
first of all that this affix is in complementary distribution with, and in all respects other than morphophonology identical to, either the free word *had* or
the free word *would*. Second, there seem to be no cases of a lexicalized form
with unpredictable meaning consisting of a word and the clitic [əd].

As to phonology, this clitic is a suffix whose agglutinative phonological realization is invariably stressless [əd]. Only automatic processes such as the
flapping of preceding dental stops (e.g., *Pat'd* = [pærəd]) apply to forms
containing this clitic.

Semantically it is clear that *'d* is indeed a function, presumably taking as a
semantic argument the proposition expressed by the elements of the remainder
of the sentence. That *'d* is an independent element of syntax and combines
syntactically with VPs like *have done it* is clear for the reasons already dis-

cussed in section 1 above: a vast and undesirable complication of the syntactic component of English, and the addition of otherwise unnecessary mechanisms to universal syntax, would inevitably follow from assuming that *Pat'd* is a syntactic atom in examples like (20).

Turning to the morphology, we can easily verify that *'d* is a bound form—a suffix. It can never occur phonologically isolated from other words in a sentence; it cannot appear sentence initially (**'D Pat have done it*), or after pause, and so on. It is attached to inflected forms and never to stems (*Linguists'd do it*, **Linguist'ds do it*). Otherwise, the clitic is productively joined to any word without regard to the morphological class or identity of its host:

(21)   a. The guy I bought it from'd buy it back.
        b. He's who I think'd probably want it.

The clitic does not support further derivational or inflectional morphology, as per (Ic), and does not seem to allow a subsequent suffixal clitic either. Thus corresponding to the sequence of free words *Pat would not*, we have either *Pat'd not* or *Pat wouldn't*, but not *Pat'dn't*.

In the present theory, clitics are lexical items that participate in a particular sort of morphological process—that specified by rule MF3 of chapter 2—but are lexically listed as elements of the syntax. The auxiliary clitic *'d*, for example, would receive a lexical entry like (22), allowing it to appear in mismatched syntactic and morphological trees like the following:

(22)   *'d:*
        morphology $= [_{W[-2]}X[-1]\text{\_\_\_\_}]$
        syntax $= [_{VP[FIN]}\text{\_\_\_\_}VP[BSE]]$

(23)

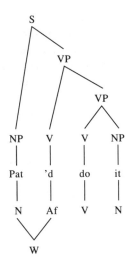

According to the list of properties in I through V above, clitics have a super-ficial quality that the standard theory, with its superficial postsyntactic cliticization component, is supposed to capture. Indeed, some of these proper-ties would seem to follow from the architecture of this model, or from this architecture supplemented by a few fairly reasonable assumptions. The post-syntactic theory of clitics would thus seem preferable to the present account in which none of these typical features is predicted by the form of the model alone.

The fact of the matter is, though, that otherwise clear examples of clitics can be found in the world's languages that differ in respect to almost any one of the behaviors listed in I through V. In that some of these properties follow from the very architecture of the theory diagrammed in figure 3.1, such a the-ory is untenable. Several of the examples discussed in chapter 5 demonstrate that bound morphemes can shade almost imperceptibly from prototypical clitics like English *'d* to normal derivational morphemes, on the one hand, and to inflectional morphemes, on the other, a state of affairs that is utterly incompatible with a theory whose components are arranged as in figure 3.1. (See also Sadock 1988a.)

As it turns out, theories with separate cliticization components are actually not very good predictors of the properties we associate with clitics, at least not directly in virtue of the fact that clitics are handled in a separate postsyntactic component. Such theories must be supplemented with special assumptions concerning the substance of the putative cliticization component, and are thus not very different from the present theory with regard to how much of the behavior of clitics must be stipulated.

3.3 Separate Cliticization Components

Of the various characteristics of clitics listed in I through V, only two actually follow directly from the fact that a grammar has a postsyntactic cliticization component. Under morphology, there is only the notion that clitics inhibit fur-ther morphology that falls into this category. Since derivational and inflec-tional morphology are handled by a higher-level component, such morpho-logical processes will all have occurred before cliticization. Note that the arrangement of components in figure 3.1 does nothing to block clitics from applying to clitics, a result that is a mixed blessing for the hierarchical theory, since there are cases, such as the English clitics, that do seem to inhibit even further morphology of the same kind, but there are also languages where clitics can pile up (see chapter 6, section 3.2, for one example of this). Under syntax, there is the important observation that clitics count as ele-ments of syntax. This is guaranteed by the fact that a component that inter-prets syntax would have only syntactic structure and its elements available to it as input.

Capturing any of the remaining putative properties of clitics requires at least a little enrichment of the theory. For example, if a "bracketing erasure" principle (Kiparsky 1982a) is appended to the theory, then the idea that clitics follow inflection is predicted, since the internal morphological structure of words would be lost to the syntax and to all subsequent components. The same principle could conceivably be made to capture the fact that clitics usually attach promiscuously to words of any morphosyntactic class, but only if it were interpreted to mean that syntactic category labels are erased at the end of syntax.

Specifying the other prototypical characteristics of clitics would require other assumptions. The general failure of clitics to occur in lexicalized combinations could be made to follow if the lexicon were hierarchically arranged so as to have no interaction with levels beyond the syntax. The fact that clitics tend to be semantic functions of the phrase they combine with in the syntax would be predicted if the semantic component operated only on levels as deep as, or deeper than, the syntax. The phonological properties in IV could be derived by making rather specific assumptions about the power of postlexical phonology.

The observation that clitics will generally attach to peripheral words is emphasized by Zwicky (1977) and Klavans (1980), working within a theory in which clitics are the responsibility of a special component of the grammar. Kaisse (1985, 82), following Zwicky (1977), stipulates this in the form of a purely descriptive law: "A clitic originating as an immediate daughter of X[n] may be adjoined only to the leftmost or rightmost node of X[n]." [2]

The most detailed of the theories that deal with clitics in a single component is that of Klavans (1980), and like Kaisse and Zwicky, Klavans stipulates many of the properties that these elements can display. Before turning to an examination of her work, though, I will offer an account of this phenomenon in terms of a theory that radically separates syntactic and morphological structure. I will then be in a position to show that much of what has to be stipulated in Klavans's theory issues from more general principles in mine.

3.4 Improper Clitics

Few clitics are actually as well behaved with respect to the list of properties in I through V as the English auxiliary clitic *'d*, and it is easy enough to find an item in some language or another that fails to conform to almost any one of these properties but is otherwise a good exemplar of the class of clitics.

I know of several cases of clitic-like elements that do not attach outside of inflection, and thus violate Ib above. Jerry Morgan (p.c.) brought out one such case from Albanian to my attention. (See Buchholz and Fiedler 1987.)

Albanian inflects indicative verbs for person and number of the subject, and imperatives for number of the (second person) subject:

(24)   *sjell* 'bring'

	Singular	Plural
1	sjell	sjellim
2	sjell	sillni
3	sjell	sjellin
Imp	sill!	sillni!

(25)   *shikoj* 'look'

	Singular	Plural
1	shikoj	shikojmë
2	shikon	shikoni
3	shikon	shikojne
Imp	shiko!	shikoni!

Dative and accusative pronouns are cliticized to the verb, very much as in Romance languages. They are proclitics to indicative forms (written as separate words), but enclitics to the imperative. In the imperative, however, the pronominal clitics *precede* the plural inflection, as shown in (29):

(26)   Më sjell një libër.
         'You (s) bring me a book.'

(27)   Sillmë një libër.
         'Bring (s) me a book.'

(28)   Më sillni një libër.
         'You (p) bring me a book.'

(29)   Sillmëni një libër.
         'Bring (p) me a book.'

A surprisingly similar set of facts (but with a twist) characterizes Platense Spanish, the dialect area including Montevideo and Buenos Aires. The facts below were described to me by Elisa Steinberg.

In these dialects, stress can shift to enclitic pronouns in the imperative. Note that this is a violation of characteristic IVc.

(30)   Tíre! 'Throw!'

(31)   Tíren! 'Throw (p)!'

(32)   Tíremelo! 'Throw it to me!'

(33)   Tiremeló! 'Throw it to me!'

Now as is well known, the clitic pronouns of Spanish are clitic-like in attaching outside inflection. But just in the case of the stress-shifted imperatives, forms with the plural inflection AFTER the clitic pronouns are possible in Platense:

(34)   Tiremenló! 'Throw (p) it to me!'

(35)   Tiremelón! 'Throw (p) it to me!'

What makes this case somewhat different from the Albanian situation is that the plural inflection can actually be found in several places at once—after the verb, and after each of the clitic pronouns:

(36)   Tirenmenlón! 'Throw (p) it to me!'

Steinberg suggests (p.c) that this is a case of autosegmental spreading of a nasal autosegment such that it associates with any syllable coda to its right. If this is the correct treatment, then the Platense Spanish pronominal clitics are not agglutinatively added to the inflicted word, thus constituting a violation of IVb, but in any case, they are not added strictly outside inflectional material.

The fact that clitics normally block all nonclitic morphology (characteristic Ic), not just inflection, follows from the fact that they regularly occur outside inflection, and inflection regularly occurs outside of derivational morphology. But an interesting exception occurs in Eskimo where there is a small class of clitics that are themselves stem-forming derivational affixes. They attach to inflected forms, but create stems that may then be further derived and inflected. Note particularly that the interpretation of the nonreflexive (3s) and reflexive (4s) inflections is unaffected by the attachment of the clitics in (38) and (40), proving the independent syntactic status of the inflected words that serve as the hosts of cliticization.

(37)   Illu-anut   ingerla-voq.
         house-3s/ALL go-INDIC/3s
         'He$_i$ is going to his$_j$ house.'

(38)   Illu-anu-kar-poq.
         house-3s/ALL-go-INDIC/3s
         'He$_i$ is going to his$_j$ house.'

(39)   Illu-minut   ingerla-voq.
         house-4s/ALL go-INDIC/3s
         'He$_i$ is going to his$_i$ house.'

(40)   Illu-minu-kar-poq.
         house-4s/ALL-go-INDIC/3s
         'He$_i$ is going to his$_i$ house.'

Many clitic forms are totally unselective with regard to the part of speech of their hosts, but a great many that I have found also exercise some degree of preference. Romance and Albanian pronominal clitics attach only to verbs; definite article clitics in Bulgarian and Macedonian (see chapter 5, section 1.2, below) attach only to nouns or adjectives; Danish definite articles only to nouns, and so on. In French the prepositions *de* and *à* attach to the masculine singular definite article and to the plural definite article to form four lexical portmanteau forms. Yet the perturbation of syntax evident in such construc-tions as *l'auteur du "Rouge et le Noire"* (Grevisse 1980) makes it abundantly clear that some of the most important properties of clitics must be attributed to the unproductive formations *du*, *des*, *au*, and *aux*. (See chapter 7, sec-tion 1.1.)

Even within English there is a range of selectivity, varying from none, for the auxiliary clitics *'s*, *'ll*, *'ve*, *'d*, to selection of a small, finite, lexically listed class of hosts for the negative clitic.[3] The possessive clitic of English presents an intermediate degree of selectivity. For all speakers it freely at-taches to nouns at the end of the possessive noun phrase, as in (41), and for all speakers it will not combine with demonstratives, as shown by the contrast in (42). (See McCawley 1988, 112.)

(41)   I object to the Senator from Arizona's question.

(42)   *I am surprised at its/*that's getting so much attention.

There is great vacillation in other cases. Most speakers tolerate examples where the clitic attaches to verbs, prepositions, and adverbs, but feel such ex-amples to be distinctly colloquial. Most speakers reject examples in which the clitic attaches to genitive pronouns that end in *s*, but some accept these as well. The judgments below are my own.

(43)   ?the man I told you about's book

(44)   ??the man who arrived's book

(45)   ?*a friend of his's apartment

What we see, then, is that neither total promiscuity of attachment, nor total productivity are necessary characteristics of elements whose behavior is otherwise like that of clitics.

Numerous languages present emphatic clitics that attach at a periphery of a phrase that they focus on. As a class these constitute an exception to the prin-ciple that clitics should be syntactic formatives, for their distribution is quite unlike that of any genuine elements of syntax. The Latin focal clitic *ne* can attach to any major constituent of a question, bringing that constituent into focus:

(46)   Bonusne est puer?
        'Isn't the boy **good**?'

(47)   Puerne bonus est?
        'Isn't the **boy** good?'

(48)   Estne puer bonus?
        '**Isn't** the boy good?'

It is technically possible, of course, to include this clitic somewhere in the syntactic structure of examples like these, but questions as to where it should occur, and what constituent type to assign it to are daunting.

Sometimes it is clear that such discourse-oriented clitics cannot be made part of the syntax. In the West Flemish dialect of Veurne, for example, the finite verb attracts a large number of clitic elements that adhere to it in an order determined by a template. One of these is clearly outside of syntax as ordinarily understood. In the cogent description of this dialect by Smessaert (1988), examples such as (49) are discussed:

(49)   *K-èn-t-ik-èm*   *èzonden.*
        1s-AUX-3sN-1s-3sM/DAT sent
        'I have sent it to him.'

Smessaert points out that the second occurrence of a first person singular clitic pronoun, *-ik-*, serves the discourse-pragmatic function of emphasizing the subject, and is optional. The first element is the obligatory subject itself. Smessaert suggests that the focusing pronoun does not belong in the syntax itself, but rather in an autonomous, parallel component where discourse-oriented properties such as topic, focus, and comment are represented. The result is a quite elegant description of a set of facts which, if dealt with in the syntax alone, would be anything but elegant.

The Veurne dialect also provides a clear counterexample to an otherwise widespread tendency for clitics that clearly are part of ordinary syntax to occur in a position adjacent to their usual slot. Neuter objects of prepositions may be cliticized to the verb, leaving a stranded preposition behind at some remove from the clitic:

(50)   K-èn-der-ik-èm   ol   van overtuugd.
        1s-AUX-3N-1s-3s/DAT already of   convinced.
        'I have already convinced him of it.'

The rules I shall formulate below require clitics to be as close to their syntactic points of origin as their morphological requirements allow, but for the prepositional object clitic *-der-*, which must occur in the clitic complex following the finite verb, this is not very close.

Finally, let me take up the relation between cliticization and the lexicon. Because of the productivity with which clisis ordinarily takes place, the meaning of a clitic and its host is usually not lexicalized. But, *pace* Zwicky and

Pullum (1983), it can be. Latin contains such items as *atque* 'and' (<*at* 'but'), and *-cunque* '-soever', itself a clitic, (<*cum* 'with'), both formed with the productive clitic *-que*, which otherwise means 'and'. Likewise formed with a clitic that in its productive use is a conjunction is West Greenlandic *soor-lu* 'for example', *aamma-lu* 'once again', and others. Similarly, English free-word conjunctions are unlikely to enter into two-word idioms, but they nevertheless can (cf. *And how!*).

So frequently are clitics not matched by independent words with related form that Zwicky (1977) suggests a fundamental division between "simple" clitics, that alternate with free words, and "special" clitics, that do not. Criterion Vb might be a sufficient reason to call something a clitic, but it is by no means a necessary one.

The various properties that clitics often display belong to different modules, and on the present theory ought therefore to be independent of one another. As we have seen, that is the case. However, there is a strong tendency for these properties to go together, a tendency that an adequate theory of cliticization should be able to express. I turn now to the development of such a theory.

3.5 An Autolexical Theory of Cliticization

My aim in this section is to develop a theory in which the properties of clitics flow from the fact that they have the morphological and syntactic properties that they would have to be given in any theory, plus natural interface constraints on the allowable association of the elements of two modular representations, in this case the syntax and the morphology. Because different languages handle clitics differently, I will not be completely successful in this, but will have to postulate two parameters that serve to distinguish various kinds of clitics.

The basic idea that will be pursued in the analysis of clitics and other sorts of mismatches between representations in independent grammatical dimensions is this: I assume that any two modular representations of the same expression are constrained to be as topologically similar as possible, up to the point where more specific features of the language prevent conformity with this general principle. Unless more circumscribed factors override, this basic constraint will not allow simultaneous parsings to count as representations of the same expression if they fail to match in certain ways that will be made more precise below. Of particular interest to us here is the fact that the structural demands of a lexeme in two dimensions frequently make it impossible for its position in those two dimensions to match as closely as the general constraint requires.

There are two facets to this general preference for parsings in two dimensions to align, one dealing with linear order and the other with constituent structure. The former is intuitively easier to grasp and will be taken up first. I state it provisionally as follows:

(51)   Linearity Constraint (LC)
        All lexemes that are projected on two dimensions must occur in the same linear order in both.

A simple case of a clitic that conforms to this principle is that of the French definite article preceding words beginning in vowels. We know from the behavior of the nonclitic articles in this language that they precede the phrases with which they combine. Thus the skeletal syntax of the expression *l'ancienne ville* will be as in (52):

(52)

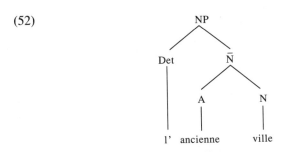

The string of terminal items in the syntax, namely Det-A-N is the same as the string of items in the morphology, namely *l'*, *ancienne*, and *ville*, though the bracketing is different in the two components. The clitic *l'* attaches to a word in its $\bar{N}$ complement, and the Linearity Constraint correctly requires this to be the first word, in this case an adjective. The various English auxiliary clitics, including *'d* discussed above, also conform to the Linearity requirement, occurring in the same order in the string of morphemes as do their syntactic counterparts in the string of syntactic terminals.

Besides linear order, constituency also plays a role in determining whether structures on distinct grammatical planes can qualify as simultaneous representations of the same expression. Because it is not generally to be expected that the constituency at every level will be identical, a much weaker sort of constraint than the Linearity Constraint is required. The intuitive idea is that a lexeme may combine with a complex expression at one level, and with the correspondent to only a part of that complex expression at another. More formally,

(53)   Constructional Integrity Constraint (CIC)[4]
        If a lexeme is in construction with P on dimension D_1, and is in construction with Q on dimension D_2, then Q', the correspondent

to Q in D_1, is dominated by P, or the correspondent to P in D_2 is dominated by Q.

I will first illustrate how this principle works in a case of a mismatch between syntax and semantics before considering its applicability to the treatment of clitics.

According to the treatment of English full-word negation with *not* suggested in chapter 7, section 1.1, the semantic value of this word will occur in semantic structures such as (54) and in simultaneous syntactic structures such as (55).

(54)

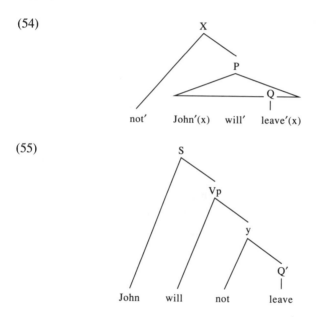

(55)

If we take the somewhat simplified semantic structure of (54) to be D_1 in (53), and the somewhat simplified syntactic structure of (55) to be D_2, we can see that this pair of trees conforms to the Constructional Integrity Constraint in that Q', the correspondent to Q in D_1, is indeed a D_1 descendant of P.

The principle would rule out the association of a (simplified) semantic structure like (56) with a (simplified) syntactic structure like (57) because in this semantic structure the negative element does not combine with a semantic constituent that includes lexemes corresponding to the syntactic VP *bite*, and because in the syntax *not* combines with VP *bite*, that does not include lexemes whose semantics is bark'(x). Thus *The dog that barks doesn't bite* is not a sentence that could mean 'the dog that doesn't bark bites'.

(56)

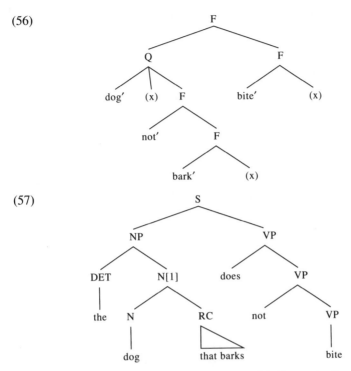

(57)

The implication of the Constructional Integrity Constraint for clitics is that they will tend to combine with a word of their syntactic complement phrase, and by the Linearity Constraint, with the nearest word of that phrase.

As an example of the operation of the CIC, consider the well-known case of the Latin clitic-conjunction *que*. Let us assume that this lexeme has just the syntactic properties of an ordinary conjunction in Latin, but that it also is subject to an independent morphological requirement to the effect that it attaches as a suffix to a fully inflected word. Note that the LC and the CIC cannot simultaneously be maintained in a case like this. If *-que* attaches as a suffix to the preceding word, in conformity with the LC, then there is a violation of the CIC, since the phrase that *-que* is in syntactic construction with follows it. If, on the other hand, *-que* attaches to the word that follows it, the CIC is met, but the LC is violated since *-que*, a suffix, would follow the first word of its co-phrase.

In this case, the clitic attaches to the first word of the phrase the follows it, violating the LC minimally, but satisfying the CIC. Thus for a phrase such as (58), we would have the dual tree given in (59).

(58)   boni pueri pulchraeque puellae

(59)

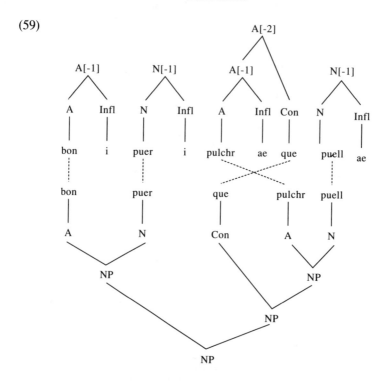

Latin *-que* is added to a peripheral word of its syntactic complement. So is the French clitic article in (52), which additionally occurs in the same order in both morphology and syntax. But it is not always the case that clitics conform to the CIC in preference to the LC. In English auxiliary cliticization, as we have seen, the host word is in a preceding phrase, not in the VP complement of the auxiliary. In Kwakwala, case adpositions and demonstrative lexemes (among others) attach with spectacular abandon to whatever word precedes them, as in the following example drawn from S. Anderson 1984. In (61), I borrow Anderson's essentially autolexical analysis and present it in the notation of the present work, some details aside.

(60)   la-i   ax ʔed-ida ts ʔədaqa-x̣-a   ɬu ʔəlqʷ ʔi
        AUX-PRO takes-the woman-OBJ-the dishes
        'The woman takes the dishes.'

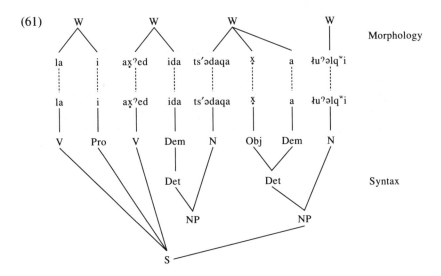

(61)

In both English and Kwakwala there is a general tendency throughout the language for leftward cliticization. (Think of examples like *doesn't*, *wanna*, *would' ya*, *lookit*, some of which will be discussed below.) I speculate that this tendency is an option that some languages exercise, though it might conflict with the requirement that a clitic occur on a word of the phrase it combines with in the syntax. Furthermore, it seems that we can say at least a little bit about the languages that display this tendency toward leftward cliticization without regard for syntactic boundaries. They will be a subset of those languages that put function words first in their phrases. Since these function words are members of closed classes (see Carlson 1983), their occurrence can be anticipated and they may be suffixed morphophonologically earlier than their syntax would call for. There is nothing like the opposite of this anticipatory cliticization in function-word-final languages, however. So far as I know, such languages never delay a function word and cliticize it, out of its own phrase, to the next word that comes along.

Thus there is an asymmetry between rightward and leftward cliticization and between cliticization inside and outside a clitic's syntactic complement. For clitics that are syntactically initial in their phrase, there is the possibility for them to attach as prefixes to the next word, or to be anticipated as suffixes to the preceding word, to which I will return below.

In the following sections, I will show how the properties of the known classes of clitics can be naturally treated by separating the syntactic and morphological properties of lexemes.

3.5.1 Simple Clitics

If the entry for a lexical item specifies it as combining syntactically with a phrase, but as morphologically bound, then according to the LC and the CIC, it will automatically have one of two behaviors: either it will precede the phrase it is in syntactic construction with and will attach as a prefix to the first word of that phrase, or it will follow its phrase in the syntax and will attach as a suffix to the last word thereof. These two situations are diagrammed in figures 3.2 and 3.3, where Cl represents the clitic. I will call lexemes with either of these behavior patterns "simple clitics."[5]

Figure 3.2

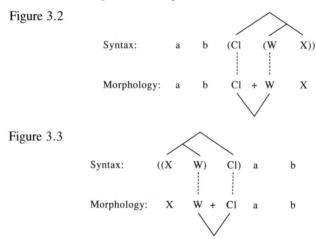

Figure 3.3

The situation diagrammed in figure 3.3 is exemplified by article and prepositional clitics in Greek, Hebrew, and Italian, and that illustrated in figure 3.4 by case, topic, and speech-act particles in many verb-final languages like Japanese and Korean. The Modern Greek definite article in the masculine and feminine accusative singular is illustrated in (62) and (63). Note that while it agrees with the head noun in gender and case, it is the first word of rest of the noun phrase that determines its phonological form:

(62)   to-filo
         the(M/ACC)-friend

(63)   tom-balyo   filo
         the(M/ACC)-old friend

(64)   tim-borta
         the(F/ACC)-door

(65)   ti-xrisa   porta
         the(F/ACC)-golden door

But besides the phrase-initial prefixes and phrase-final suffixes, there are other patterns that are frequently encountered. There are, for example, anticipatory clitics such as English auxiliaries, and Kwakwala and Yagua (Payne 1986) determiners, and second-position clitics such as Latin and Eskimo conjunctive particles. A class of penultimate position clitics has also been reported, one example of which will be discussed below.

3.5.2 Anticipatory Clitics

Anticipatory clitics often show agreement with what follows, rather than with what they are attached to, or determine characteristics of the phrase they precede rather than the phrase they are phonologically associated with. The phrases that follow them are sometimes not phrases that would otherwise occur in similar positions in the language. For all of these reasons, they are properly handled as phrase-initial function words in the syntax that just happen to be attached morphologically to the word that precedes them.

In Yagua, for example, as in Kwakwala, determiners occur as suffixes on the word that immediately precedes the noun phrase, whatever that happens to be, as examples (66) and (67) from Payne 1986 show. Furthermore, as these examples also show, the clitics agree with the N̄ that follows them in animacy and number.

(66)   Sa-sạạy Alchico-níí Rospita-rà   pạ́ạ.
        3s-give Alchico-3s Rospita-INAN bread
        'Alchico gives Rospita the bread.'

(67)   Sa-sạạy Alchico-rà   pạ́ạ-níí Rospita.
        3s-give Alchico-INAN bread-3s Rospita
        'Alchico gives Rospita the bread.'

There seems to be little doubt then, that anticipatory clitics are represented as units of the syntax that occur in the same linear order in both the morphological and syntactic strings. Anticipatory clitics thus follow the LC as it applies to the two ordered representations of morphology and syntax, but fail to conform to the CIC. As opposed to simple clitics, whose attachment is predictable both as to morphological host and as to whether they will be prefixes or suffixes, anticipatory clitics are somewhat special and require a richer lexical specification to get their properties right.

3.5.3 Second-Position Clitics

There are clitics with very much the same grammatical behavior as anticipatory or simple clitics, but which occur as suffixes to the first word of the phrase that they are syntactically associated with. We have seen one example of this in the form of the Latin conjunction -que. Another example is found in

Amharic, which has clitic determiners that agree with the head noun in gender but attach as suffixes to the first word of the NP that they determine (Gene Gragg, p.c.).

(68)   bet-u
        house(M)-DET/M

(69)   tillik'-u   bet
        big-DET/M house(M)

(70)   tillik'-u   k'äyy bet
        big-DET/M red house(M)

The clitic definite articles of Amharic thus contrast minimally with the Greek or Yagua articles. All of these are syntactically initial in their phrases. The Greek articles conform to both the LC and the CIC; the Yagua articles conform to the LC but violate the CIC; and the Amharic articles conform to the CIC but violate the LC.

3.5.4 The Eight-Fold Way

The properties uncovered so far can be summarized in a compact theory of clitics in the present framework:

(71)   If a lexeme is in construction with a phrase in the syntax and is an
        affix in the morphology, then
        a. it is an affix to an inflected word (i.e., it bears the morphological
           rule feature [M3]), and
        b. it may violate at most one of the homomorphism conditions (51)
           and (53).

When I say that a lexeme has a certain property in a certain module, what I mean is that the component of its lexical entry relevant to that module has the stated property. Thus the English auxiliary clitic *'d*, whose lexical entry is given in (23) above, can be said to combine with a VP in the syntax, or to combine with an inflected word in the morphology.

Condition (71b) amounts to a three-valued dimension of variability that has to do with the degree of deviance from perfect congruence between the syntactic and morphological trees: a lexeme may violate neither homomorphism constraint, or either one, but not both. There are two other dimensions of variation, both of them two-valued, and both quite independent of the phenomenon of cliticization per se. They are simply the independent syntactic and morphological properties implied by the definition above. If a lexeme is in syntactic construction with a phrase, it must either occur before that phrase, or after it, in a phrase-structure grammar. Since the morphological component is also assumed to be a phrase-structure grammar, affixal lexemes will be either prefixes or suffixes.

This would seem to give a twelve-way classification of clitics in a space with two two-valued dimensions and one three-valued dimension. Of these twelve points in morphosyntactic space, however, four are actually logically impossible. There are only two consistent types of simple clitics, i.e., those that violate neither homomorphism constraint. Because they occur in the same linear sequence and in the same maximal phrase in both representations, they are either prefixes, if phrase initial, or suffixes, if phrase final. A clitic cannot be simple, phrase initial and suffixal, or simple, phrase final and prefixal.

There are also only two types of clitics that violate the CIC, rather than four, the other two types necessarily violating the LC as well, a behavior that is forbidden by (71). Consider a hypothetical clitic that is phrase-initial in the syntax, a prefix in the morphology, and violates the CIC. Since it begins its phrase and violates the CIC, it will have to combine with the preceding word. But if it is a prefix to that word, it will also violate the LC, contradicting the theory of clitics embodied in (71). The same reasoning makes it impossible for there to be phrase final syntactic items that attach morphologically as suffixes in such a way as to violate the CIC but not the LC.

These observations are summarized in figure 3.4, where the crossed-out cells of the matrix indicate an impossible combination of values. In the cells representing possible clitics, the upper line represents the syntactic bracketing and order, and the lower line the morphological bracketing and order.

Figure 3.4

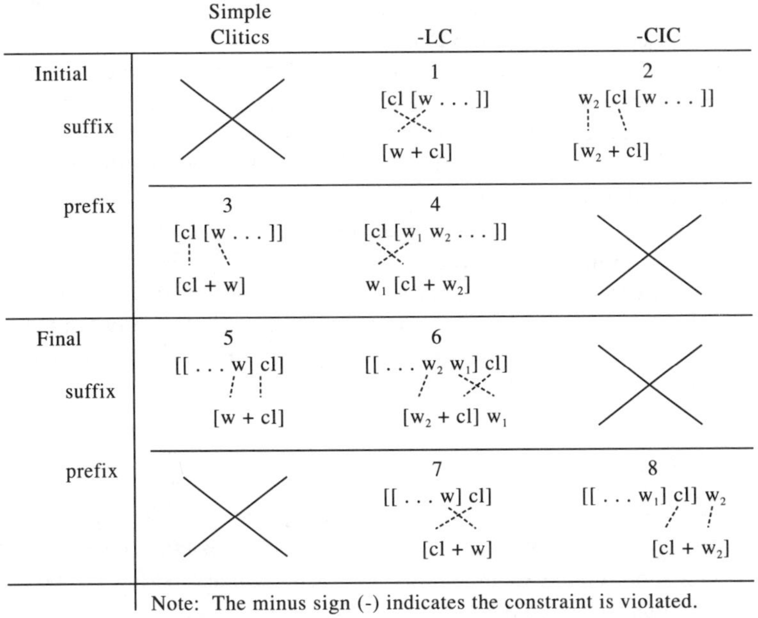

Note: The minus sign (-) indicates the constraint is violated.

The various determiner clitics discussed so far would have lexical entries such as the following:

(72)   *ton* (Modern Greek):
        syntax = [$_{NP[ACC]}$[____N̄[MASC]]
        morphology = [$_w$____W]   (M3)

(73)   *nii* (Yagua):
        syntax = [$_{NP}$[____N̄[3SG, ANIM]]]
        morphology = [$_w$W____]   (M3)
        interface = −CIC

(74)   *u* (Amharic):
        syntax = [$_{NP}$[____N̄[MASC]]]
        morphology = [$_w$W____]   (M3)
        interface = −LC

The Greek determiner can have the simple lexical form it does because the two principles of congruence suffice to predict both the morphological attachment and the word to which it will attach. Since its lexical form mentions nothing to the contrary, both the CIC and LC will hold. In virtue of the former it will have to attach to a word that follows it, since that is where its syntactic sister lies, and in virtue of the latter, it will have to be a prefix to the word that immediately follows it. No mention needs to be made of its prefixal status. The other two types that appear above have slightly more complicated entries, but still have some of their properties determined not directly, but indirectly through the agency of the LC and CIC.

In specifying the more complex behavior of these latter two clitics, I have chosen simply to mention which of the two interface conditions they fail to meet. In conjunction with the stipulated morphological fact of their being suffixes, their distribution is correctly predicted. The Yagua clitic will attach to the previous word because it is a phrase-initial suffix constrained by the LC, and the Amharic clitic will attach to the following word because it is a phrase-initial suffix constrained by the CIC. This method of stipulation, however, ignores the observation that some head-initial languages tend generally toward leftward cliticization. If this is a property of Yagua itself, and not of the lexeme in question, and if this property is lacking in Amharic, then the interface statement in (73) and (74) might well be suppressible.

3.5.5 Three Missing Types

It is easy to find examples of only two of the remaining five logically possible clitics in figure 3.5. Besides the simple, initial clitics like the Greek example, the anticipatory clitic exemplified by the Yagua article, and the second position clitic that we see in the Amharic suffix -*u*, I have only been able to find convincing cases of simple final clitics (class 5 of figure 3.5) and penultimate word suffixes (class 6 of figure 3.5). These two extant types are represented by an illuminating phenomenon in Tongan[6] and by another example from Modern Greek.

As described in Poser 1985, Tongan regularly places stress on the syllable containing the second vowel mora from the end of a word. The only regular exception is presented by definite NPs, where the last syllable is always stressed.

(75)   *fakatáha* 'meeting'

(76)   *he fakatahá* 'the meeting'

(77)   *fakatáha láhi* 'big meeting'

(78)   *he fakatáha lahí* 'the big meeting'

This stress shift can be neatly handled by postulating a word-final morpheme consisting of an abstract vowel that appears on the last word of any definite NP. It is, in other words, a suffix to the final word of a phrase, i.e., a simple, final clitic. (See chapter 5, section 1.3 for a fuller discussion.)

Modern Greek cliticizes not only articles, but also possessive pronouns to words of the NP they are found in. The clitic may appear on the last word of the NP (the head noun), but it may also appear as a suffix to the preceding word.[7]

(79)   o-filos-mu
        the-friend-my

(80)   o-kalos-mu filos/o-kalos filos-mu
        the-dear-my friend

(81)   o-kalos   palyos-mu filos/o-kalos palyos filos-mu
        the-dearest old-my   friend

(82)   *o-kalos-mu palyos filos

I have not seen any good examples of the remaining types, namely phrase-final clitics that are prefixes to the following word; phrase-final clitics that are prefixes to the preceding word; and phrase-initial clitics that are prefixes to the second word of its phrase. There is a simple generalization that binds these three missing types together—they are all prefixes and they violate one or the other of the homomorphism constraints. We may state this observation as a further interface constraint in the present framework:[8]

(83)   A lexeme that violates a homomorphism constraint is a suffix.

That the Greek possessive clitic illustrated in (79)–(82) is not an example of a final word prefix is easily shown. Modern Greek does not allow stress more than three syllables from the end of a word. When the unstressed clitic *-mu* occurs on a word like *kalíteros* 'dearest', that already has stress that far from the end, the stress is shifted to the penult. Thus in the following example it is clear that *-mu* is a suffix to the second-to-last word, not a prefix to the final word:

(84)   o-kaliterós-mu   filos
         'the-dearest-my friend'

In her otherwise convincing discussion of clitic types, Klavans offers three examples that are purported to be examples of these three prefixal, mismatched clitic types. All three examples are flawed. She observes, for example, that ordinarily proclitic prepositions and the negative *ou* in Classical Greek can sometimes appear sentence finally. Ordinarily they are atonic, but sentence finally they bear stress.

(85)   ou lúei
         'He does not loose.'

(86)   pós gár óu
         'For why not?'

In the latter example, she suggests that in *ou* we have a delayed clitic, but it is very difficult to accept these facts as indicating that. First of all, we would have to believe that this element is cliticized TO A WORD OF THE NEXT SENTENCE, and second, we have to neglect the fact that it is stressed, usually an indication of independent word status.

Klavens's examples of the remaining two prefixal types are from Proto-Indo-European (PIE) and from a stage in the development of Tepecano that she reconstructs. That is probably as much as one needs to say about these examples, but in the case of the PIE example, even the reconstruction (taken from P. Anderson 1979) does not seem to exemplify the missing type she claims it does.

Assuming Anderson's reconstruction of PIE syntax according to which preverbs occurred either as separate words before the verb, or as proclitics to a stressed verb, Klavens argues, somewhat tentatively, that this is an example of what in my terms would be a phrase-final clitic prefixed to the last word of the phrase. The flaw, of course, is that as a free word, the preverb does not occur phrase finally at all, but immediately before the verb. Thus the clitic is clearly in syntactic construction with the verb alone, and precedes it. It is, in other words, a simple, initial clitic.

3.6 Klavans's Theory of Clitics

There are several theories of clitics in the current literature (S. Anderson 1987; Kaisse 1985; Marantz 1988; Zwicky 1977, 1985, to name a few), but the most carefully worked out is that of Judith Klavans. In her dissertation (1980) and in some subsequent papers (1983, 1985), she develops an intriguing and empirically rather successful view of the behavior of clitics that in some respects resembles the one offered here. Her theory predicts, for example, the existence of eight different classes of clitics, in fact exactly the same eight that are logically possible under the treatment presented in the previous section. What I want to show here is that much of what is axiomatic in Klavans's theory in fact follows from more basic facts when an autolexical view is adopted.

In its most refined version, Klavans's theory postulates that the behavior of clitics is to be understood in terms of the fixing of three independent binary parameters, called Dominance, Precedence, and Phonological Liaison, all three of which are specific to the handling of clitics.

3.6.1 The Dominance Parameter

In Klavans's words (1985, 97), Dominance "expresses the possibility that a clitic attaches to the initial or final constituent dominated by a specified phrase." It should be obvious how this variability arises spontaneously in the theory of autolexical syntax: normal clitics have independent syntax. In a phrase-structure grammar, this means that they will either precede or follow the phrase with which they are syntactically associated. The Linearity Constraint requires that they will attach to a neighboring word and if that word is in the syntactic complement of the clitic (i.e., if it is in the specified phrase mentioned by Klavans), then it will have to be either initial or final in that phrase. If, on the other hand, the clitic violates the CIC, and joins a word that is not a descendant of its syntactic co-phrase, then it will again have to be a neighboring word which will be either an initial or final word of some other constituent. Thus the effect of this "parameter" is achieved without having to stipulate it as part of a special theory of clitics.

Whereas Klavans's Dominance parameter is freely fixable, the range of variation is limited by other facts of a language system under the autolexical theory. If there is independent evidence concerning the syntactic position of the element that shows up as a clitic, then that should bear on the question of which periphery it winds up on. Thus it is no accident under the autolexical theory that Latin *que* is specified as initial for Klavans's Dominance parameter. It is a conjunction, and conjunctions *precede* the phrases they are associated with in Latin. Likewise, it is not surprising that the French clitic article occurs on the first word of the $\bar{N}$ that it combines with syntactically, for it is a determiner, and determiners in French are initial in NP.

Sometimes, of course, the position of a clitic cannot be shown on independent grounds to match its syntax because there are no other elements in the language with syntax that we can presume to be similar. The conjunctive clitics of Eskimo work exactly like the Latin clitic conjunction, showing up as suffixes to the first word of the conjunct they introduce:

(87) Kaalip   ataataa   Maaliallu   anaanaa
      Kaali-p   ataata-a   Maalia-p-lu   anaana-a
      Karl-ERG father-3s Maalia-ERG-and mother-3s
      'Karl's father and Maalia's mother'

But there are no independent conjunctions per se in West Greenlandic and most varieties of Eskimo. There are adverbs with conjunction-like meanings, as in (88), and these do indeed occur initially in the phrase they introduce, but we may well doubt that their distribution is necessarily the same as that of the true clitic conjunctions.

(88) Kaalip   ataataa   aamma Maaliap   anaanaa
      Kaali-p   ataata-a   aamma Maalia-p   anaana-a
      Karl-ERG father-3s also   Maalia-ERG mother-3s
      'Karl's father as well as Maalia's mother'

Thus while there is nothing stopping us from assigning a clitic such as *-lu* in (87) a syntactic position such that Klavans's Dominance parameter automatically comes out right (initial, in this case), there is also not much in the way of positive argument for doing so.

Even if the position of the clitic within its host phrase is at odds with what would be expected on the basis of the syntax of apparently similar free syntactic items, the autolexical theory is capable of handling the facts, but only by straining to do so. Consider a language that obligatorily cliticizes pronominal elements to some constituent. Let us further imagine that their position is not the one that would be predicted from the position of full NP arguments. This is the situation we find for Romance clitics. We could describe such a language in autolexical terms by positing distinct syntax for pronominal arguments and for full NP arguments. Languages sometimes do, after all, position their pronouns differently from their full NPs (cf. German).

So the autolexical theory does not absolutely demand that Klavans's first parameter of cliticization be independently fixable on the basis of external syntax, but it does lead to such a correlation as the default expectation. In the best case, nothing new needs to be said about a clitic in the grammar of a specific language. Which word it attaches to will simply be a function of the syntax that it would have to be assigned anyway. In the worst case, a special syntactic rule would have to be postulated, a rule that cannot be independently shown to characterize the syntax of the language. In Romance languages, for example, a special LP rule ordering pronominal elements in the syntax immediately before the finite verb would need to be added to the grammar. In either case, though, there is no need for an independent binary parameter that functions only to distribute clitics.

3.6.2 The Phonological Liaison Parameter

While Klavans's first parameter of cliticization turns out to correspond to the independent syntactic characterization of an autolexical element in the theory I am investigating, her third parameter, Phonological Liaison (which I consider out of order for the purposes of exposition), is very close to being the same thing as the independent specification of the morphological properties of such a lexeme. As she describes it (Klavans 1985, 98), this third parameter "gives the direction of phonological attachment. . . . [T]he values are binary . . . PROCLITIC/ENCLITIC." Since, by assumption, clitics are autolexical elements with independent syntactic and morphological reality, the autolexical theory will have to specify whether an affixal clitic is morphologically a prefix or a suffix, thus making otiose any special statement to this effect.

But again there are differences between Klavans's special parameters and the reduction of them to ordinary principles of syntax and morphology. Here too we see that the autolexical view leads to constraining expectations concerning the realization of the parameter, whereas the highly phenomenon-particular parameters do not. For example, if the choice between suffixation and prefixation is not free in the morphology of a language, but covaries with other facts of the language, then we should expect that clitics would covary in the same way. A very simple but telling kind of case is that of a language with a strong preference for suffixation over prefixation, or vice versa. Eskimo is such a language. All dialects are exclusively suffixing in the productive parts of their highly developed derivational and inflectional systems, and all of them have only enclitics.

As pointed out in Greenberg 1957, there is a general preference in natural languages for suffixing over prefixing. Languages that are exclusively prefixing are rare. But if such can be found, the prediction from an autolexical theory of clitics is that this tendency will manifest itself without regard to the distinction between derivational, inflectional, and clitic morphology. Similarly, this theory predicts that if the choice between prefixation and suffixation is dependent on other facts of the language, say the part of speech of the word, then whether clitics are prefixes (proclitics) or suffixes (enclitics) will be predictable, and not a matter of free choice, as it is in Klavans's theory.

A very big difference between the postulation of a binary proclitic/enclitic parameter and the reduction of this aspect of the behavior of clitics to general principles of morphology is that the former approach strictly limits (albeit by stipulation) the possible morphological realization of clitics to concatenative morphology, and even there excluding the possibility of clitic infixes, or "endoclitics," as Klavans points out. The unadorned autolexical theory does not impose this restriction, though it could be made to do so by brute force. It is thus weaker then Klavans's theory to a certain extent, but its permissiveness, as I shall show in chapter 5, is warranted by the facts.

3.6.3 The Precedence Parameter

This binary parameter, with values "before" and "after," determines whether a clitic is positioned to the left or the right of the initial constituent of the phrase that is the "domain" of cliticization in Klavans's theory and the syntactic co-phrase in mine. It has no direct analog in the autolexical theory, its effect arising from the interaction of the two congruity constraints and the stipulation that a lexeme can violate at most one of them. An important difference, again, is that the autolexical theory makes use of features of the grammar that are independently needed, whereas Klavans's theory, with its separate subsystem for clitics, postulates an otherwise unneeded mechanism.

In any case, though the mechanisms are quite different, Klavans's three-parameter system and the autolexical system predict exactly the same eight classes of possible clitic types. The chart below presents these eight types arranged according to Klavans's three parameters:

Figure 3.5

	After	Before
INITIAL Enclitic	$[Cl [W \ldots]]$ $[W + Cl]$	$W^2[Cl [W_1 \ldots]]$ $[W^2 + Cl]$
Proclitic	$[Cl [W_1 W_2 \ldots]]$ $W_1 [Cl + W_2]$	$[Cl [W \ldots]]$ $[Cl + W]$
FINAL Enclitic	$[[\ldots W] CL]$ $[W + Cl]$	$[[\ldots W_2 W_1] Cl]$ $[W_2 + Cl] W_1$
Proclitic	$[[\ldots W_1] Cl] W_2$ $[Cl + W_2]$	$[[\ldots W] Cl]$ $[Cl + W]$

A final difference between Klavans's three-parameter theory and the autolexical one concerns the treatment of the three vanishingly rare clitic types. The parametric values of these missing types are:

1. Initial, After, Proclitic
2. Final, After, Proclitic
3. Final, Before, Proclitic

Aside from the fact that all of them are proclitics, it is difficult to see that they constitute a natural class on Klavans's analysis, let alone that this theory suggests why they should be so hard to find. On the autolexical view, however, these three types are precisely those prefixal clitics that violate one or the other of the interface constraints. They can be expected to be rare because of their having two strikes against them: that they are prefixes, is one; and that their positions in syntax are at odds with their positions in morphology is the second.

4

Incorporation

4.1 Historical Background

For purposes of the present chapter, I will use the term "incorporation" to refer to phenomena in natural languages (other than cliticization as described in chapter 3), where a proper subpart of a word can be shown to have the function of a formative, i.e., an atomic element, in the syntax. The details of the morphological joining are immaterial to my definition. The incorporated item may be a stem, either compounded with another stem or used as a base for affixation. It may be an affix or even a symbolic process, and may, in either case, be classified as derivational morphology or as inflectional morphology.

In chapter 6, I will broaden the notion of incorporation to include examples of discrepancies between semantic organization and either morphological or syntactic structure, but for now my attention will be restricted to cases where it is clear that part of a morphological word is to be represented as a formative in syntax. In the absence of positive syntactic arguments to the contrary, I will assume that pieces of words are not to count as independent elements of the syntax. By itself, no purely semantic principle, such as Baker's 1988 Uniformity of Theta Assignment Hypothesis, will be taken as requiring an analysis in terms of noncoincident morphosyntactic bracketing, and thus the range of phenomena that will be discussed in this chapter will be considerably narrower than that of those phenomena labeled incorporation in Baker 1988.

By far the most discussed putative instance of nonclitic interpenetration of morphology and syntax is noun incorporation, so called because a noun stem representing a syntactic argument of a verb (typically the object) is found as a part of the morphological verb. This phenomenon is frequently encountered in North American languages, but it is not found either universally or exclusively there. Noun incorporation was introduced into the modern literature as evidence against the strict lexicalist hypothesis in work by Rischel (1971, 1972) and myself (Sadock 1980). In those languages where it has a clearly syntactic face, noun incorporation offers excellent evidence against the hierarchical model of the relation between morphology and syntax, and it was primarily as an attempt to handle this striking phenomenon that I originally suggested the model of autolexical syntax.

It has recently been reasserted, however, that noun incorporation is, after all, a strictly morphological process with no important syntactic ramifications (Mithun 1984; Hopper and Thompson 1984; Di Sciullo and Williams 1987; and most recently Rosen 1989), thus resurrecting a debate that took place early in this century. The term "incorporation" was first employed by Humboldt ([1836] 1988) who applied it to Nahuatl examples like *ni-naca-qua* 'I-meat-eat'. Humboldt's argument was the distinctly nonrelativistic one that languages like Nahuatl confuse syntax and morphology and are thus less perfect than those like Classical Greek or Sanscrit that clearly separate the two.

> [T]he METHOD OF INFLECTION in all its completeness, . . . alone imparts true inner fixity to the word for both mind and ear, and likewise separates with certainty the parts of the sentence, in keeping with the necessary ordering of thought. . . . Compared with the INCORPORATIVE PROCEDURE, and that of loose ADDITION without true word unity, the METHOD OF INFLECTION appears as a principle of genius, born of a true intuition of language. (Humboldt [1836] 1988, 145)

In apparent reaction to the by-then unpopular glottocentricity of the Humboldtian view, Kroeber (1911) attempted to ban the notion on general principles:

> In short, the term "incorporation" is a delusion, whether applied to pronoun or to noun. It must be relegated to the same category as other antiquated catch-words such as "agglutination," which have originated in the assumption that the languages of so-called uncivilized people must contain certain features of a kind totally different from those characteristic of Europeans—and incidentally features of an inferior order,—and which have found their chief vogue and employment not among serious painstaking students of language but among doctrinaires, compilers, and those false popularizers who think to diffuse knowledge by giving a phrase instead of an idea. (Pp. 582–83)

Kroeber (1909) offered the following definition of noun incorporation, and then proceeded to argue that the phenomenon did not (indeed, could not) exist:

> Noun incorporation is the combination into one word of the noun object of the verb and the verb functioning as the predicate of the sentence. It is essential that the resultant of incorporation is a single word, else the process is without limit and all syntactical relation may be construed as incorporation. (P. 37)

Note that Kroeber's straw-man definition is essentially antilexicalist; it assumes (as I do) that the phenomenon of incorporation is definitionally one that straddles the border between syntax and morphology. Soon after Kroeber published the brief paper from which the above passage is quoted, Sapir (1911) criticized him precisely because of the transmodular nature of his definition. Displaying a strikingly modern prejudice, Sapir argued that general considerations required that the definition of noun incorporation be either morphological, or syntactosemantic, but not both at the same time.

> Examining this definition, we find that two things are required—a noun must combine with the verb-predicate into a word-unit, and the noun so combined must function as the object of the verb. The first requirement is morphologic in character, the second purely syntactic; in other words, the first calls for a certain type of word formation, while the second demands that a particular logical relation subsist between the two independent elements that enter into this word formation. Without denying the abstract right to set up such a definition, it would seem that the combining of a morphologic requirement with an independent syntactic one yields, on general principles, a definition of too narrow a scope for the discussion of as fundamental a problem as noun incorporation is felt to be. Noun incorporation is primarily either a morphologic or syntactic process; the attempt to put it under two rubrics at the same time necessarily leads to a certain amount of artificiality of treatment. (P. 255)

In denying that it was useful to talk directly about the "logical" (read: syntactic) function of pieces of words, Sapir was the first lexicalist. His own proposed definition of noun incorporation was purely morphological:

> It is this process of compounding a noun stem with a verb that it is here proposed to call noun incorporation, no matter what the syntactic function of the noun logically is. The type of verb, "to song-write," that Dr. Kroeber alone regards as illustrative of noun incorporation, is best considered a particular class of the more general type of noun-verb compound verb. (P. 257)

Since Sapir took the morphological means (compounding) by which the nominal and verbal element are joined as the criterion for noun incorporation, he was able to argue that it was well attested in American languages. In fact he argued that it exists covertly in what Bloomfield (1933) was to call synthetic compounds (Roeper and Siegel's (1978) verbal compounds), like *man-eater*. These Sapir took to be agentive nominals derived from fictitious compound verbs such as **man-eat*, itself an example of noun incorporation.

This entirely morphological definition of noun incorporation as compounding made Sapir unable to count the Eskimo phenomenon that now goes by that name as a genuine example of the type, since in Eskimo the morphological facts are quite different. There we find straightforwardly derivational means being used to derive verb stems from noun stems. In fact, the Eskimo languages have no (original) compounding of any kind.

> Eskimo, a language particularly rich in suffixes that verbify nouns, has been termed polysynthetic, but has not been employed by serious students as a source of examples of noun incorporation. (P. 254)

Though Sapir spoke of the "syntactic function" of the incorporated noun, his actual idea was that a logical relation that could be expressed syntactically can also be expressed morphologically. The syntax is "sacrificed" in favor of the morphology, and only the logical relation remains. This is very nearly the same idea that recent work attempts to formalize in terms of theta-role assignment either in the syntax, or in the morphology, but not both (Rosen 1989).

Sapir won his theoretical point, and Kroeber quickly and completely capitulated (Kroeber 1911); noun incorporation was to be understood as nothing other than the morphological compounding of a noun with a verb. Nevertheless, throughout his article, Sapir seems to equivocate, speaking as if it is a necessary feature of noun incorporation that the equivalent of SOME syntactic relation is expressed. The last footnote in his article is telling; it reads:

> Since this was written (June, 1910) Mr. J. P. Harrington [Harrington 1910] has published sketches of two Tanoan dialects, Tiwa and Tewa. In Tiwa both direct and indirect objects may be incorporated in the verb complex, coming between the pronominal prefix and the verb stem; such incorporation is obligatory for singular direct objects. (P. 282)

The direct object relation is syntactic. It is therefore difficult to see how it makes any sense to say that the incorporation of a certain syntactic relation is obligatory in a theory in which incorporation is purely morphological. It is also hard to understand how Sapir could reconcile his claim that the logical relation of the incorporated element is of no consequence with the demonstration that a certain syntactic function (that of direct object) is treated specially. The explanation for this apparent inconsistency between Sapir's methodological pronouncements and his descriptive behavior lies, I believe, in the fact that noun incorporation in American languages like Tiwa often is of such a character as to demand a description that is simultaneously morphological and syntactic, theoretical prejudices to the contrary notwithstanding. The closing sentence of Sapir's important article in fact reveals that this really had been his opinion all along. Note that here he even relaxes the erstwhile morphological sine qua non, admitting that derivation can be an instance of the "process" (of noun incorporation).

The characteristic fact about the process is that certain syntactic relations are expressed by what in varying degrees may be called composition or derivation. (Sapir 1911, 282)

It is just this point that I tried to make in Sadock 1980 concerning noun
incorporation in West Greenlandic. Though Greenlandic noun incorporation
and Tiwa noun incorporation are morphologically dissimilar processes, the
former derivational and the latter compositional, their transmodular nature
binds them together and makes them different in kind from run-of-the-mill
compounding, or run-of-the-mill derivation, where indeed, syntax is irrelevant. In an English form like *pan-fry*, for example, we have the same sort of
morphological style that we find in Tiwa incorporation, and in the formation
of denominal verbs like Sapir's neologism *verbify* we find the same morphological relation as in Eskimo incorporation. But we would not be tempted to
call either of these English formations "incorporation," for neither has anything like the syntactic ramifications that noun incorporation in Tiwa or
Greenlandic has, as we shall see.

Since a great deal more is known about the details of incorporation than was
the case eighty years ago, I suggest that we reopen the Kroeber-Sapir debate. I
believe it ought to be called a draw: Kroeber was right at the outset in providing a transmodular definition of noun incorporation, but wrong in claiming
that it did not exist; Sapir was correct in his contention that noun incorporation
is a fact of language, and also that various syntactic relations can be involved,
but wrong in his claim that it can be understood in purely morphological
terms.

4.2 The Nature of Noun Incorporation

We should not be at all surprised to find that in some particular languages
some word-building process displays all of the characteristics that we have
come to expect of lexical relationships: incomplete productivity, phonological
and semantic unpredictability, syntactic identity with underived forms, and
discourse opacity to the word-internal morphemes. We should not even be
surprised if these traits show up in noun incorporation, a word-building process that would seem to be amenable to a syntactic treatment, if any is; for the
null hypothesis clearly ought to be that any individual word-building process
does not interact with the syntax.

In the past few years several authors have asserted that noun incorporation
(and presumably then, all nonclitic morphological constructs) are properly
treated without reference to syntax cf. Mithun 1984; Di Sciullo and Williams
1987; Rosen 1989). The copious citation of facts from various languages compelling a lexical treatment for noun incorporation IN THOSE LANGUAGES
simply demonstrates that such a treatment is correct FOR THOSE LANGUAGES.

But the crucial issue for linguistic theory is whether there are ANY cases of noun incorporation that must be viewed as simultaneously morphological and syntactic. A single well-documented example will make the positive case, whereas the negative case can never be proved absolutely. It appears to me that there are languages, in particular Eskimo, the very same Tiwa mentioned by Sapir in 1911, and probably some South Munda languages such as Gta?, that present compelling evidence that their particular version of noun incorporation has a syntactic face. The ramifications of such a demonstration are considerable, for once the syntactic reality of some morphological entity is recognized and a constrained theory of its properties is set up, the door is open to the treatment in similar terms of other sorts of morphological operations, where the recognition of the syntactic nature of the phenomenon is not necessary but merely highly desirable from a descriptive point of view.

Following Sapir's lead, it might be assumed, since the morphological technique for incorporating noun stems in Eskimo is derivational rather than compositional, that the Eskimo morphological process called noun incorporation is just not relevant to the debate. But we must not lose sight of the larger issue—whether morphology is always irrelevant to syntax or not. The claim that internal morphology never has any syntactic value would be falsified by derivational incorporation, such as is found in Eskimo, every bit as easily as by an example of the compositional type. If anything, we should be more surprised to find syntactic interactivity in straightforward cross-categorial derivation than in compounding, since compounding is a morphological phenomenon that prima facie seems to straddle the border between two major components of grammar. At any rate, Southern Tiwa and Munda incorporate by compounding and still display characteristics that compel a transmodular analysis.

In what follows I will show that in some languages there are properties of incorporating structures that are inconsistent with a purely morphological view of the phenomenon, *pace* those who have claimed that such properties never exist. I will show, in other words, that there are languages where the syntactic relevance of noun incorporation cannot be denied.

4.2.1 Productivity

There are frozen syntactic constructions like *battle royal*, or *all of a sudden* that are usable with only a limited range of lexically specified words, but by and large, syntax is productive. A syntactic construction ordinarily has a form and a meaning that are entirely predictable on the basis of the form and the meaning of its elements and the manner in which they are joined. The only limits on whether some particular set of instantiations of the elements of a syntactic construction can be so combined are usually semantic and/or pragmatic.

However, as Chomsky (1970) pointed out, this stands in striking contrast to the situation in morphology, where there are often restrictions of an arbitrary sort, having nothing to do with meaning or import, making only certain combinations possible. There are frequently irregularities of form that arise when morphological elements are joined, and the meaning of the result often follows no general rule. Complex morphological forms are, in other words, frequently listed rather than constructed.

In her survey of noun incorporation, Mithun asserts that "N[oun] I[ncorporation] may be highly productive, but it is not free in the sense that syntactic operations can be" (1984, 889). She offers anecdotal evidence supporting the claim that in Mohawk, "speakers know not only whether a derivationally complex word is possible, but also whether they have heard it before. . . . They have no trouble understanding the new words, but they recognize that they are not part of their own (vast) lexicon" (p. 889). Thus according to Mithun, speakers of Mohawk (Greenlandic, Tiwa, etc.) must have much larger vocabularies than we do. Strangely, these very same languages are burdened with productive derivational processes that could serve to reduce the memorized vocabulary, but according to Mithun, this richness has just the opposite effect. One would think that such productivity would be made up for by a savings in storage space, rather than a requirement for more.

My own experience with a polysynthetic language, West Greenlandic, tells me that Mithun's claim is exaggerated. A great many fully transparent derivational forms are indeed lexicalized, bringing the lexicon up to roughly the same level as what we find in a less synthetic language (which after all will contain a relatively larger number of lexicalized phrases), but speakers do not have perfect memories with regard to what they have heard. The mathematical possibilities make it incredible that speakers could know every productive combination they have heard. There are approximately one hundred productive denominal verb-forming affixes in West Greenlandic. If there are (conservatively) five thousand lexical nouns in the language, there are half a million simple verbs formed from nouns. But there are about fifty fully productive noun-modifying suffixes in the language, and any of the nouns so formed can be incorporated. With just these two affix classes, then, there are twenty-five million possible forms. Taking into account the fact that verbs are also modifiable with the aid of approximately one hundred productive derivational suffixes we now have two and a half BILLION forms of a very common kind, involving only three derivational processes.

The fact is, though, that there are infinitely many possible forms involving noun incorporation, since verbs can be nominalized, and the resulting noun incorporated. Examples such as the following, demonstrating iterated incorporation, are by no means uncommon in spoken or written West Greenlandic.

(1)   Apeqqutissa-qar-to-qar-poq
        question-have-NOM-have-INDIC/3s
        'There is someone with a question.'

The few truly productive morphological processes of English have much the same quality. Productive noun-noun compounding, for example, has yielded a huge number of transparent but lexicalized forms. From the realm of computer jargon, where such forms abound, there are examples like *disk drive*, *printer port*, *database management*, *word processor*, etc., etc. These are all part of my vocabulary and I know that I have heard them before. But what about *display shape*, *color flashing*, *printer resources*, *network chip set*, *non–von Neumann single-chip image processor*, *bar-code-reader port*, and *1-bit processor elements*, all of which (among others) I found on a single page of *Byte* (10, no. 1 [1985]: 9)? I have no idea whether I have heard any of these terms before, and even though I am writing them down and thinking about them, I seriously doubt if any is worth committing to memory.

The extreme of productivity is obligatoriness. Mithun (1984) therefore found it important to assert that noun incorporation never has this quality:

> [A]ll languages which exhibit such morphological structures [as noun incorporation] also have syntactic paraphrases. . . . The fact that productive morphological constructions of this type never exist in a language without syntactic analogs indicates that the morphologization itself must be functional. A comparison of the process across languages reveals that, in fact, speakers always incorporate for a purpose. (Pp. 847–48)

However it is clearly untrue that the productivity of morphology is always unlike that of syntax, as is shown by the fact that some morphology in some languages is the only means, or the only normal means, available for the expression of certain notions. In a great many languages, sentential negation can only be expressed by means of a verbal affix, for example. If some morphological processes are the obligatory means for the expression of certain concepts, why should noun incorporation be any different?

In fact, as was noted above, Harrington (1910) claimed obligatoriness of noun incorporation in Tiwa, a group of closely related Tanoan dialects of the American Southwest, a claim that has been recently confirmed in a revealing article by Allen, Gardiner, and Frantz (1984).

The fact of the obligatoriness of incorporation in certain languages immediately creates a problem for any theory that fails to recognize the syntactic reality of the process. It is difficult to imagine how one could even state that noun incorporation is obligatory if the morphological process is conceived of as having no connection with the syntax.

4.2.2 Referentiality

Following Postal (1969), we do not expect pieces of words to have independent referential or discourse properties and it was for this reason that I pointed out in Sadock 1980 that incorporated nominals in Greenlandic have the same kind of semantic/pragmatic status as independent nominals would be expected to have. While it is frequently the case that noun incorporation is accompanied by lack of semantic/pragmatic autonomy of the incorporated nominal (particularly where there is no indication of the syntactic independence of the nominal), it is not always so, *pace* Hopper and Thompson (1984). Those authors say, "In a number of languages, a non-referring N is bound to the stem of a V, forming a compound with the V as its head" (p. 711). And later, concerning N-N compounding, "Just as with incorporation into V's, the compounded N in such examples is non-referring; it can play no further discourse role unless it is re-introduced with full categorial status. It is insulated from reference to syntactic processes or anaphoric rules" (p. 714).

The observation that noun incorporation is more frequent when there is no independent reference to be found in the object goes back to Sapir (1911), who remarked concerning Nahuatl and Paiute:

> [I]n both languages the objective relation is more often expressed by syntactic means than by noun incorporation, the latter method being employed, it would seem, in expressing "general" or "characteristic" acts as contrasted with "particular" or "accidental" acts. (P. 267)

But it is clear that this statement was not intended to cover all cases in all languages. Sapir observed that some of the Yana examples he mentioned "seem capable of being regarded as of the 'particular' type." Indeed, his Yana texts (1910) contain examples such as the following, where an incorporated noun refers to a particular thing on a particular (though here as yet unrealized) occasion:

(2)   ba´i-rusi`   k!u´nusik!u wê´tk'iᶜiᴱ
         deer-will.hunt and.I.shall fetch.it.home
         'He will go to hunt deer, and I shall fetch it home.'
         (181, line 12; translation on 183)

In Sadock 1980, I offered two Eskimo examples of incorporated nominals that serve to introduce new topics. The examples were purposely chosen from a children's story in order to drive home the point that this is possible even in very simple, unaffected styles. So as to make it perfectly clear that this was not an aberration of the text that I chose, I offered five more examples in Sadock 1986a, which were found within the space of 223 words of connected text in a recent book of reminiscences. Here, I will provide one more, this from the fourth and fifth lines of a novella by my friend and Greenlandic consultant, Inooraq Olsen (1980). Such usages are extremely frequent in both written and spoken Greenlandic of all styles. They are, in fact part and parcel of the language.

(3)   . . . kisiannimi usi   nassata-qar-punga—
              but   in.fact baggage-have-INDIC/1s
         'but I just remembered I have some luggage—'

(4)   katersoriar-lugit   ingerlaannarlunga . . .
         collect-CONTEMP/3p I.just.go
         'I'll just go and collect them.'

Here *nassataq* 'baggage' (a count noun in West Greenlandic) is incorporated in the verb *nassataqarpunga* 'I have baggage'. Nevertheless, it is referential and specific, and introduces a discourse topic, whose reference is then picked up anaphorically in the agreement on the transitive verb *katersoriarlugit*.

Certain of the noun-incorporating affixes of West Greenlandic even allow the incorporation of definite forms, in which case, of course, there is no question of their referentiality. Two such are *-leri(voq)* 'be involved with', as in *Amaalialerivoq* 'he is very much interested in Amaalia', and *-pallap(poq)* 'to strongly resemble, behave just like,' as in *Paaviarpallappoq* 'that's just like Paavia'.

The reason that examples of incorporated nouns with high referentiality and discourse salience are so frequent in West Greenlandic is that many of the most ordinary verbs that would be used for introducing a new topic—"to have," "to get," "to make," "for there to be," etc.—occur only as denominal suffixes. Any circumlocutory method of avoiding them would carry a heavy load of Gricean implicatures stemming from the abnormality of the construction. (Cf. the discussion of the difference between *pink* and *light red* in McCawley 1978.)

Thus we should not be surprised that in Tiwa, where incorporation is sometimes grammatically obligatory, the incorporated nominal can also introduce a discourse topic. Even in the very brief Tiwa text that Harrington recorded in 1910, there is one very clear instance of this, as I pointed out in Sadock 1986a. The internal nominal is an inanimate object, an argument type that is obligatorily incorporated. (See also Allen, Gardiner and Frantz 1984 and Sadock 1985b.)

The story concerns Old She-Wolf and Old She-Deer. She-Wolf goes to where She-Deer lives and suggests to her that they live together. One day, as they are out gathering wood, old She-Wolf playfully bites Old She-Deer, who realizes that the reciprocal arrangement is fraught with danger. She tells her little ones that she might soon be killed by the wolf and warns them that if the wolf brings them some pieces of meat and if, when they roast it, it makes a sizzling sound, they should not eat it. This last part goes as follows, in Harrington's notation and gloss:

(5)   Hu xu   'ǎĭxä^n hi   ja
        So then in case perhaps hither

        'uma^{n}na^{n}m-tǔǎ-ka^{n}la^n
        them.2+INAN.she.for.you.2+-meat-brings

        n,   ma^{n}n-xa-k'ǔĭ   t^{s}iɬiɬi-m-ɬö ja-mä^n,
        when you.2-roast-put s-s-s.sound-sizzle. goes,

        'ǎĭta^n xu   ma^{n}n-na-k'al-pu^n
        in.that.case then you.2-not-eat-shall

(Here reference to the meat, introduced as an incorporated stem, is continued in terms of zero-pronominal anaphors, the normal anaphoric device for definite third-person subject and object reference (Harrington 1910). Harrington lists the root *xa* as a verb, so the reference in the next two verbs must also be to the meat.)

Thus we must conclude that there is only a weak relation in general between incorporation of nominals and loss of referentiality. In those cases where noun incorporation gives evidence of its syntactic nature, for example by being obligatory under certain circumstances, there is very little in the way of semantic bleaching. Logic decrees that it could hardly be otherwise. If the conditions that make noun incorporation unavoidable had nothing to do with the referential properties of the incorporated nominal, and incorporated nominals were always lacking in reference, the language would be unable to express certain essential things. Since in Tiwa nonhuman objects must be incorporated, then one could not say the equivalent of "I bought a shirt," where the reference is supposed to be to a specific shirt!

4.2.3 Syntax

Neither the fact that noun incorporation is sometimes as productive as syntactic phrase formation, nor the fact that it does not necessarily create referential islands is really proof of its syntactic nature. There is no reason in principle why morphological operations must be limited, unless they are always restricted to the lexicon (as a list of occurring forms), a proposition that I think no one today would subscribe to. If some morphology is fully productive, why not noun incorporation? Similarly, no theory of grammar that I am aware of automatically requires that proper parts of words have less robust semantics than whole words or phrases. Thus Postal (1969), who first described the anaphoric islandhood of words, had to add a special stipulation to his theory, which otherwise made exactly the wrong predictions.

The crucial evidence for the syntactic nature of certain varieties of noun incorporation would have to come from syntax itself. A variety of testable predictions flows from the assumption that a proper part of a word actually represents a syntactic formative, the most important of which are the following:

1. The presence of a word-internal syntactic formative should be inconsistent with the presence of an external syntactic formative in the same presumed syntactic role. For noun incorporation in particular, a word-internal noun stem that counts as, say, the direct object of the clause (or the head of the direct object) should be mutually exclusive with the presence of an external direct object (or one with an overt head N). Thus instances of noun incorporation with so-called "doubling" of the object in the form of an external NP clearly cannot be instances of syntactic noun incorporation, while those where doubling has not occurred might be, and those where doubling is impossible would seem to be.

2. The incorporation into a word of a piece of an external phrase ought to leave behind, or "strand," other possible constituents of the phrase. The stranded elements ought to have precisely the morphosyntactic form that they would have if the incorporated word were in the phrase, and to the extent that semantic organization mirrors syntax, the external phrase ought to be understood as having the incorporated element in it. In the case of noun incorporation, tell-tale remnants of the external NP ought to be left behind, including adjectives, relative clauses, possessors, articles, and so on.

3. Most important, the result of incorporation might yield a syntactic pattern that does not otherwise exist in the language. In other words, the word containing the incorporated element might have surface syntax distinct from any underived word in the language. As for noun incorporation, this could mean, for example, that the remnant left behind by incorporation might not be a phrase that occurs otherwise in the language in that particular syntactic configuration. The existence of otherwise impossible arguments of verbs that contain incorporated nouns is a sure sign of the syntactic relevance of the phenomenon.

Let us consider first the possibility of doubling objects under noun incorporation. It is well known that this is sometimes allowed and sometimes not. West Greenlandic and Southern Tiwa are both languages in which an overt copy of the incorporated noun in the position of the argument that the noun is supposed to represent is ungrammatical. If the incorporated nominal is taken to BE the direct object, then this restriction is immediately explained, whereas if it is not taken to be the syntactic object, some other sort of restriction must be invented to account for the lack of doubling. Rosen (1989), for example, suggests the following sketchy account for the failure of doubling of an incorporated N in certain languages:

> A second possible explanation of the lack of doubling within the lexical approach concerns the selectional restriction placed on the verb by the incorporated noun. . . . It is possible that the selectional restrictions placed on the verb in Southern Tiwa and West Greenlandic exemplify the other extreme: The head of the direct object must not duplicate any of the information in the incorporated noun. The restriction may be so strict as to rule out any instance of doubling. (P. 307)

This restriction, if actually formalizable at all, is first of all ad hoc, and second, quite unlike selectional restrictions of the familiar sort. Ordinary selectional restrictions that predicates impose are not such as to disallow the repetition in arguments of information that is predictable from the meaning of the verb. A sentence such as "My wife is pregnant" is more normal, in fact, than "My spouse is pregnant," even though the femaleness of the subject is selected for by the predicate. There are even verbs like *devein* and *diagonalize* that exert selectional pressures on their objects so strong that one can practically predict what head noun will occur. The first of these requires objects in the category of shrimp and prawns, the second requires mathematical objects called matrices. Yet they certainly allow overt expression of an object that just duplicates the information implied by the selectional restriction: *devein shrimp, diagonalize a matrix*. Selectional restrictions are just not the right sort of mechanism to appeal to in accounting for the lack of doubling of incorporated arguments in certain languages.

Rosen is, I believe, on the right track when she suggests that in some languages the incorporated noun merely restricts the meaning of the verb, but in Southern Tiwa and West Greenlandic "the incorporated noun carries with it a full specification of noun head features." This would follow if the noun occupied a syntactic position in the sentence. Rosen, however, gives no reason why this should be so in some languages and not in others. Furthermore, just saying that the noun is rich in nominal features is not enough to account for the lack of doubling, since there is no connection between this "richness" of the internal noun and the direct object slot outside the verb. There is obviously nothing wrong with having an argument in a DIFFERENT syntactic position that duplicates an incorporated object, e.g., Greenlandic *Meeqqat meeraqarput* 'Children have children'. So the lexical account requires some further statement (presumably involving either thematic or grammatical relations to be appended to the treatment in order to get the facts right. If, on the other hand, the incorporated nominal is taken actually to be the object, the mutual exclusivity of the appearance of an incorporated noun and a full direct object falls out directly.

A lexical account thus provides no real explanation for the failure of doubling in languages like Southern Tiwa and West Greenlandic, and must resort to ad hoc and unmotivated statements to account for it. Viewed autolexically, undoublable incorporated N's are (parts of) syntactic arguments, and doubled incorporated N's cannot be (parts of) syntactic arguments.

4.2.4 Stranded Elements

I turn next to the question of stranded elements. Grammatically or pragmatically obligatory noun incorporation virtually demands that modifiers of the incorporated nominal be allowed to occur outside of the verb form, lest the language's expressive power be intolerably diminished.

The first question bearing on the syntactic reality of the incorporated noun is whether the form of the external argument to an incorporating verb is precisely what one would expect if a single element, namely the head noun, were missing. In Greenlandic this is clearly borne out by several facts. For example, only the head noun of a Greenlandic NP may be inflected for possession; modifiers, though formally nominals, are inflected only for case and number.

(6)   qatannguti-n-nik
        sibling-1s-INST
        'my sibling (INST)'

(7)   qatanngutinnik arna-mik
        sibling-1s-INST female-INST
        'my sister (INST)'

(8)   *qatanngutinnik arna-n-nik
        sibling-1s-INST female-1s-INST

This restriction extends to modifiers of incorporated nouns. Just like modifiers of overt head nouns, they may not be possessed:

(9)   Arna-mik   qatanngu-seri-voq.
        female-INST sibling-be.occupied.with-INDIC/3s
        'He is occupied with (someone's) sister.'

(10)   *Arna-n-nik   qatanngu-seri-voq.
        female-1s-INST sibling-be.occupied.with-INDIC/3s
        presumably: 'He is occupied with my sister.'

Another indication of the status of the stranded elements, discussed in detail in Sadock 1980 and repeated in Sadock 1986a, is this: incorporating verbs, and only these, may impose restrictions on the formal plurality of an external NP, which they do when the internal N is lexically specified as to formal plurality. Though some verbs may select a semantically plural complement (e.g., *katersor(pai)* 'collect (them)'), only incorporating verbs select for SYNTACTIC plurality. For example, the noun *qamutit* 'sled', is formally plural, being derived historically from a no longer extant root meaning 'sled runner'. Despite the fact that it is now semantically singular (one can talk about one sled), its formal plurality is reflected in the fact that it demands plural agreement. When incorporated, the stem still requires a formal plural outside of the verb, construed as a modifier of the incorporated noun:

(11)   Ataatsinik   qamuteqarpoq.
         ataaseq-nik qamut-qar-poq
         one-INST/p sled(p)-have-INDIC/3s
         'He has one sled.'

(12)   *Ataatsimik   qamuteqarpoq.
         ataaseq-mik qamut-qar-poq
         one-INST/s   sled(p)-have-INDIC/3s
         'He has one sled.'

But even in languages where incorporation is not obligatory, it is sometimes the case that constituents outside the verb are understood as modifying the internal nominal.

This possibility is accounted for by proponents of a lexical account of all incorporation (e.g., Mithun 1984; Di Sciullo and Williams 1987; and Rosen 1989) by assuming that in some languages the incorporated noun serves as a sort of "classifier," restricting the range of sortal applicability of the verb, without actually specifying the object. On this analysis, an external argument to an incorporating verb represents a more specific entity of the kind selected for by the incorporated noun stem. The idea is that the incorporated noun can be taken as a qualifier of the activity expressed by the verb, and the external argument as the real argument, the effect of modification of the incorporated nominal being a product of the semantics rather than the syntax. Analogously, a sentence like *Three senators are pregnant* is understood as referring to a group of three women senators, but there is no need to postulate an NP containing "woman" in the syntax of the sentence. The predicate *pregnant* selects for female subjects, so whatever the subject properly refers to, it must also be understood as referring to females.

While such a semantic theory might be plausible in the case where the incorporated nominal is quite general and the external argument is necessarily a more specific entity of the same kind, as in English *compose a cantata*, *sing an aria*, *drink beer*, and so on, it is much less plausible where the two sets have no necessary relationship to one another. This is the case in (13), a Mohawk example, taken from Mithun (1984, 870) and in general where the external nominal is a quantifier, as in Mithun's Caddo example (14), the Greenlandic example (11) above, or the Southern Tiwa example (15), taken from Allen, Gardiner, and Frantz (1984, 297). It is not at all clear that "polka-dotted" in (13) is more specific than "dress," and it is surely not the case that "a lot" in (14) and "two" in (15) are types of grass and cats, respectively. The classifier theory of incorporation in such cases requires a profoundly different theory of quantification from any that exists at present, whereas the syntactic theory can rely on ordinary quantification theory, since (14) and (15) would contain phrases meaning "much grass" and "two cats"—phrases that exist with the correct meanings in the languages in question anyway.

(13)   Kanekwarúnyu wa'-k-akya'tawi'tsher-ú : ni.
        it.dotted.DIST   past-I-dress-make
        'I made a polka-dotted dress.'

(14)   Wayah hák-k'uht-'í'-sa'.
        a.lot   PROG-grass-be/grow-PROG
        'There is a lot of grass.'

(15)   Wisi ibi-musa-tuwi-ban.
        two   AGR-cat-buy-PAST
        'They bought two cats.'

Mithun, Rosen, and others who wish to maintain a lexical account of noun incorporation analyze examples like (13)–(15) as containing headless, or empty-headed nominal objects. But empty headed arguments generally require a discourse antecedent in every language that I have researched.[1] Thus English *I sang three*, or German *Ich habe ein Schönes gesungen* are quite grammatical, but cannot begin discourses, even though we know from the meaning of the verb what sort of entity the object must be. The class of songs (or Lieder) must already have been introduced into the discourse for these sentences to occur appropriately.

Now in Greenlandic, this is also by and large true. Thus a sentence like (16) can only be used appropriately if the sort of thing that the object is supposed to refer to has already been established as a discourse topic.

(16)   Marlunnik nerivunga.
        marluk-nik neri-vunga
        two-INST/p eat-INDIC/1s
        'I ate two.'

The sole exception that I am aware of (other than that mentioned in note 1) is provided by noun incorporation. An example like (17) can be used to initi-

ate a discourse. It can be used, in other words, under exactly the same circumstances as (18), which has a free object.

(17)   Marlunnik ammassattorpunga.
        marluk-nik ammassak-tor-punga
        two-INST/p sardine-eat-INDIC/3s
        'I ate two sardines.'

(18)   Ammassannik marlunnik nerivunga.
        ammassak-nik marluk-nik neri-vunga
        sardine-INST/p two-INST/p eat-INDIC/1s
        'I ate two sardines.'

Mithun's 1984 glosses suggest that exactly the same collection of facts
characterizes even Mohawk. Her gloss of (13) as 'I made a polka-dotted
dress' suggests that no prior antecedent is required, while her gloss of the syntactically parallel (19), which includes *one* suggests the opposite.

(19)   Kanekwarúnyu wa'katkáhtho.
        it.dotted.DIST   PAST.I.see
        'I saw a polka-dotted (one).'

The upshot of all of this is that it is simply not the case that existing semantic rules will account for the interpretation of sentences with external modifiers of incorporated nominals. We would minimally require a special rule of
interpretation that gives a complete interpretation to free quantifiers and adjectives as complements of all and only verbs containing incorporated nominals.

A rather different case demonstrating the strict parallelism that can characterize the interpretation of incorporated nouns and free syntactic alternatives
can also be found in West Greenlandic. A few affixes incorporate not the head
noun, but specifically a quantifier. Thus *marloraarpoq* means 'He caught
two', (<*marluk* 'two'). But if the quantificational expression contains more
than one phonological word, e.g., *marluk affarlu* 'two and a half', part of the
expression is stranded by incorporation:

(20)   Marlo-raarpoq affar-mil-lu.
        two-he.caught half-INST-and
        'He caught two and a half.'

(Note the instrumental case of the stranded expression, for which see
Sadock 1980.)

There are also a few nominal modifiers in West Greenlandic that have a
different sense when used as modifiers than they do when used as head nouns.
As Anthony Woodbury (1989) has observed, this includes the class of mate-

rial terms like *qisuk* 'wood', *marraq* 'clay', and so on. When used directly as modifiers, these terms describe the material of which something is largely made: *illu qisuk* 'wooden house', *tiitorfik marraq* 'china cup'. When used as independent nominals, however, these terms designate an aggregation of the substance itself, not something made of it. *Qisummik takuvunga* means 'I saw a piece of wood', and cannot possibly be used to mean 'I saw something made of wood'. When used as modifiers of incorporated nouns, such expressions always have their modificational sense, not their independent nominal sense:

(21)   Qisum-mik illo-qar-poq
        wood-INST house-have-INDIC/3s
        'He has a wooden house.'

Here again, the nonsyntactic account of the meaning of external modifiers that takes them to be ordinary arguments and intersects that meaning with the selectional restrictions imposed by the verb will not work. But the assumption that there is a syntactic phrase *illumik qisummik* in (21) gets the meaning right automatically, since that phrase means 'wooden house'. Furthermore, since any intransitive verb in West Greenlandic that means roughly what the suffix *-qar* means takes its object in the instrumental case, and since modifiers agree with their heads in case, the form of (21) is predicted as well. (See Sadock 1980; 1985a for details of this aspect of the syntax of West Greenlandic.)

The semantics of the classifier theory of the meaning of noun incorporation clearly needs to be complicated in various ways in order to account for examples like these. But that semantic theory collapses utterly, it seems to me, where the external modifier is what in the semantic literature is called an intensional adjective. Thus while a polka-dotted dress is a dress, counterfeit money is not money at all. Yet adjectival nouns with meanings like 'counterfeit' can perfectly well occur external to an incorporating verb in Greenlandic, with precisely the same semantic effect that they have when they occur as modifiers of independent nouns.

(22)   peqquserluutinik aningaasiortoq[2]
        peqquserluut-nik aningaasaq-lior-toq
        false-INST/p   money(p)-make-NOM
        'one who makes false money, a counterfeiter'

In such a case, the suggestion that the incorporated modifier simply restricts the range of arguments of the verb fails. Finally, it is quite unclear how the classifier theory is supposed to work in the case of incorporated interrogatives, such as the sampling of Greenlandic examples below.

(23)   Kinaavit?
        'Who are you?'

(24)   Sutorpit?
        'What did you eat?'

(25)   Susivit?
        'What did you buy?'

(26)   Susunnippa?
        'What does it smell like?'

   While the interpretation of stranded modifiers is strongly suggestive of syntax, it is not entirely convincing as a demonstration of the syntactic reality of
the incorporated noun for the simple reason that interpretation is a matter of
semantics. If, as I shall argue in chapter 6, semantic representation is profita-
bly viewed as an autonomous level, parallel to, but not the same as syntax,
then what has really been shown is that the incorporated N can, in certain
languages, and under certain circumstances, be a SEMANTIC argument of the
verb. The key fact that argues for the syntactic reality of some incorporated
nouns is that the remnant of an argument phrase left by incorporation is sometimes not a possible argument in the language at all. In general, any unique
syntactic property of verbs containing incorporated nouns, as compared with
all other verbs in a language, counts as an extremely strong demonstration of
the syntactic reality of incorporation, particularly if the unique structure can
be reduced to ordinary syntax coupled with ordinary morphology, as in the
cases discussed above.
   In my 1980 article I laid great emphasis on the fact that the external syntax
of Greenlandic verbs with incorporated nominals is not identical to that of
basic verbs of the language. I repeated these arguments in Sadock 1986a,
adding a new one. Because of their centrality to the argument at hand and to
the general thesis of this book, I will rehash them here, too.
   Perhaps the most important fact is that incorporating verbs (and no others)
may have external possessors in the ergative case.

(27)   kunngip panippassuaqarpoq³
        kunngi-p panik-passuaq-qar-poq
        king-ERG daughter-many-have-INDIC/3s
        'There are many king's daughters (i.e., princesses).'

   Here the external ergative NP *kunngip* is taken as a possessor of the incorporated nominal *panik*, exactly as in the NP *kunngip pania* 'princess'. What
is important about this particular construction is that otherwise, ergative NPs
CANNOT POSSIBLY SERVE AS ARGUMENTS OF INTRANSITIVE VERBS. Unlike English, and many other languages, a possessor can never be construed as such
without an overt possessum. Therefore, the following example is completely

ungrammatical, and cannot mean, for example 'I saw the King's (something or other)'.

(28)) *kunngip takuvunga
       kunngi-p taku-vunga
       king-ERG see-INDIC/1s

There is one transitive noun-incorporating affix in West Greenlandic, -gE, an extremely frequent and characteristic morpheme which is usually translated 'have it as N'. A much better translation of a sentence of the form NP[ERG] NP[ABS] N+gE is "NP[ABS] is NP[ERG]'s N":

(29)   Jerry-p   Biinia erneraa.
                         erneq-gE-vaa.
       Jerry-ERG Ben   son-gE-INDIC/3s/3s
       'Jerry has Ben as a son.' or
       'Ben is Jerry's son.'

Now if the incorporated noun in such a sentence is possessed, stranding the ergative possessor, there results a sentence with TWO ERGATIVES, something that occurs nowhere in the language outside of incorporation constructions.

(30)   Hansi-p   puisi-p   neqaati-gi-vaa.
       Hans-ERG   seal-ERG   cache.of.meat-gE-INDIC/3s/3s
       'It is Hans's cache of seal meat.'

If the incorporating verb is transitivized, say by the addition of a causative morpheme, it is also possible to produce clauses with two ergatives, one the subject, and the other the possessor of the incorporated noun. Once again, such examples are not even grossly like anything that occurs independently of noun incorporation in West Greenlandic.

(31)   Hansi-p   qimmi-p   ame-qar-tip-paa.
       H.-ERG   dog-ERG   skin-have-cause-INDIC/3s
       'Hans let him have (gave him) a dog's skin.'

Impossible arguments understood as modifiers of incorporated nouns are also found in the South Munda language Gta?, which was brought to my attention by Norman Zide. According to Zide's field notes, the directional adjective mb&?sia? 'left' never stands alone, but is always combined with the word for 'hand'. All by itself it does not constitute a NP meaning 'the left one'. But the noun meaning 'hand' can be incorporated, stranding what is an unambiguous modifier in the language:

(32)   n&N mb&?sia? gwe?-ti-ke[4]
       I   left   wash-hand-PAST
       'I washed (my) left hand.'

Returning to West Greenlandic, a second feature that gives rise to otherwise impossible sentence patterns (at least in the older language)[5] is found with verbal affixes that incorporate a predicate nominal (Sadock 1980; 1986a). Such verbs, and no others, may have an additional absolutive case NP associated with them that obligatorily follows the verb. Thus such sentences have two absolutives, one the subject, and the other a modifier of the incorporated predicate nominal.

(33)   Joorut   palasi-u-voq   tusaamasoq.
        Jorgen(ABS) priest-be-INDIC/3s famous(ABS)
        'Jorgen is a famous priest.'

The final example of a unique configuration in which incorporating verbs of West Greenlandic are found is what we might call polysynthetic gapping.

(34)   Maani amerlasuunik   qaqqaqarpoq
        maani amerlasuu-nik   qaqqaq-qar-poq
        here   many-INST/p   mountain-have-INDIC/3s
        'Here there are many mountains

        aamma tatsinik   amerlasuunik.
        aamma taseq-nik   amerlasuu-nik
        also   lake-INST/p   many-INST/p
        as well as many lakes.'

Here the verb is understood as occurring in a second conjunct, just as in the case of gapping in more familiar langauges. What is remarkable here is that the gapped verb is morphologically a derivational suffix and not an independent word.

For reasons that I do not understand, this sort of gapping requires a quantifier in both conjuncts.[6] The enabling quantifier can itself be incorporated if the affix is one of those that specifically incorporates quantifiers (for which see the discussion surrounding (20) above).

(35)   Marlo-riar-punga pingasu-nil-luunnit.
        two-do-INDIC/3s three-INST/p-or
        'I did it two or three times.'

In all three of these cases of a unique structure that occurs with incorporating verbs, the configuration we find arises naturally from the assumption that the incorporated noun is syntactically part of an argument phrase.

First of all, notice that removing the possessum from a phrase like *kunngip pania* 'king's daughter (princess)' would strand the ergative *kunngip*, giving rise to just the sort of sentence exemplified by (27).

Next, consider the construction represented by (36), with a postverbal absolutive understood as a modifier of an incorporated predicate nominal. Besides incorporated structures such as this, there are double-absolutive predicate-nominal sentences of West Greenlandic that contain nonverbal copulas, such as the demonstrative *tassa* or the cliticized pronoun *una*:

(36)   Joorut   tassa palasi   tusaamasoq.
        Jorgen(ABS) that priest(ABS) famous(ABS)
        'Jorgen is the famous priest.'

(37)   Joorun-una   palasi   tusaamasoq.
        Jorgen(ABS)-it priest(ABS) famous(ABS)
        'It's Jorgen who is a famous priest.'

The assumption that the incorporating suffix -*u* is the verbal analog to the nonverbal copular elements in (36) and (37) immediately explains the form of (33), including the fact (which is unexpected in this SOV language) that the modifier of the predicate element must follow the verb. In (36) and (37) the order is also fixed, with the predicate following the copular element.

Lastly, gapping of a full verb (to the right only, despite the word order of the language (cf. Ross 1970) is possible in West Greenlandic:

(38)   Maani qaqqanik   amerlasuunik takuvoq
        maani amerlasuu-nik qaqqaq-qar-poq
        here many-INST/p   mountain-have-INDIC/3s
        'Here he saw many mountains

        aama   tatsinik   amerlasuunik.
        aamma taseq-nik   amerlasuu-nik
        also   lake-INST/p many-INST/p
        as well as many lakes.'

Thus the unusual sentence pattern in (34) would likewise be explained if its syntax were the same as that of a comparable sentence with an independent verb, such as we have in (38).

4.2.5 Summary

Because the point seems to have been misunderstood (e.g., by Rosen 1989), let me first make clear what I have NOT done. I have not proved that everything that has been termed noun incorporation in the literature is always and only a morphological process that interacts with syntax. What I have shown is that surely in West Greenlandic, and most likely in Southern Tiwa and Gta?, a noun stem contained within a morphological verb sometimes has all the syntactic and semantic properties of an independent head noun. Even in these languages, though, there is nothing in the argument to suggest that every morphologically included noun is syntactically real. Indeed, I know that is not the case in West Greenlandic, where there are a great many lexicalized incorporations that give no evidence whatsoever of interactivity with the syntax.

As an example, consider the lexicalized form *nunaqarpoq* 'to dwell in a certain locality', which is transparently *nuna* 'land' plus *-qar(poq)* 'have'. Despite the morphological composition of the word, doubling of the incorporated noun is perfectly allowable in this case:

(39)   Nuna-mi tassa-ni nunaqarpoq.
        land-LOC that-LOC he.lives
        'He lives on that land.'

Note also that the argument of this verb is not in the instrumental case, which is what we would expect of a modifier of the incorporated noun, but rather in the locative, as befits the meaning of the verb. Furthermore, unlike the other examples of the use of *-qar(poq)* discussed above, the morphological noun in this case does not set up a discourse topic.

(40)   *Kalaallit-Nunaanni   nunaqarpoq, kisianni takunngilara.
        Greenlanders-land.LOC he.lives   but   I.have.not.seen it.

The existence of items like this, with all the expected properties of syntactically inert derivational morphology makes it that much clearer that the syntactic reality of the productive examples has to be recognized.

What I have demonstrated beyond any doubt, I believe, is merely that there exists some morphological structures whose parts must be visible to the syntax. I use the word "merely" with hesitation, because theories of grammar allowing for the manipulation of syntactic elements by the morphology (and vice versa) will inevitably turn out to be very different from those that do not.

There is a precedent for this, of course, in cliticization, where at least the host to which the clitic attaches regularly counts as a syntactic formative, i.e., an element of the syntactic parsing. In chapter 3 I showed that a grammar allowing simultaneous and possibly discrepant syntactic and morphological bracketings yielded an elegant and empirically successful theory of cliticization. What I shall turn my attention to next is an account of incorporation along similar lines.

4.3 Incorporating Incorporation

I will use the word "incorporation" very generally to refer to any morphological process (other than cliticization) that produces morphological units in which some of the morphological constituents can be shown to have independent syntactic reality. The term is neutral as to the morphological technique that is employed: affixation, symbolic change, reduplication, and compounding could all potentially provide examples of incorporation. Likewise, it is of no consequence to this definition whether we would call the morphological operation in question derivation or inflection; either could provide examples of incorporation. The definition also does not imply anything about the categories involved, either in the morphology, or in the syntax. Nouns, verbs, adjectives, prepositions, and so on, could all participate in incorporation. The West Greenlandic phenomenon that was discussed in detail in the foregoing sections was just that particular instantiation of the general case where a syntactic nominal is the derivational base for a suffixal verb-forming morphological process.

According to this construal of the term, incorporation is, like cliticization, a phenomenon with both a syntactic and a morphological face, for in both, a proper subpart of a word-sized unit counts as an independent element of the syntax. Both phenomena, then, involve lexemes that are realized as morphology of some kind, and yet have the syntactic status of formatives. In all cases that I know of, both clitics and incorporating lexemes are syntactic functors, i.e., syntactic atoms that combine with phrases to form larger phrases, or more simply, lexical heads.

In the foregoing sections of this chapter, I have tried to provide arguments necessitating a syntactic treatment of certain nonclitic morphological operations by paying attention to the details of their behavior. An entirely different sort of argument, which is almost as persuasive, regards the relation of incorporative morphology to other kinds of morphological juncture, in particular, cliticization.

As I document in detail in Sadock 1988, there are no clear boundaries between the two phenomena. Bound morphemes that are syntactically active shade by degrees from those that display the constellation of properties that we associate with clitics through incorporators, to those that are typical of syntactically inert morphemes. In fact, all of the traditional classes of morphology—derivation, inflection, and cliticization—have unsharp boundaries on all sides, as several of the examples discussed in chapter 5 will serve to show.

One of the important lessons to be drawn from the existence of such clines is that it is impossible to consign the various traditional morphological types to different areas of the grammar. In that they shade into one another, all types of morphology must be dealt with in a single component. Their differences lie partly in their associations with other autonomous dimensions of grammatical organization. In answer to Stephen Anderson's (1982) question, "Where's morphology," I would not respond as did Jensen and Stong-Jensen (1984) that it is in the lexicon, but rather, "It's in the morphological component, where it belongs."

But a lesson of more immediate concern to us here is that there is no single criterion that sets cliticization apart from other morphological operations. Thus the syntactic activity of clitics should not be viewed as in and of itself criterial. For an element to be comfortably labeled a clitic, it should display a whole host of phonological, morphological, semantic, AND SYNTACTIC properties that are, in principle at least, independent of one another, so where a grammatical phenomenon conforms to only part of this list, we should not demand a preexisting pigeonhole to put it in.

Nevertheless, there seem to be relatively stable associations of properties from various components of the grammar that correspond closely to the traditional categories. Indeed, there is a frequently observed set of behaviors from various modules that seems to characterize one particular intermodular phenomenon that we may call incorporation, and another that we may call cliticization. In chapter 5 I will survey a number of disparate examples from an assortment of languages that serve to illustrate both that the association of certain intermodular clusters of properties occurs with much greater than chance frequency, and also that the clustering is not necessary.

Incorporation and cliticization share a number of features, including the fact that both compose formatives of the syntax into morphological structures, that the pivotal element—the clitic or incorporator—is a lexical head in the syntax, and that it has robust semantics, including referentiality, where that is applicable. The two principal differences between canonical cliticization and canonical incorporation are these:

1. Clitics apply morphologically to full words, but incorporating lexemes attach morphologically to stems.
2. Clitics attach to syntactically nearby words, but incorporators attach to heads of syntactic phrases, regardless of proximity.

The attachment of clitics to nearby words was handled in chapter 3 by the Linearity Constraint, which requires that the elements of the morphological string and the elements of the syntactic string occur in the same order. As was demonstrated in that chapter, however, individual clitic morphemes, such as Latin *-que*, could be lexically exempt from the LC, and occur out of order in the string of morphemes with respect to their expected positioning in the syntax. But the fact that clitics that violate the LC attach as soon as they can, while still fulfilling their morphological obligations (i.e., as second position, or penultimate position clitics) indicates that the LC is still partially in effect.

Thus there are actually two versions of the LC—a strong one requiring absolute identity of ordering of matching elements in morphology and in syntax, and a weaker one, allowing minimal discrepancies of order, but otherwise requiring the order of elements in the two representations to be the same.

Now incorporation, as mentioned in several places above, and as will be documented below, involves heads of syntactic phrases (cf. Baker 1988; Marantz 1984; Hoeksema 1984), and is thus at odds with the Linearity Constraint, since there is no guarantee in the abstract that a lexical head and the head of its complement will occur in adjacent positions in syntax. The Linearity Constraint might thus be overridden by the requirement of headship that governs cases of incorporation.

Recall from chapter 3 that there is a trade-off between the LC and the CIC in that both may not be violated at the same time. When what we now see to be the strong form of the LC is violated by a particular clitic, the CIC must be obeyed, and the clitic will attach to an element of its syntactic co-phrase.

Turning our attention to incorporation, we may notice that the balance between the two types of homomorphisms generalizes. The total relaxation of the Linearity Constraint that is typical of incorporation is counterbalanced by a strengthening of the CIC. With regard to clitics, the CIC requires only that they preferentially attach to some unspecified element of the phrase that they are in syntactic construction with; with regard to incorporators, it demands attachment to a uniquely identifiable, central element of that phrase, namely its head. Functionally, this trade-off between the two homomorphism conditions on the syntax-morphology interface assures that the syntactic function of a mismatched element is reconstructible.

So just as there are strong and weak conditions on the degree of correspondence of the linear order of elements between representations, there are strong and weak conditions on the degree of structural correspondence between syntax and morphology:

(41)   Linearity Constraints
    a. Strong
       The associated elements of morphological and syntactic representations must occur in the same linear order.
    b. Weak
       The associated elements of morphological and syntactic representations must occur in as close to the same linear order as the morphological requirements of the lexemes allow.

(42)   Constructional Integrity Constraints
    a. Strong
       If a lexeme combines with a phrase P in the syntax and with a host in the morphology, then the morphological host must be associated with the head of the syntactic phrase P.
    b. Weak
       If a lexeme combines with a phrase P in the syntax and with a host in the morphology, then the morphological host must be associated with some element of the syntactic phrase P.

We may now think of the limitation on allowable discrepancies between syntactic and morphological representations in the following terms:[7]

(43)   Morphosyntactic Homomorphism Condition
Let each of the strong homomorphism constraints count as two degrees of similarity, and let the weak homomorphism constraints
count as one. The total degree of similarity betwen autonomous
syntactic and morphological representations must be at least two.

Thus if a particular morphosyntactic association violates the weak Linearity
Constraint (and hence also the strong Linearity Constraint), it must obey the
strong version of the CIC and count as incorporation as the term is used here.
The types of clitics that violated the Linearity Constraint of chapter 3 still
obeyed the weak Linearity Constraint, and the CIC which they obeyed was
also the weak variety. Those clitics that did not obey the CIC at all, obeyed the
strong form of the LC. These two varieties of cliticization are contrasted with
incorporation in the following diagrams.

(44)   Nonlinear Cliticization
Obeys weak LC and weak CIC.

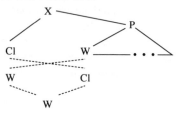

(45)   Nonconstructional (Anticipatory) Cliticization
Violates weak CIC and obeys strong LC.

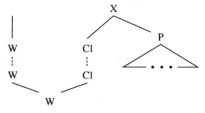

(46)   Incorporation
Violates weak LC and obeys strong CIC.

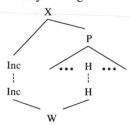

The formulation in (43) sets a lower bound on the degree of morphosyntactic similarity, but is quite consistent with the existence of associations of greater similarity than this minimum. The simple clitics of chapter 3, for example, obey the strong LC and the weak CIC. It is also possible for a lexeme to have both a syntactic and a morphological representation and to conform to both of the strong homomorphism conditions (41a) and (42a).

This situation in fact frequently occurs in languages that conform rather strictly to Greenberg's Type III class (Greenberg 1966a), i.e., verb-final languages in which the heads of nested phrases are adjacent. In such languages, postpositions will immediately follow the head noun of their object NPs, auxiliaries will immediately follow the main verb of their complement VPs, complementizers will immediately follow the finite verb of their clauses, and so on. Function lexemes in languages where lexical heads are uniformly final in their phrases strongly tend to be phonologically dependent suffixes on the preceding word, which is both the head of their own syntactic co-phrase, and immediately before them in syntax. Such bound morphemes thus obey both the strong LC and the strong CIC. They are simultaneously clitics and incorporators, at least morphosyntactically.

But as mentioned at the outset of this section, there is something else besides the question of whether or not the strong CIC is obeyed that sets incorporation apart from cliticization. In the data that I have examined, the great majority of lexemes that conform to the strong CIC combine morphologically with stems, rather than fully inflected words. Such lexemes are derivational or inflectional affixes (or morphological modifications) or pieces of compounds. On the other hand, the great majority of lexemes that conform to the weak (or the strong) LC, and not the CIC, combine morphologically with inflected words. Such lexemes are classical clitics.

These correlations are good, but as we shall see in chapter 5, they are not perfect. I will state them as morphosyntactic defaults which can be overridden by lexical information that imposes requirements that differ from what these principles would otherwise demand. In the absence of such overriding features, a lexeme will have some of its morphosyntactic properties determined on the basis of others according to the following two principles.

(47)   Incorporation Principle
        If a lexeme combines with a stem in the morphology and with a phrase in the syntax, its morphosyntactic association will conform to the strong CIC.

(48)   Cliticization Principle
        If a lexeme combines with an inflected word in the morphology and with a phrase in the syntax, its morphosyntactic association will conform to at least the weak LC.

If a language in which syntactic heads are regularly adjacent lacks clear inflectional morphology, as is the case, for example, in Japanese and Korean, then the distinction between cliticization and incorporation collapses, since the definitions above refer to inflection. In fact, it is sometimes not possible to distinguish sharply between either of these kinds of morphology and inflection, especially where the morpheme in question is syntactically obligatory. Inflectional morphology is distributed according to the Head Feature Convention (Gazdar et al. 1985), and will thus wind up in the same place as either a phrase-final clitic or a head-incorporating morpheme in a language of this type. The collapse of such distinctions is understandable in a model in which all morphology per se is attributed to a single component, but would be surprising in any system that segregated the various types of morphology into separate subcomponents.

4.3.1 The Direction of Incorporation

Through the strong CIC, the Incorporation Principle requires that when a lexeme L combines syntactically with a phrase HP and morphologically with a stem H^{-0}, then H^{-0} is associated with the head of HP in the syntax. There are two ways that this could happen. Either the complex lexical expression $L+H^{-0}$ occurs in the position that L itself would be expected to occupy in the syntax, as in (49), or $L+H^{-0}$ occurs in the position that H, the syntactic correspondent to the stem H^{-0}, would be found in, as in (50).

(49)

(50)

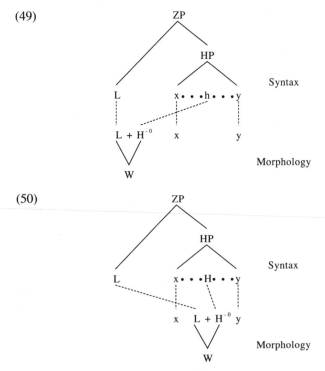

In Sadock 1985a I attempted to approach the question of the direction of incorporation by counting the number of crossing association lines between the two representations. The idea was that a diagram with fewer crossing lines was to be preferred to one with more. I now think that this effort, which met with only limited success anyway, was misguided. Steven Lapointe (1987, 1988) has argued forcefully for an autolexical system in which association lines never cross, making the morphosyntactic interface obey a fundamental constraint of the allied discipline of autosegmental phonology (Goldsmith 1976). If Lapointe is right, then we must abandon the attempt to account for ordering in such terms. As it turns out, the facts concerning the direction of incorporation seem to yield easily to a straightforward and intuitively sensible principle that makes no appeal to line crossing.

Returning to the problem at hand, note that if the language in question is one in which L and H both occur on the same periphery of the phrases they form (as is quite often the case with incorporative phenomena), it will be impossible to tell the difference between these two cases, at least on the basis of word order alone. But linear order ought to reflect the direction of incorporation if L and H are not adjacent, giving rise to either (49), (50), or their mirror images.

Now any of these morphosyntactic associations have a certain air of implausibility about them. The configuration in (49) (or its mirror image) corresponds to a raising analysis under a transformational treatment such as Baker's (1988); the element H is found in a higher position in the tree, namely in association with the higher element L. Such a structure would be licit on Baker's account in that the trace of movement of H would be properly governed by the element that has been moved to a c-commanding position. But such a process could also easily lead to the production of new superficial structures, not found outside of incorporation, since there is no guarantee that the remnant of HP, namely x-y, is an otherwise occurring phrase type in the language. Even if x-y is a possible phrase in the language, it must be a possible complement of L, in other words, a null-headed HP, for the association to be structure preserving (assuming that the complex morphological entity L+H counts as an L).

The sort of association we find in (50) is also less than plausible looking, for the lowering of L to H would (in transformational terms) leave an ungoverned trace. On the other hand, this direction of association would seem to have an easier time producing a surface order of morphemes that resembles what otherwise occurs in the language. For it to do so, the sequence x-L+H-y would have to resemble an HP, and thus all that would have to be true is that L+H is an H in the language.

But despite their initial implausibility, there seem to be good examples of the type of association shown in both (49) and (50) in the data surveyed in chapter 5. Therefore, structure preservation is not a necessary characteristic of incorporation. Indeed, if it were, some of the most important evidence for the syntactic reality of the process would not have existed. Furthermore, government does not seem to play a prominent role in licensing incorporation of the kind I am dealing with, though it might in the case of analogous mismatches between semantic and syntactic representations, which form the bulk of the cases that Baker treated in his work.

All examples of noun incorporation that I know of are either compatible with (49), or must be analyzed in that way. In West Greenlandic, for example, the normal order of a stranded modifier with respect to an incorporating verb matches the normal order of an instrumental case object with respect to an intransitive verb:[8]

(51) Angisuu-nik qimme-qar-poq
      big-INST/p   dog-have-INDIC/3s
      'He has big dogs.'

(52) Meeqqa-nik asannip-poq
      child-INST/p love-INDIC/3s
      'He loves children.'

Since the order of elements in a West Greenlandic NP is N+modifier, this clearly shows that the incorporated N-stem is attracted to the verb (as in the mirror image of (49)), rather than the verbal affix being attracted to the N-stem.

As a case of the opposite kind, consider the incorporating determiners of Icelandic, as analyzed in chapter 5, section 1.1. If, as I suggest there, the determiner is "lowered" from the position that ordinary demonstratives occupy (example (54)) to the head noun, then we have the situation diagrammed in (50).

(53) rauði hestur-inn sem   týndast
      red   horse-DET which got.lost

(54) sá   rauði hestur sem   týndast
      DEM   red   horse which got.lost

The survey in chapter 5 contains a near minimal pair of phenomena with respect to the direction of incorporation which is instructive to consider in more detail. Both Hungarian (chapter 5, section 4.2) and Crow (chapter 5, section 4.3) contain incorporating postpositions, but those of Hungarian descend to the head of their NP complements (if the derivational metaphor may be excused), while those of Crow rise to combine with the head of the phrase that governs them.

(55) János bement a   nagy ház-ba.
      J.   entered the big house-into
      'Janos went into the big house.'

(56)   Húuleesh Jerry-sh Chichúche ku-ss-dée-k.
        yesterday J.-DEF   Hardin   it-GOAL-go-DECL
        'Jerry went to Hardin yesterday.'

One might think that the difference has something to do with what item is responsible for the incorporation, but this notion is falsified by the pair of cases at hand, since in both languages the incorporating power is a lexical feature of the adposition, some of which do not participate in incorporation at all. We may also compare the Eskimo situation, where the lexeme that must be specifically marked as triggering the incorporation is clearly the suffixal verb, with Gta? (and other south Munda languages such as Sora) where most nouns have special incorporating forms, but those that do not cannot incorporate (Ramamurti 1931). In either case, the noun-verb combination occurs in the position where the simple verb would be found.

The actual difference resides in the relationship between the morphological and syntactic rules that the autolexical element participates in. In both Crow and Hungarian we are dealing with an element that combines with NPs in the syntax to form adpositional phrases. But the morphological combinatorics of the postpositions differ greatly between the two languages. In Hungarian they participate in a morphological rule that combines a noun and a postposition to form a noun,[9] whereas in Crow they combine with verb stems to form verb stems. What we can now observe is that the complex noun of Hungarian occurs where the noun would, and the complex verb of Crow occurs where the verb would. In general, then, the complex morphological item occurs where its head occurs in syntax. The reason that all noun incorporation involves raising is simply that noun incorporation, among other things, is the morphological combination of a nominal and verbal form to form a verb, which by the principle just adumbrated will occur in the position of the syntactic verb.

The situation can be understood by examining the following diagrams, which resemble those argued for by Lapointe (1987; 1988) in that nonterminal nodes of the morphological tree are associated with the syntactic tree.

(57)

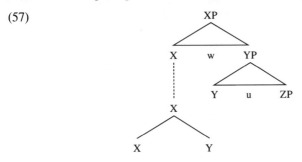

(58)

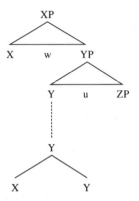

The diagram in (57) corresponds to the Crow situation, where X = V, and Y = P; The diagram in (58) analyzes the Hungarian facts, where X = P, and Y = N.

Though it is quite possible, and certainly desirable, for the principle governing the direction of incorporation to follow from the architecture of the system, I do not see that it does at present, and so I will state it as an observational law to be explained by further research:

(59)   Direction of Incorporation
         The syntactic position of a complex morphological expression is the
         same as the syntactic position of its morphological head.

Thus in (57), the morphological expression [X,Y] is headed by X, and so it occurs in the syntactic position of X, in the syntactic tree, namely before w-u-ZP. In (58), the morphological phrase [X,Y] is headed by Y, and so the complex occurs in the syntax where Y does, namely between w and u-ZP.

5

A Survey of Morphosyntactic Mismatches

The interface principles discussed so far greatly limit what kinds of discrepancies are allowed to exist between syntactic and morphological bracketings, and therefore the possible types of incorporative and clitic-like phenomena that can exist, but they still allow quite a range of them. As described above, incorporation involves morphology to a stem, but it is neutral as to whether this will be inflectional or derivational morphology, compounding, affixation, or modification. Clitics generally manifest themselves as affixes, but in at least one case, that of Tongan discussed below, an argument can be made for the existence of a clitic that shows up as an effect on stress.

Saussure (1959) and Sapir ([1921] 1949) emphasized that the same notional category can be expressed in terms of a variety of formal means. Such categories as tense and aspect are manifested in some languages (e.g., various creole languages) in the form of a verb that takes a verb-phrase complement, but in others as an inflection on main verbs (Latin), and in others (e.g., Eskimo), as derivational morphology. We might take Chinese to be a language in which aspect is realized as a clitic. If there is evidence that tense or aspect is to be represented in the syntax of a language as a V with a VP complement, and the formal expression of this category is in terms of some morphological operation, then we would have a case of incorporation, regardless of the specific morphological means that are employed. The Kirundi example discussed in section 3.2 below is an inflectional example of incorporated tense.

Another dimension of variation for morphosyntactic mismatches concerns the syntactic substance of the incorporating element. For each syntactic rule in natural language that introduces a lexical category and a complement, the IP and CP allow for there to be incorporative and clitic instantiations of the category of the head. We will be able to recognize such morphemes by the fact that they leave behind what is left of an ordinary complement phrase after its lexical head has been removed, have the semantics that we would ordinarily expect of syntactic formatives, and are mutually exclusive with the actual occurrence, in the form of an independent formative, of a duplicate of the syntactic category they instantiate. If such a morpheme is expressed as morphology to a stem, it should obey the IP and be found in morphological association with the head of its complement phrase, and if it is realized as morphology to an inflected word, it should obey the CP and form a morphological structure with a word in a neighboring syntactic position.

Suppose we take the following as a reasonable sample of the rules of natural languages that introduce lexical categories. The list is, of course, incomplete, but it does include some of the most frequently encountered syntactic rules of this kind. (The numbering refers to the section in this chapter in which each rule is discussed.)

(5.1) $NP \to Det, \bar{N}$
(5.2) $VP \to V, NP$
(5.3) $VP \to V, VP$
(5.4) $PP \to P, NP$
(5.5) $\bar{S} \to Comp, S$
(5.6) $\bar{N} \to N, NP$
(5.7) $\bar{N} \to A, \bar{N}$
(5.8) $AP \to A, NP$

The prediction is, then, that the lexical category in each of these rules can incorporate the head of its complement, or cliticize to a nearby word. In fact, it is easy enough to find both clitic and incorporating instantiations of the head introduced by most of these rules.

There is one quite major class of exceptions. Clitics always seem to represent closed lexical classes. They are frequently encountered among determiners, auxiliary verbs, prepositions, complementizers, conjunctions, and pronouns, but I have no good examples of clitic main verbs, clitic nouns, or clitic adjectives. I will refrain from speculating here as to why this should be so, and simply state this as an observed law of morphosyntax.

(1)   Law of Clitics
        A lexeme whose morphological and syntactic nature is such that it falls under the CP is a member of a closed lexical class.

I shall proceed straightaway to catalog a variety autolexical instantiations of the lexical categories in the rules above.

5.1 $NP \to Det, \bar{N}$

Suppose a language presents a determiner with ordinary syntactic properties, but with the peculiarity of being an affix. Such an affixal determiner could be a clitic that combined with a peripheral word of its $\bar{N}$ complement, as in Modern Greek, or it could be governed by the IP, in which case it would be an affix to the head noun of its $\bar{N}$ complement. Presuming that the morphological character of the affixal determiner is such as to create inflected nouns, then by the IP and (57) of chapter 4, it should be found on the head noun of the determined phrase in the position that noun would ordinarily occupy. Various Scandinavian dialects contain "postpositive" definite articles and in Icelandic, we find a definite article with almost exactly the predicted properties just mentioned.

5.1.1 Scandinavian Definite Articles

The definite article in Icelandic must appear suffixed to the head noun when no adjective precedes the head in a definite N̄:

(2)   hesturinn 'the horse'

(3)   *hinn hestur

(4)   hesturinn sem týndast 'the horse that got lost'

(5)   *hinn hestur sem týndast

When an adjective precedes, it is still possible to suffix the article to the head noun, but it may also appear as a free determiner. Einarsson (1949, 48) says, however, that this latter use of the free article is "very rare in the spoken language":

(6)   rauði hesturinn sem týndast
       'the red horse that got lost'

(7)   hinn rauði hestur sem týndast
       'the red horse that got lost'

The idea that the suffixed article actually counts as a piece of syntax can be supported in several ways. First of all, the suffixed article is mutually exclusive with a genuine overt determiner such as a demonstrative or prenominal genitive:

(8)   sá hestur 'that horse'

(9)   *sá hesturinn

(10)   Jóns hestur 'John's horse'

(11)   *Jóns hesturinn

(12)   minn hestur 'my horse'

(13)   *minn hesturinn

A complication here is that the postnominal genitive of personal pronouns can be used with a definitized noun, but in that case, there is sometimes the sense of the genitive being in apposition to a definite NP, rather than being a determiner. Thus compare:

(14)   maðurinn minn
         'my husband' (i.e., 'the man of mine')

(15)   maður minn 'my (good) man'

Genitives of personal names can be used following the possessum, but when the possessum bears the definite suffix, the genitive requires a genitive pronoun as well as the name, again an indication of apposition:

(16)   hestur Jóns 'John's horse'

(17)   hesturinn hans Jóns 'John's horse'

The second argument for the syntactic reality of the suffixed article has to do with the so-called strong and weak forms of the adjective in Icelandic. A weak form such as *rauði* 'red [MASC, SG, NOM]' is used with definite, overt determiners such as demonstratives, OR WITH A NOUN WITH A SUFFIXED DEFINITE ARTICLE. Otherwise the strong form is used:

(18)   sá rauði hestur 'that red horse'

(19)   rauði hesturinn 'the red horse'

but

(20)   rauður hestur 'a red horse'

(21)   einn rauður hestur 'one red horse'

If the suffixal article of Icelandic could be treated as syntactically identical to an overt, free demonstrative, this generalization would be captured automatically.

One morphological complication needs mentioning before the Icelandic definite article can be treated as a straightforward instance of an autolexical element governed by the IP. It would appear that it is added to fully inflected words, rather than to stems, and therefore would not come under the IP at all, but rather under the CP. Thus the definite form of the nominative *hestur* 'horse' is *hesturinn*, while the definite form of the genitive *hests* is *hestsins*. This suggests that the article is a clitic and should display rather different properties.

However, there is some fairly persuasive evidence that the definite suffix is actually part of the inflection of the noun, or at least displays tendencies in that direction. First of all, there are some morphologically exceptional formations. For example, masculine nominatives ending in -*ur* simply add the suffixed article, as in the example of *hesturinn* above, but feminines and neuters that end in -*ur* are subject to a syncope process: *lifur* 'liver'—*lifrin* 'the liver'. Even more telling is the fact that there are a few lexically exceptional forms.

The nominative plural of *maður* 'man' is *menn*, but the definite form is *mennirnir* as if derived from *mennir. Similarly, the genitive singular of *faðir* 'father' is *föður*, but the definite form is *föðursins* rather than *föðurins. This indicates that a form like *hestsins* should be analyzed as the stem *hest-* plus the definite, masculine singular nominative inflection *-sins*, rather than the full word *hests* plus clitic *-ins*. I conclude that the definite article of Icelandic is added to stems in the morphology, but to N's in the syntax and is therefore subject to the IP, which correctly predicts its appearance on the head of N̄.

As opposed to the highly incorporative behavior of the definite article in Icelandic, the other Scandinavian languages present either inflectional or clitic-like forms. In all the major Scandinavian languages, a noun phrase consisting of just a definite noun shows up as a noun with a suffixed article, but other considerations militate for different solutions from the one suggested for Icelandic.

In Danish, the behavior of the suffixed article leans strongly toward a clitic analysis, since any other material intervening between the position of the article and the noun itself blocks the cliticization, as shown in the paradigm below:

(22)   et hus 'a house'
         huset 'the house'
         *det hus
         *det huset

(23)   et stort hus 'a big house'
         *store huset
         det store hus 'the big house'
         *det store huset

The fact that this is positional blocking is confirmed by the fact that a few adjectives with universal senses either obligatorily (example (24)), or optionally (example (25)) precede the presumed position of the article, as shown by their position with respect to possessive determiners.

(24)   alle mine børn 'all my children'
         *mine alle børn

(25)   hele mit liv 'all my life'
         mit hele liv 'all my life'

These very adjectives do not block the cliticization of the definite article, presumably because they do not necessarily intervene between it and the noun host:

(25)   alle børnene "all the children'

(27)   hele tiden 'the whole time'

Complicating this straightforward situation is the fact that restrictive relative clauses also block the cliticization of the definite article:

(28)   et hus som jeg købte 'a house that I bought'
     det hus som jeg købte 'the house that I bought'
    *huset som jeg købte
    *det huset som jeg købte

But if the definite article in Danish is a clitic that precedes $\bar{\text{N}}$ in syntax, why
should either a preceding adjective or a following relative clause block the
cliticization? The free article is initial in the noun phrase, and the simplest
theory of the clitic form would position it there as well, predicting correctly
that an adjective would block cliticization, but incorrectly that a relative
clause would not.

It is conceivable that it is the distance in depth of the head noun and determiner that a structure like (31) implies, rather than their distance in the linear
string, that blocks the cliticization in this case. A parallel for this is the fact
that the host-clitic sequence *you'll*, pronounced [jUl], cannot occur if the pronoun is embedded at any depth within the subject NP. Thus in (29) and (30),
you'll must (in my speech) be pronounced as two syllables: [juwl]

(29)   Either Bill or you'll be chosen.

(30)   The student I mentioned to you'll be here today.

(31)
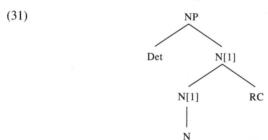

In any case, nonrestrictive relative clauses do not block the cliticization of
the definite article, which makes perfect sense if their syntactic position is outside the NP (see McCawley 1988, chap. 13), and therefore do not intervene
between the article and the noun.

For the most part, then, the Danish article behaves as a second position
clitic with highly restricted affinity. Its distribution (except for the blocking of
the process by restrictive relatives) can be handled by assigning the article a
lexical entry such as the following, for the neuter singular:

(32)   *et* (Danish):
morphology = $[_{N[-2]}$ N$[-1]$, NEUT, SG] ____]
syntax = $[_{N[2]}$ N$[1]]$
interface = $-$SLC

This lexical entry allows the article to violate the strong Linearity Constraint and attach out of position with respect to the syntax. But if a word other than a noun immediately follows the syntactic position of the determiner, it will block cliticization, since the determiner requires a noun host in the morphology.

5.1.2 Macedonian Postpositive Articles

A similar second-position clitic, but with somewhat less finicky taste in hosts, was brought to my attention by Victor Friedman.[1] The article in question is to be found in Macedonian (Koneski 1967; Lunt 1952). The Bulgarian article is similar, but not identical in its distribution.

The definite article in these languages is a suffix, as in Scandinavian. Its integration into the word is demonstrated by a number of facts. For example, words in Macedonian may not end in a voiced stop or fricative, so the alternation in (33) demonstrates the wordhood of a form containing the postpositive article.

(33)   zap 'tooth'
zabot 'the tooth'

Second, the article counts in determining the antepenultimate stress of the Macedonian word.

(34)   vodénica 'mill'
vodenícata 'the mill'

(35)   sínovi 'sons'
sinóvite 'the sons'

Third, it sometimes triggers syncopation of a medial-syllable vowel, as also happens under inflection.

(36)   nokot 'fingernail'
nokti 'fingernails'
noktot 'the fingernail'

Finally, the allomorphy of the definite article is determined by the word it attaches to. This determination is partly morphological and partly phonological. Thus masculine nouns that end in a consonant take *-ot* ((33) above), while feminine nouns take *-ta* (34). On the other hand, any noun that ends in *-a*, be it a masculine or feminine singular, or a neuter plural, takes *-ta*.

(37)   sudija 'judge' (M/s)
         sudijata 'the judge'

(38)   žena 'woman' (F/s)
         ženata 'the woman'

(39)   sela 'villages' (NEUT/pl)
         selata 'the villages'

While such facts as these might lead one to call the article an inflection in
Macedonian, it is distributed more along the lines of second-position clitics,
as described in chapter 3, section 5.3 above. In particular, the article is not
always attached to the head noun, but is attached to any single adjective that
precedes the noun, or to the first of a series of adjectives:

(40)   dobr-iot čovek
         good-the man
         'the good man'

(41)   dobr-iot mal čovek
         good-the little man
         'the good little man'

The following example from Koneski (1967, 327) clearly demonstrates
how much like ordinary second-position clitics the positioning of the Macedonian article is, since in this case the article is attached to a form that is not
even a modifier of the head noun.

(42)   četiri-stotini lug'e
         four-hundred people
         'four hundred people'

(43)   četiri-te stotini   lug'e
         four-the hundred people
         'the four hundred people'

Assuming that definite articles are found in the syntax of Macedonian in the
same place as demonstratives (there are no indefinite articles), namely to the
left of N̄, and assuming that the articles are lexically listed as suffixes and not
marked as violators of the CIC, their placement in all of the above examples is
assured.

But despite the rather ordinary clitic-like distribution of these morphemes,
the articles of Macedonian depart from ordinary clitics in the morphology. As
we have seen, they are integrated with the word more strongly than we would
typically expect. Indeed, if the article happens to attach to an adjective, then it
is the nature of the adjective, rather than the head noun, that determines the
allomorph of the article that is used. Compare (45) with (37).

(44)   dobar sudija
        good judge
        'a good judge'

(45)   dobri-ot sudija
        good-the judge
        'the good judge'

The adjective in this example has masculine form, in agreement with inherent features of *sudija* (rather than its phonological desinence), and thus it might be said that the masculine form of the article is a matter of agreement with the phrase *dobar sudija* 'good judge'. But this cannot be, for there are a few adjectival forms with an unusual [a] ending, and these demand the *-ta* form of the article. The numeral "two" is one such example. It has three agreement forms: *dvajca* for masculines referring to persons, *dva* for nonpersonal masculines, and *dve* for all other nouns. Regardless of the form of the noun, the adjective determines what allomorph of the article is used, the two [a] final adjectives taking the *-ta* article, and the other taking the *-te* form.

(46)   dvajca-ta vojnici
        two-the   soldiers (M/p)

(47)   dva-ta   volci
        two-the wolves (M/p)

(48)   dve-te ženi
        two-the women (F/p)

A second thing about the article that gives it the appearance of something other than a clitic is that it sometimes selects a special form of the adjective. Instead of the expected consonant-final form that most masculine adjectives take in isolation, the article *-ot* is added to adjectives expanded with *-i*, a form that otherwise occurs in the vocative. Thus the definite form of the noun *vetar* 'wind' is *vetrot*, whereas the definite form of the adjective *dobar* is *dobriot*, not **dobrot*. (Cf. example (45) above.)

Also unlike typical cliticization is the fact that the host of the definite article is morphosyntactically restricted. Only adjectives and nouns (namely those parts of speech that have gender and number morphology) may take it. This is shown by the unacceptability of attaching the article to an adverb, as in example (49), collected by Victor Friedman (p.c.).

(49)   *Mnogu-ot/ta/to/te golem čovek
        very-the   big   man
        (supposedly: 'the very big man')

Neither can the article occur on the subsequent adjective, as shown by (50) (also due to Victor Friedman), so instead, an independent demonstrative, as in (51), must be used.

(50)   *Mnogu golem-iot covek
         very   big-the   man
         (supposedly: 'the very big man')

(51)   Onoj mnogu golem covek
         that very   big   man
         'that very big man'

Let us assume that the adjectives and nouns in Macedonian have the value of a special gender/number feature [GN] redundantly assigned to them on the basis of a combination of morphological and phonological considerations, as in (52), a rule which states that nouns and adjectives ending in /a/ belong to the A gender.

(52)   If $X = [+N]$ and $/X/ = /. . . a/$
         then $X = [GN\ A]$

The properties of the clitic definite article can then be captured by assigning lexical entries to them such as the following:

(53)   *-ta* 'the' (Macedonian):
         morphology $= [_{X[-2]} X[GN\ A] \underline{\quad}]$
         syntax $= [_{N[-2]} \underline{\quad} N[-1]]$
         interface $= -SLC$

Since the Macedonian article is a suffix in the morphology and precedes its sister phrase in the syntax, it must violate either the strong LC or the CIC. The fact that it is the former that is violated is therefore registered in its lexical entry. Unlike Greek and Yagua articles, the Macedonian clitic requires a specific kind of morphological host, namely one bearing the feature [GN A], and since that feature is only assigned to nouns and adjectives, the use of the clitic article will be blocked if the $N[-1]$ it combines with in the syntax does not happen to begin with a noun or adjective.

5.1.3 Tongan Definitive Accent

William Poser (1985) has discussed an interesting problem in Tongan morphosyntax for which an elegant solution is available in the framework of autolexical syntax. The problem has to do with the fact that definiteness in Tongan is marked partially by means of NP-initial articles, but partially in terms of an accent shift on the last word of a definite noun phrase. The trigger for this shift can be analyzed in the present framework by postulating a simple final clitic that attaches to the last word of the definite NP. The case also provides important evidence for the phonological integration of this clitic with ordinary word-level phonology, thus challenging once again the conception of grammar that relegates cliticization to a separate, post-syntactic component.

Normally, accent in Tongan falls on the syllable containing the penultimate vowel mora, and thus on the last syllable if it contains a long vowel (indicated by a following colon), but on the penultimate syllable otherwise:

(54)   kumá: 'rat'
        fále   'house'
        faléni   'this house'

There is also a rule of resyllabification in Tongan that causes two like vowels to coalesce into a single long vowel unless the second of these would be stressed by being the penultimate vowel mora:

(57)   fakahá: 'to show'
        fakahaá'i 'to show completely'
        fakaha:'ía 'to show completely (polite)'

It appears, then, that Tongan phonology includes two ordered rules, one which assigns accent to the penultimate vowel mora, and a subsequent one that collapses two like vowels unless the second is stressed:

(60)   Stress Assignment
        $V \rightarrow [+STRESS] /$___ $C_0V\#$

(61)   Resyllabification
        $V_1V_2 \rightarrow V_1[+LONG]$
        where V_1 and V_2 are alike in all features
        except $[+/-STRESS]$ and V_2 is $[-STRESS]$

But just in case a word is the last word of a definite NP, the accent shifts to the right as if there were an additional vowel mora at the end of the word:

(62)   fakatáha 'meeting'

(63)   he fakatahá 'the meeting'

(64)   fakataha láhi 'big meeting'

(65)   he fakataha lahí 'the big meeting'

Suppose, then, that words that end definite NPs have an additional final vowel mora when they enter the phonology, that (63) and (65) are segmentally as in (66) and (67), where @ represents a vocalic segment that will invariably be deleted:

(66)   he fakataha+@

(67)   he fakataha lahi+@

The stress in these forms will now be correctly assigned by the normal stress assignment rule (60).

Definitive accent shift also interacts with resyllabification in the same way as does affixation:

(68)   pó: 'night'

(69)   poó 'night (definitive form)'

(70)   maáma 'lamp, light'

(71)   ma:má 'lamp, light (definitive form)'

This fact is also predicted by the treatment suggested here since the definitive accent is actually treated as a special case of affixation.

The problem is this: We normally expect the phonology of individual words to be determined independently of syntax. But clearly, whether a word is the last word of a definite NP can only be determined if one has access to the syntactic structure in which it is found. We are thus led to suppose that contrary to an otherwise valid principle of lexical phonology (Kiparsky 1982a; Mohanan 1986), the rules of stress assignment and resyllabification are not rules of lexical phonology, but rules that apply after syntax.

But as Poser points out, even this weakening of the theory will not work in the present case for there is compelling evidence that Resyllabification is a lexical phonological rule and that Stress Assignment must therefore also be a rule of lexical phonology, since it precedes Resyllabification.

The first piece of evidence arguing for the lexical nature of Stress Assignment that Poser presents has to do with the fact that reduplication inhibits the operation of Resyllabification. In (72) we would not expect resyllabification, since the second [o] vowel is stressed by Stress Assignment, but in (73) we would expect *ongo:ngóa.

(72)   ongoóngo 'news'

(73)   ongoongóa 'famous'

If we assume that a strong boundary intervenes between the reduplicated prefix and the stem in such forms and interpret Resyllabification as not applying over such a boundary, we can accommodate this inhibition of resyllabification. But if the rule is a postsyntactic rule, then we are faced with a most serious sort of violation of the autonomy of morphology and syntax; this postsyntactic rule would have to be able to examine the internal structure of a word, contrary to the Lexicalist Hypothesis (Chomsky 1970), the Generalized Lexical Hypothesis (Lapointe 1980), and similar otherwise valid empirical claims concerning the relationship between syntax and morphology.

A very similar argument for the lexical nature of Resyllabification rests on the fact that a particular prefix, causative *faka-*, also inhibits resyllabification:

(74)   fakaafá: 'bring a hurricane upon' (< afa: 'hurricane')

(75)   *faka:fá:

Once again, if Resyllabification were a postsyntactic rule of phonology, it should not be sensitive to the internal structure of a word.

Poser's final argument has to do with the fact that there are lexical exceptions to Resyllabification. In certain cases where we would expect two heterosyllabic vowels, the second of which has been stressed by Stress Assignment, we find instead a single short vowel:

(76)   ó: 'to go'

(77)   ómi 'to come' (*oómi)

The vowel shortening occurs only where we would expect a sequence of like vowels, the second of which is stressed, and hence can be determined only after Stress Assignment has applied. But this is a minor rule, one that applies only to certain lexically listed forms, and hence not the sort of rule that we should expect to find operating postsyntactically. Again the evidence indicates that Stress Assignment must be a lexical rule.

Poser has suggested a treatment of these facts within the framework of GPSG. His solution involves a foot feature (Gazdar et al., 1985, 79ff.) [/def] introduced by an ID rule NP[+DEF] → NP[/DEF] and an LP statement: X < [/DEF]. The effect is to guarantee that the last, and only the last, word of a definite NP bears the feature [/DEF], a feature which will trigger the accent shift under scrutiny here. (Compare Zwicky and Nevis's (1986) feature [+First].) I do not propose to criticize Poser's treatment here beyond pointing out that it involves yet another mechanism for handling transmodular paradoxes. Rather, I wish to show that a solution is available within the framework of ALS that makes use of the very same principles that are motivated by considerations of quite different phenomena.

The crux of the treatment I wish to suggest is that there is a morpheme with independent syntactic and morphological properties that is responsible for the definitive accent. Syntactically, this morpheme follows definite NPs, but morphologically, it is suffixed to fully formed words. That is to say, it is a phrase-final, suffixal clitic, which in the unmarked case will attach to the last word of its syntactic complement. That is, of course, exactly where we find it.

The phrase in (67) above would receive the dual analysis in (78), an analysis in which the subcategorization requirements of the definitive accent lexeme are satisfied in both components.

(78)

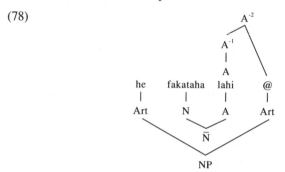

The crucial feature of ALS that resolves the ordering problem that Poser pointed out is that the morphological and syntactic analyses are simultaneous, rather than ordered with morphology preceding syntax. From the point of view of the autonomous morphological component, the expression *lahi*+@ is indistinguishable from any morphological construct since the syntactic properties of the lexeme @ are represented only in the syntax, where they belong.

5.2 VP → V, NP

Since the head of the phrase introduced by this rule is a member of the open class of transitive verbs, we should expect no clitic instantiations of it, by (1) of this chapter, the Law of Clitics. An affix or head of a compound that counts as the V in the rule above should therefore fall under the IP and form verbs by attaching to the head noun of the object phrase, leaving the rest of the phrase intact. If the affix forms morphological verbs, then it should be found where the verb in the rule above is ordinarily found, and leave behind a headless NP as a complement. This is, of course, exactly the behavior of the West Greenlandic object-incorporating suffixes, and Southern Tiwa, and Gta? compounding verb stems, about which enough has been said already.

5.3 VP → V, VP

5.3.1 Miscellaneous Cases

One of the most frequent categories of derivation and inflection in natural languages includes processes that add modal, aspectual, or temporal significance to verbs. Semantically, such operations frequently appear to be operations on propositions rather than on the meanings of the verbs themselves, the semantic scope of the verbal affix often extending beyond the meaning of the verb to which it is attached. In numerous languages ordinary productive negation is expressed by means of a verbal affix. It is often clear that the scope of this negative morpheme extends to the entire verb phrase of which the negated verb is the head, and is not restricted to the verb itself. Consider the following kind of construction in West Greenlandic (Fortescue 1984, 137).

(79) Aatsaat   tikeraa-nngi-laq
      for.first.time visit-NEG-INDIC/3s
      'It's not the first time he has visited.'

The scope of the single negation here extends over the adverbial *aatsaat* 'for the first time', so the sentence does not mean 'This is the first time he has failed to visit'.

Consider also the Japanese derivational suffix -*sugiru* 'excessively', which is added to verbs and adjectives, as discussed in Sugioka 1984, from which the following examples are drawn.

(80) Taroo wa tabe-sugi-ta.
      T.   TOP eat-excessively-PAST
      'Taroo ate too much.'

(81) Taroo wa kasiko-sugiru.
      T.   TOP clever-excessively
      'Taroo is too clever.'

The meaning of this suffix is something like that of the English derivational prefix *over-* in *overeat*, but as emphasized by Sugioka, there are notable differences between the two. The meaning of the English prefix modifies only the meaning of the verb that it is morphologically associated with. The Japanese suffix, on the other hand, clearly has the whole verb phrase in its scope, not just the verb to which it is morphologically joined:

(82) Taroo wa aisukuriimu o   tabe-sugi-ta.
      T.   TOP ice cream   ACC eat-excessively-PAST
      'Taroo ate too much ice cream.'
      (Cf. *John overate ice cream.)

(83) Taroo wa hayaku tuki-sugi-ta.
      T.   TOP early arrive-excessively-PAST
      'Taroo arrived too early.'
      (Cf. *John overarrived early.)

If it could be shown that -*sugiru* is a syntactic verb that takes a VP complement, as its meaning suggests it is, then this is clearly an example that conforms to the IP, since the suffix appears on the main verb (or adjective) of the predicate phrase, regardless of whether that verb exhausts *-sugiru*'s semantic scope or not.

The evidence so far is entirely semantic, and in view of the fact that I will suggest in chapter 6 that semantic organization is essentially independent of both the morphological and syntactic dimensions, one could easily locate the scopal discrepancies of Eskimo negation and Japanese *-sugiru* in the semantics and morphology, but not in the syntax at all, saying that the suffix attaches morphologically to the semantic head of its semantic argument phrase.

There is, however, some slim evidence that supports the syntactic, rather than semantic account of the distribution of *-sugiru*, namely the fact that the suffix need not attach to an item whose semantics it modifies at all. For example, subject honorifics (Harada 1976) are formed by prefixing an honorific particle *o-* to the infinitive of the verb, which is then used as the object of the locative preposition *-ni*. The resulting pseudo-adverbial is then verbalized with the aid of the auxiliary verb *nar*, which otherwise means 'become', but is presumably empty in this usage:

(84)   Sensei   wa hon o   o-yomi ni   nari-sugiru.
        professor TOP book ACC HP-read LOC AUX-excessively
        'The professor reads too many books.'

The position of *-sugiru* makes sense on the syntactic incorporative theory, for regardless of semantics, the SYNTACTIC head of the honorific VP *hon o o-yomi ni nar-* is the verb *nar*. If *-sugiru* is a morphological derivational suffix to verbs, and a verb that takes VP complements in the syntax, the IP predicts its location in (84).

5.3.2 Kirundi Future Marker

Sometimes there is incontrovertible grammatical evidence that verbal morphology counts as an independent, complement-taking verb in the syntax, (thus matching the semantics). An interesting example from the Bantu language Kirundi was brought to my attention by John Goldsmith.

In Kirundi, as in other Bantu languages, the verb consists of a number of morphemes in a fixed order. For our purposes it will be sufficient to consider the verb as consisting of a subject prefix, a tense prefix, a verbal stem, and an aspectual suffix. For the most part, the tense morphemes in the verbal complex have no particular relevance to the syntax and may be given a lexical specification that mentions their morphological and semantic properties alone. But the future-tense marker *-zoo-* is different in at least the following three ways: (1) unlike all other tense markers, which occur with the bare stem of the verb, *-zoo-* requires an infinitive form of the verb stem, if the verb-stem begins in a vowel; (2) the aspect marker must be *-a*, just as it must in an independent infinitive; and (3) if the verb-stem is defective and lacks an infinitive, it also lacks a future form. Yet it is clear that *-zoo-* is morphologically part of the verb, not just because it fills the tense-morpheme slot in the canonical verb template, but also for various phonological reasons. For one thing, no independent word of Kirundi can end in a long vowel as *-zoo-* does.

These facts indicate that the syntax of the marker *-zoo-* is just that of a verb that takes an infinitive complement, as several independent auxiliary verbs in the language do. Its morphology is just that of an ordinary verb-internal tense morpheme. The oddity is that these two behaviors are not usually associated with the same lexeme. We have here a kind of verb incorporation for which the evidence of syntactic relevance is telling.

Goldsmith suggests (p.c.) an autolexical representation for a word like *bazookuandika* 'they will write' as in (85). Note how the feature [INF] is inherited in this dual structure. It is found on the verb stem in the syntax because *zoo* selects complements with this feature and *andik* is the head of its complement. It also found on the morphological occurrence of that verb by (21) of chapter 2. Assuming that only morphological complements of the infinitive morpheme *ku* can bear this feature in the morphology, then that morpheme must be found in the morphological tree, but not in the syntactic tree, since *ku* has no syntactic representation.

(85)

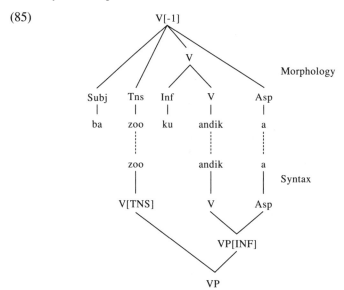

This case also falls under the Incorporation Principle; the element *-zoo-*, which has distinct syntax and morphology is required to combine with the head of its complement, which it clearly does in this example and even more clearly does in corresponding transitive sentences or sentences with auxiliary verbs. In all cases the autolexical element appears on the head of the phrase it is associated with:

(86)   Bazookuandika igitabo.
        'They will write a book.'

Verb incorporation, like much of what can be called incorporation, is often arguably a matter of derivational morphology, as in the Japanese example above, but it need not be. In Kirundi it is clearly an inflectional affix that is independently represented in both the syntax and morphology.

5.3.3 Hungarian Verb Compounding

Examples of verb compounding, where one of the members of the compound has the status of an auxiliary, and the other functions as the head of a VP are also fairly easy to come by. Donka Farkas and I (Farkas and Sadock 1989) have argued that the complex distribution of preverbs in Hungarian can be rather simply accounted for by postulating a morphological rule that composes finite and nonfinite verb forms into a single morphological entity. Thus the morphological structure of a sentence such as (87) is as indicated in the lower tree in (88).

(87)   Mari fog próbalni énekelni.
        M.   will try(INF) sing(INF)
        'Mary will try to sing.'

(88)

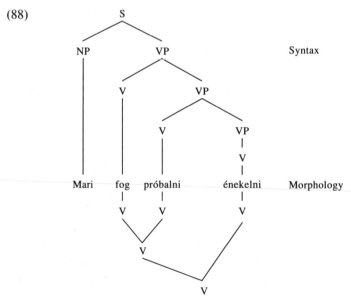

When and only when such a compound verb is present, a preverb that originates in association with a lower verb is found with the compound verb as a whole, since there is no room inside the compound for such a morphological constituent. In example (89), *fel-olvasni* 'to read out loud' (lit. 'read up') is a lexicosemantic unit (see chapter 7, section 3), but the preverb *fel* is associated with the entire compound verb *fog próbalni olvasni* in the autonomous morphological representation.

(89)   János fel fog próbalni olvasni.
           J.   up will try(INF) read(INF)
           'János will try to read out loud.'

The details of this analysis go well beyond the present point, which is simply that verb compounding of this sort is an additional example of incorporation. The interested reader is referred to Farkas and Sadock 1989. The finite verb is always attached to the head of its syntactic complement, i.e., the main verb of the immediately following VP.

Shifting attention now to cliticization, we need look no farther afield than English. The well-studied auxiliary clitics like the one in example (90) are clear instances of anticipatory clitics as described in chapter 3, section 5.2, governed by the CP.[2] A lexical entry for the present copular auxiliary, third person singular, is given in (91).

(90)   The girl sitting next to Jay's going to try first.

(91)   *'s* (English):
          syntax = $[_{VP\ [PRES,\ 3,\ SG]}$ —— VP [VFORM PPL]]
          morphology = $[_W$ W ——]
          interface = −CIC

5.4 PP → P, NP

5.4.1 Miscellaneous Cases

An autolexical element obeying the IP and instantiating P in this rule would convert unmarked noun phrases to the adverbial-like status of adpositional phrases, but would surface as morphology added to the stem of the head noun. A corresponding clitic would attach adjacent to the first word of an NP, if the language is prepositional, and adjacent to the last one, if it is postpositional.

Now it is extremely frequent to find the indicator of the oblique status of a noun phrase turning up as morphology on the stem of the head noun of the phrase, but ordinarily we would call this sort of situation case marking. If the morphology of the language does not provide a clear method of discrimination between stems and full words, and if furthermore the head is peripheral in the phrase, then the syntactic adposition that is realized as a morphological marker on the phrase-peripheral head of NP would simultaneously have all of the characteristics of a clitic, an element of an incorporative structure, and an inflection. This is the situation we find in languages like Japanese and Korean, for example in a Korean phrase like (92):

(92)   i   khal-ilo
        this knife-with
        'with this knife'

In such a case there is no reason (and, in the present theory, no need) to say whether the morpheme *ilo* is a case marker, clitic, or incorporating post-position.

But there are languages that present evidence to the effect that oblique head-marking is really the incorporation of an adposition. Baker (1988), for example, argues that Mohawk prepositions incorporate the head noun or their complement phrase, exactly as the IP would predict, and offers examples such as the following (from Hewitt 1903) to demonstrate his claim:

(93)   Wa'-hati-nawatst-a'rho' ka'-nowa-ktatie'   ne
        AOR-3Mp-mud-placed   PRE-carapace-along the
        Rania'tẹ'kowa'
        Great Turtle
        'They placed mud along the Great Turtle's carapace.'

Others (e.g., Chafe 1970), however, would analyze Mohawk morphemes such as *ktatie* as verbs, and if this is so, then (93) would simply be another example of noun incorporation and not an example of genuine preposition incorporation.

5.4.2 Hungarian Case Marking

But consider Hungarian, a language with both free postpositions and suffixes with relational meanings.[3] The suffixes are phonologically integrated with the noun to which they are attached and undergo vowel harmony determined by the vocalism of the stem, and participate in other obligatory phonological alternations such as the lengthening of a stem-final short [a] or [e]:

(94)   Magyarország-ról 'from Hungary'

(95)   Budapest-ről 'from Budapest'

(96)   utcáról 'from a street' (cf. utca 'street')

The postpositions, however, remain separate words and do not harmonize with the noun that precedes them or undergo rules of internal sandhi.

(97)   Magyarország mellett 'beside Hungary'

(98)   Budapest mellett 'beside Budapest'

(99)   utca mellett 'beside a street'

Despite the fact that some of these relational items are suffixes and some
separate words, they share so many syntactic and morphological (not to mention semantic) properties with the independent postpositions as to demand
treatment as the same thing at some level. Though the suffixes are frequently
called case endings in traditional descriptions of Hungarian, they are unlike
typical case endings in other languages in that they occur only once in a noun
phrase; they do not demand concord on determiners and adjectives, as do the
otherwise similar Finnish cases for example. In occurring in just one place in
the noun phrase they mark, the Hungarian relational suffixes are just like the
postpositions in this language, and indeed, are like adpositions in general.

(100)   egy fehér ház 'a white house'

(101)   egy fehér házról 'from a white house'

(102)   egy fehér ház mellett 'beside a white house'

One exception is the demonstrative construction in Hungarian, which consists of a demonstrative plus a definite noun phrase. In this construction the
suffix is required on both the demonstrative and on the head noun of the following NP:

(103)   ez   a   ház
          this the house
          'this house'

(104)   er-ről   a   ház-ról
          this-ről the house-ról
          'from this house'

But the independent postpositions are no different; they must also appear in
both places:

(105)   e⁴ mellett a   ház   mellett
          this beside the house beside
          'beside this house'

In addition to these syntactic similarities, the bound and free relational morphemes show morphological resemblances as well. A number of both the free
postpositions and the relational suffixes are bimorphemic. Using the termi-

nology of cognitive grammar (Langacker 1987 and the references there), they consist of a base denoting the landmark and a suffix denoting the path. Compare:

(106)   -bAn[5] 'in'; -bA 'into'; -bÓl 'out of'

(107)   mellett 'beside'; mellé 'to beside'; mellől 'from beside'

From the point of view of internal morphology, then, the suffixal postpositions and free postpositions also constitute a single category.

The most impressive proof of the syntactic reality of the Hungarian relational suffixes, however, is the fact that under certain circumstances, these morphemes turn up as stems rather than affixes. When the object of a free postposition is a pronominal,[6] the pronominal object shows up as personal inflection on the postposition:

(108)   mellettem 'beside me'

(109)   melletted 'beside you'

(110)   mellette 'beside him'

Remarkably enough, when those forms that would otherwise be relational suffixes have pronominal objects, the erstwhile suffixal morpheme is used as a stem, with its own internal vowel quality, and the personal endings are added to it:[7]

(111)   bennem 'in me'

(112)   benned 'in you'

(113)   benne 'in him'

These Hungarian facts can be treated straightforwardly within the framework developed here. The independent postpositions will be lexemes with the syntax of adpositions (hence postpositions, in this postpositional language) and the default morphology of stems. The personal affixes will be lexemes with the syntax (and semantics) of noun phrases. Morphologically they will be obligatory affixes to stems. The relational suffixes will be syntactic adpositions with the optional morphological status of suffixes to stems.

The independent adpositions are the easiest. If we describe them as syntactic adpositions, then by Sapir's Rule ((145) below) it is correctly predicted that they will be morphological stems. Thus (114) is a sufficient autolexical description of the morphosyntactic status of *mellett* 'beside', assuming that the word order is handled by an independent statement that governs other phrase types as well:

(114)   *mellett*:
         syntax = [$_{P[1]}$N[2], ——]
         morphology = default

I assume that the inflectional indicators of pronominal objects of adpositions in Hungarian really count as noun phrases in the syntax, the motivation for this claim being that there is complete complementarity between their appearance and the appearance of overt arguments:

(115)   mellette 'beside it'
         benne 'in it'

(116)   a ház mellett 'beside the house'
         a házban 'in the house'

(117)   *mellett
         *ben

(118)   *a ház mellette
         *a ház benne

But despite their syntactic reality, the suffixal pronouns have nondefault morphology; they are not stems, but necessarily combine with the stems of prepositions.[8] Their lexical entries ought therefore to be something like the following one for the first-person singular member of the family:

(119)   *Am*:
         syntax = NP [1, SG]
         morphology = [$_{P[-1]}$ P ——]

Given this sort of lexical entry for the personal suffixes, the syntactic representation of an "inflected preposition," as they are sometimes called, will be just that of an ordinary postpositional phrase—like *Béla mellett* 'beside Bela'—but of course will be different morphologically:

(120)

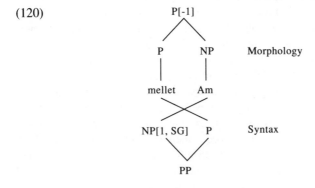

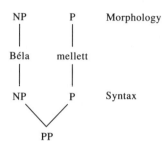

Turning finally to the autolexical adpositions of Hungarian, i.e., the suffixal forms, we may note that their behavior is accounted for if they have just the same syntactic entry as the independent adpositions, but are listed as having OPTIONAL nondefault morphology. Here "optional" means just that the morphological requirement is not always in force. The conditions determining whether the morphological subcategorization statement is in effect or not will be discussed presently.

(122)   *ben*:[9]
          syntax = [$_{PP}$, NP, ____]
          (morphology = [X[0], ____])

Now when a lexeme like (122) has a nonaffixal argument (i.e., anything but a pronoun like that in (119)), it will appear as an affix to a stem[10] and thus be governed by the IP. Thus it will attach to the head noun of the object phrase, regardless of where in the phrase this head appears, as in the following example, which I owe to Donka Farkas.

(123)   a   szép   kép-ről   amit   tegnap   látt-unk
          the beautiful painting-ről which yesterday saw-we
          'from the beautiful painting that we saw yesterday'

The preposition and the pronominal argument cannot both be affixal at the same time; there is a direct conflict between the morphological requirements of the one morpheme and those of the other. As we have seen, it is the adposition that gives up its morphological peculiarity in favor of the default morphology for a syntactic item, namely that of a stem, and for that reason its lexical entry indicates that the nondefault morphological status is optional.

But if the monosyllabic adpositions of Hungarian have the morphological status of affixes only optionally, what prevents them from occurring as free forms in phrases like *a ház ben*? Some parochial statement to the effect that the monosyllabic adpositions of Hungarian are suffixal except under duress would do the trick, but there is a more principled account of fact. As Paul Kiparsky (1973) has emphasized, more specific grammatical rules take precedence over more general ones, which apply "elsewhere." Since the lexical statement allowing certain syntactic adpositions of Hungarian to be suffixes is more particular than the general tendency for content morphemes to be expressed as stems, it will take precedence over the general rule wherever it can, viz., in all cases except where its object is itself obligatorily a suffix.

5.4.3 Crow Complex P Incorporation

There is an unusual kind of prepositional phrase incorporation in the Siouan language, Crow, brought to my attention and described by Randolph Graczyk (1989).

Crow has several simple, suffixal clitic postpositions:

(124)   Mary-sh ashtáahile is-kawúua-**n**   awáachi-k
        M.-DEF teepee   its-inside-LOC sit-DECL
        'Mary is sitting inside the teepee.'

(125)   Bill bin-náask-**etaa**   díili-k
        B. water-bank-along walk-DECL
        'Bill is walking along the shore.'

One of these, *(ku)-ss-(ee)*, expressing the goal relation, is different from the rest in that it demands incorporation into the verb. When it is not cliticized to a relational noun like *awúua* 'inside', or *píishi* 'behind', it still must cliticize to something, and is then supported by the empty noun-stem *ku-* 'it' (example (126)). When it cannot be incorporated (e.g., when there is no host (example (127)), it has the desinence *-ee/-aa*. But when it is suffixed to a relational noun, both the postposition and the relational noun are incorporated into the verb (example (128)).

(126)   Húuleesh Jerry-sh Chichúche **ku-ss**-dée-k.
        yesterday J.-DEF Hardin   it-GOAL-go-DECL
        'Jerry went to Hardin yesterday.'

(127)   Shóoss-da-lee?   Chichúche **kusseé.**
        where-GOAL-go-INTER Hardin   GOAL
        'Where are you going? To Hardin."

(128)   Charlie-sh aasúua **píishi-ss**-xalusshi-k.
        C.-DEF   house behind-GOAL-run-DECL
        'Charlie ran to the back of his house.'

There is both phonological and morphological evidence that the postposition and the relational noun are incorporated into the verb. First, the phonological facts: Crow words contain only one stress, and there is only one stress in *píishi-ss-xalusshi-k* in (128). Note particularly that in the semantically and syntactically parallel sequence *is-kawúua-n awáachi-k* in (124), there are two word stresses. Thus the division of the string into words that is given in (128) is quite secure.

Next, the morphological evidence: In Crow, first and second person arguments are expressed obligatorily as verbal prefixes, e.g., *diiwaalichí* 'I hit you', *biiláalichi* 'you hit me', *biilichí* '(he/she) hit me', etc. According to Graczyk's research, the incorporating relational noun plus postposition must occur inside these verbal prefixes, next to the stem:

(129)   Mary-sh awaasúua bii-**píishi-ss**-dee-hche-k.
         M.-DEF house   1s-behind-GOAL-go-cause-DECL
         'Mary sent me to the back of the house.'

(130)   *Mary-sh awaasúua píishi-ssee bii-lée-hche-k

What is especially important about this example is the stranding of an unmarked NP *awaasúua*, giving the sentence two unmarked NPs, the maximum number that a Crow clause can contain. But the verb is marked with the 1s object agreement prefix, and such verbs can only co-occur with one unmarked nominal. Thus *awaasúua* cannot be an immediate constituent of the clause, and we must recognize that it is still the possessor of the incorporated N *píishi*.

Since example (129) is unlike any sentence in the language that does not contain an incorporated preposition, the only reasonable analysis is an autolexical one like that given in (131), where the integrity of the prepositional phrase *awaasúua píishi-ss* 'to the house's rear' is recognized in the syntax.[11]

(131)

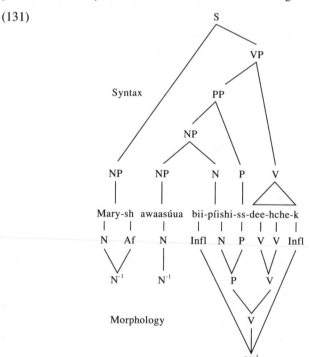

The crucial element, the postposition *(ku)-ss-(ee)*, will have to have a more complex lexical entry than any we have seen so far, since it simultaneously cliticizes and incorporates, or put more accurately, cliticizes to a relational noun to form a complex preposition of a kind that necessarily incorporates.

Crow morphology must contain the following minor rule that creates verb stems from verb stems by prefixing to them one of a small class of prepositions (arbitrarily indicated here with the feature [F]):

(132) $V[-0] \rightarrow P[F] + V[-0]$

The behavior of the postposition *-ss* can then be captured by describing it lexically as in (133).

(133)   *ss* (Crow):
        syntax $= P$
        morphology $= [_{P[F]} N[R, -1]$ ____]

The morphological field in this entry makes *-ss-* a clitic, since it attaches to a (relational) full noun. What is created by this process is a complex morphological preposition bearing the feature [F]. Assuming that the lexicon contains no underived postpositions marked [F], the only incorporating ones will be those formed from relational nouns ([R]) by the addition of *-ss*.

5.5 $\overline{S} \rightarrow$ Comp, S (Etc.)

If Comp is realized as incorporative morphology on stems, then it should appear together with main verbs of subordinate clauses, assuming (conservatively) that clauses are headed by VP. If the morphological result is a complex Comp, then it should appear where Comp would, and if it is a complex verb, then it should appear where the main verb does. In fact, the morphological modification of verbs of subordinate clauses to indicate complement status is one of the most frequent categories of inflection to be found in the languages of the world. But to count as incorporation, it must be clear that the mood morphology of a subordinate clause has exactly the SYNTAX of a complementizer and can therefore not be adequately treated by ordinary feature percolation mechanisms or in the semantics.

A convincing demonstration of the syntactic reality of a verbal marker would be its alternation with, and/or phonological resemblance to, an independent complementizer. Finnish provides such an example.[12]

5.5.1 Finnish Negative Incorporation

In Finnish the negative marker is a morphological and syntactic verb that inflects for person and number.

(134)   Hyppään.
         'I jump.'

(135)   Hyppäätte.
         'You(p) jump.'

(136)   Kello on neljä.
         'Clock is four,' i.e., 'It is four o'clock'.

(137)   En hyppää.
         'I do not jump.'

(138)   Ette hyppää.
         'You(p) do not jump.'

(139)   Kello ei ole neljä.
         'It is not four o'clock.'

Certain subordinating conjunctions in Finnish incorporate this negative verb. For some, such as *elle-* "unless, if not" the incorporation is obligatory, while for others, e.g., *että* "that" the incorporation is optional. According to Karlsson (1983, 191) both (141) and (142) are grammatical:

(140)   Elle-t   ole hiljaa, mene-n ulos.
         unless-2s be quiet   go-1s   to.outside
         'Unless you are quiet, I will go out.'

(141)   Väitätkö, että kello ei ole neljä?
         'Are you claiming that it is not four o'clock?'

(142)   Väitätkö, ettei kello ole neljä?
         'Are you claiming that it is not four o'clock?'

In (142), the negative verb, i.e., the head of the subordinate clause, has been incorporated into the complementizer. In the autolexical framework it is possible to say that (141) and (142) have exactly the same syntactic structure, but differ in that the negative verb is morphologically associated with the complementizer in one and not the other sentence, a situation that is in strict accordance with the IP. The syntactic and morphological structure of the subordinate clause with discrepant analyses, (142), are given in (143).

(143)

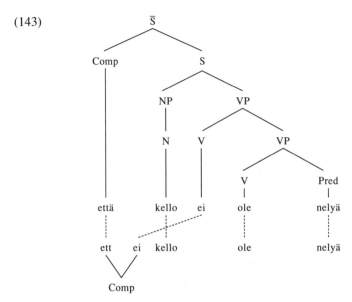

The Finnish complementizer facts make sense not only on the conservative assumption that clauses are headed by VP, but also on more speculative assumptions concerning clause structure, such as those found in Chomsky 1986. For the remainder of this section I will suppose, for the sake of discussion, that subordinate clauses are structured as in (144), where Comp heads what is traditionally S̄, and Infl heads the clause:

(144)

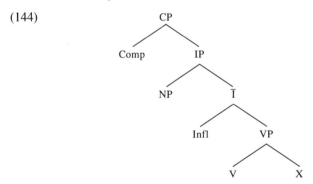

There are four possibilities with regard to which of the "nonlexical" elements Infl and Comp are incorporators: either Infl alone, or Comp alone may be an incorporator, or both may be, or neither.

The first possibility, that Infl is an incorporator—but Comp is not—would appear to be extremely common. Given a structure such as (144), an incorporating Infl will be found on the main verb of VP, if it is realized as verbal morphology. This follows from the strong CIC, (59) of chapter 4, and the IP.[13] This is such a common state of affairs that if Infl is actually an independent element of syntax, it is almost always involved in incorporation.

We may attempt to make this correlation explicit by making use of an observation of Sapir's. Sapir ([1921] 1949) organized "grammatical concepts" into a hierarchy of four classes, the endpoints being "basic (concrete) concepts" and "pure relational concepts." He said (p. 101) that basic concepts are "normally expressed as independent words or radical elements," while pure relational concepts are "normally expressed by affixing non-radical elements to radical elements . . . or by their inner modification, or by independent words,[14] or by position."

Suppose we identify concrete notions with elements that are represented in a semantics such as that outlined in chapter 2, section 1.2, i.e., F(unctions), M(odifiers), O(perators), and Q(uantifiers). Then we can come close to formalizing Sapir's insight by setting up a morphosemantic default like the following:

(145)   Sapir's Rule
         A lexeme that is represented in the semantics is a stem in the morphology. A lexeme that is not represented in the semantics is not a stem in the morphology.

But since (145) describes default correlations, it allows for the possibility of Infl (or any other noncontent lexeme) to show up as an independent morphological element. Ordinarily, independent words indicating personal information concerning arguments of a verb would be called pronouns, but there could exist facts that make such an identification impossible, in which case we would have to recognize the inflection-like character of independent words. A clear example of this kind is to be found in Huastec, a Mayan language of Northern Mexico. Here inflectional material occurs as an independent word in the syntax, the grammatical analog of a chemical free radical. The following facts and description of this language are due to Bruce Franklin (p.c.). See also Ochoa Peralta (1984).

5.5.2 Huastec Agreement

As in most Mayan languages, Huastec personal inflection is in terms of two sets of makers, called the A and B sets, that correspond closely to absolutive and ergative markers, respectively. In the transitive paradigm, the two morphemes are joined, and there is some syncretism, as shown in the following partial chart of the forms.

(146)　Huastec Agreement Forms (singular)
　　　a. Intransitive

Subject	1	2	3
	ʔin	ʔit	∅

　　　b. Transitive

Object \ Subject	1	2	3
1	—	tin	tin
2	tu	—	ti
3	ʔu	ʔa	ʔin

Whereas in most Mayan languages, such morphemes show up as prefixes and suffixes to the verb, in Huastec they are independent of the verb intonationally, and can even be separated from it:

(147)　ʔit　　cekenek
　　　2sABS tired
　　　'You are tired.'

(148)　ʔit　lej　cekenek
　　　2sg very tired
　　　'You are very tired.'

(149)　yab ki　　hayk'iʔ　k'aniiθaal
　　　NEG1p/3s ever　　appreciate
　　　'We do not ever appreciate her.'

There are at least three reasons why the little words in question cannot be considered pronouns. First of all, the transitive forms are portmanteau words, encoding, sometimes nonsegmentally, two separate referential bundles. For example, the third person singular absolutive in Huastec, as in many other Mayan languages, is signaled by the absence of a morpheme rather than the presence of one. The first singular subject, third singular object forms ʔu in the chart above is morphologically an indicator of the first-person ergative only, but since ergative subjects always imply absolutive objects, the unmarked third person is understood. While such behavior is quite common in agreement systems, pronouns do not work this way.

Second, there are independent pronouns in the language, and these have shapes quite distinct from the free agreement particles. The free pronouns apparently do not distinguish absolutive and ergative:

(150)   Huastec Independent Pronouns

	Singular	Plural
1	nan(aaʔ)	waw(aaʔ)
2	tat(aaʔ)	xax(aaʔ)
3	jaj(aaʔ)	bab(aaʔ)

Finally, the agreement particles are obligatory, even when the information they contain is explicitly represented by means of independent pronouns. It is often the case that such duplication is found in Huastec, since the syncretisms of the agreement morphemes would otherwise introduce intolerable ambiguities. The form *tu*, for example, represents the first-person singular subject, second-person singular object, as well as first plural object with any subject whatsoever. In the following sentence, which I owe to Bruce Franklin also, the five-fold ambiguity is resolved by the use of independent pronouns:

(151)   tataaʔ-cik tu   ʔucaʔ wawaaʔ
          you-p   X/1p said   we
          'You(p) said (it) to us.'

Inasmuch as the personal particles of Huastec contrast with independent pronouns, occur obligatorily, and display paradigmatic properties typical of agreement systems, I conclude that they are, in fact, agreement markers, even though they are independent words of the syntax.

I would like to suggest that the lexeme *tu* in Huastec is actually ambiguous in two ways, representing either the 1s/2s combination of ergative and absolutive arguments or the first-person plural absolutive category, combined with an ergative of unspecified person and number. On this latter reading, it would have a lexical specification such as the following:

(152)   *tu* (Huastec):
          syntax = Infl[ERG X, ABS 1 PL]
          morphology = X[−1]
          semantics = nil

In other Mayan languages, the morphological specification could be suppressed, allowing the default affixal behavior implied by (145) to emerge.

Returning to the possible behaviors of Comp and Infl, the second possibility is that Comp will be an incorporator and Infl will not. In such a case, we should expect Comp to combine morphologically with the head of its clausal complement, which under the assumptions of Chomsky 1986 that we are now exploring, is Infl.

One possible instance of this is to be found in Walmadjari, a language of Western Australia, described in Hudson 1976. A great many languages of Australia conjugate by means of auxiliaries, the conditions under which such periphrastic conjugation is obligatory, optional, or impossible differing widely. In many of these languages the auxiliary adds an increment of meaning often pertaining to Aktionsart, or aspect, but in some cases the auxiliary appears to have no such meaning, and to be what Capell (1976) called a "catalyst," a form that is required just to allow the affixation of bound morphemes such as tense and agreement to have something to attach to.

5.5.3 Walmadjari Auxiliaries

In Walmadjari, there are only two auxiliary roots, *pa-* and *nga-*, which contrast with the absence of an auxiliary. In combination with tense morphemes, which occur not on the auxiliary, but on the verb stem itself, the choice of auxiliary determines the mood of the sentence, as shown in the following chart.

(153)

	Regular Tense System	Past/Nonpast Tense System
Aux root *pa-*	indicative	implied negative
Aux root *nga-*	interrogative	implied admonitive
Aux root Ø-	hortative	imperative obligative

This mood indicating function of the inflected auxiliary can be seen in the following paradigm from Hudson 1976, where the suffixes on the main verb are from the regular tense system.

(154)   Yan-ku pa-lu.
go-FUT AUX-3p
'They will go.'

(155)   Yan-ku nga-lu.
go-FUT AUX-3p
'Will they go?'

(156)   Yan-ku-li.
go-FUT-1d.INC
'Let's go.'

If mood is determined by the nature of Comp, then Walmadjari presents an instance of an inflected, i.e., incorporating, complementizer.

5.5.4 West Flemish Inflected Complementizers

A very clear case of an inflecting complementizer has recently been carefully documented by Smessaert (1988). In the West Flemish dialect of Veurne, complementizers not only attract subject, object, and other clitics (see chapter 3, section 4), but also agree with the subject in the same manner as do verbs. The verbal paradigm in the present tense in this dialect has *-n* in the first-person singular and plural and in the third-person plural, and has *-t* every-where else, as shown by the conjugation of the verb *zou* 'will'.

(157)

	Singular	Plural
1	k-zoun	m-zoun
2	je-zout	je-zout
3M	ne-zout	
F	ze-zout	ze-zoun
N	t-zout	

The first morpheme in the forms above is a subject clitic. It appears before the verb in the indicative, and after it in the interrogative, the paradigm for which is given in (158), where inflectional *-t* is elided before consonants.

(158)

	Singular	Plural
1	zoun-k	zoun-me
2	zou-je	zou-je
3M	zout-en	
F	zou-se	zoun-ze
N	zou-t	

Remarkably, complementizers of subordinate clauses, like *dat* 'that', *o* 'whether', and *a* 'if, when(ever)', display almost exactly the same paradigm:

(159)

	Singular	Plural
1	dan-k	da-me
2	da-je	da-je
3M	dat-en	
F	da-se	dan-ze
N	da-t	

A complication that makes this case less than a perfectly straightforward example of complementizers incorporating Infl is the fact that both the com-plementizer and the verb are inflected in a West Flemish subordinate clause:

(160)   K-zou-n-t-joun   zèggen a-**n**-k-et   wist-**en**.
         I-would-INFL-it-you tell   if-INFL-I-it knew-INFL
         'I would tell you if I knew.'

In the subordinate clause *anket wisten*, the first-person inflection *-(e)n* appears both on the complementizer *a* and on the finite verb. One possibility is that this inflectional material both incorporates the head of its own complement, and is obligatorily incorporated by the Comp, two possibilities that are individually allowed by the IP. To allow this, however, would require an extension of the system developed so far such that a single node at one level can be matched with two at another, as depicted in (161).

(161)

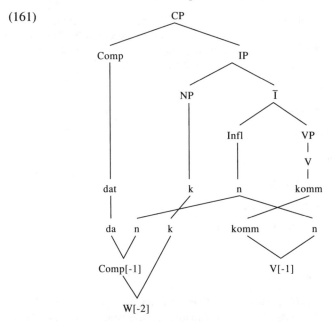

Though it might turn out to be necessary to allow such double associations,[15] doing so is not required in the present instance. I assume instead that verbal inflection is sometimes purely morphological and not associated with a syntactic formative, in which case it is properly called agreement. If this is the case here, then only the inflected complementizer is a case of incorporation, as I use the term. The bimodular structure for (160) will therefore be as in (161), but with the suffix following the verb in the morphology unconnected to the syntax.

5.5.5 Santali Clitic Infls

The Finnish and West Flemish examples discussed above are close to canonical incorporation (in the sense in which I use the term) both in that the morphological manifestation of Infl is as morphology to a stem, and in that the syntax would not otherwise put the morphemes in question adjacent to one another. Much more common than these cases of apparent incorporation of Infl are those where Infl behaves as a clitic.

Consider the case of Santali, a Munda language of India, whose relevance was brought to my attention by Knut Bergsland. Santali obligatorily references animate subjects by means of what Bodding (1929) calls an enclitic pronoun. This particle appears as a suffix to the verb in some cases, but if there is anything preceding the verb, it appears suffixed to that word. To quote Bodding (p. 165):

> If the verb stands alone, i.e., is the whole sentence, or is the initial part of a sentence, the subject pronoun naturally comes at the end of the verb (in the finite verb after the *a*); when preceded by a word, the verbal subject is generally affixed to the preceding word.

Some examples from Bodding:

(162)   calak'am 'Will you go?'

(163)   alom calak'a 'Do not go.'

(164)   *alo calak'am

(165)   calak'an 'I will go.'

(166)   hen calak'a 'Yes, I will go.'

(167)   he inin calak'a 'Yes, I will go.'

(168)   *in calak'an

(169)   *he calak'an

Note especially (166), where the subject marker is attached to a sentence adverb, demonstrating its clitic-like behavior, and the contrast between (167) and (168). In (168) *in* is an independent, uncliticized first person pronoun. The sentence is ungrammatical, however, requiring the morphologically identical particle as well (cliticized in (167) to the pronoun itself!). This clearly demonstrates the nonpronominal, inflectional function of the subject marker.

Let us suppose that Santali syntax contains the rule (170), that assures that the clausal subject inflection immediately precedes the verb. The suffixal subject markers will have lexical entries along the lines of (171), which simply state that they count as syntactic Infl and that they must be suffixes to full words.

(170) $S \rightarrow XP^n \text{ Infl VP}$

(171)   *(i)n* (Santali):
        syntax $= \text{Infl}[1S]$
        morphology $= [_{X[-2]}X[-1] \underline{\qquad}]$

Now since Infl is introduced between phrases in (170), the CIC will be satisfied regardless of the direction in which Infl attaches. If anything precedes it in the syntax, then the LC will constrain it to attach to that preceding word, but if nothing does, then the strong form of the LC simply cannot apply, and the marker will attach to the first word of VP, as required.

5.5.6 Nama (Hottentot) Clitic Infl

Another very clear example of an Infl-like element with clitic behavior is to be found in Nama Hottentot. The discussion below is based directly on Roy S. Hagman's lucid description (Hagman 1977).[16]

Nama nouns must bear a Person/Gender/Number (PGN) suffix. Gender is determined according to sex for nouns referring to people or animals, but is an arbitrary lexical fact for other nouns, with some subregularities of the kind familiar from European languages. There is also a facultative gender which any noun may bear that serves to mark an NP as indefinite.

Nama clauses contain an obligatory element preceding the verb phrase that we may identify as syntactic Infl, expressing exactly the same PGN features, and having exactly the same allomorphy as the noun–inflection marker PGN. The syntactic Infl is a suffix to whatever word immediately precedes it, and is thus a run-of-the-mill anticipatory clitic, if it is generated syntactically in a position immediately before the VP, or a run-of-the-mill second-position clitic, if it arises sentence-initially in the syntax. As can be seen from (172) and (173), the Infl replicates the PGN features of the subject, if there is one. If there is no subject present, the Infl represents the subject, at least semantically, as (174) shows.

(172) !'áa-s   !'oá-p   ke   nee 'áo-p-à   ra   !ũu
       town-3/F/s to-INFL(3/M/s) DECL this man-(3/M/s)-SB PROG go
       'This man is going to the town.'

(173) !ũu-p   ke   ra[17]   nee 'áo-p-à   !'áa-s   !'oá
       go-INFL(3/M/s) DECL PROG this man-3/M/s-SB town-3/F/s to
       'This man is going to the town.'

(174) /úí tsèe-ts   ke   nĩĩ ≠'oá !áro-p   !nãa
       one day-INFL(2/M/s) DECL FUT go.out forest-3/M/s into
       'One day you will go out into the forest.'

Declarative clauses such as these have an obligatory particle immediately following the position of Infl. Interrogative clauses have either a discontinuous particle, one piece of which goes immediately after Infl, and one at the end of the clause, or nothing, and imperative-hortatives have either no particle at all, or a softening particle at the end of the clause.

As in Santali, Infl may be suffixed to a conjunction that introduces a clause:

(175) tsií-p   ke   nee 'áo-p-à   kè   !ũu
       and-INFL(3/M/s)   DECL this man-3/M/s-SB PAST go
       'and this man went'

(176)   'oo-s   ke   //'ĩ-s-à   kè   tĩ

then-INFL(3/F/s) DECL DEM-3/F/s-SB PAST ask
'then she asked . . .'

In (172) and (173) some constituent has been fronted and the Infl attaches to the end of that constituent. In (175) and (176), nothing has been fronted, and Infl attaches to the conjunction. If something is fronted in a clause like (175), the clitic Infl attaches to the end of the fronted constituent, and not to the conjunction (cf. (177)), giving evidence that Infl is generated before the speech-act particle and not clause initially. If it were a clause-initial second-position clitic, it would be found after the conjunction in all cases.

When the conjunction is *'oo*, nothing may be fronted (Hagman 1977, 118).

(177)   xape 'ééka-p   ke   práin-à[18]   marínà kè   hòo
        but   then-INFL(3/M/s) DECL Brian-3/M/s/SB money PAST find
        'but then Brian found the money'

On the basis of these facts, I postulate that the basic structure of a declarative clause is as in (178), and that there is a topicalization rule (179) that puts one constituent in front of Infl.

(178)   S → Infl[αF] ke N[αF] VP

(179)   TP → XP S/XP

Rule (178) specifies the agreement of Infl with a nominative NP, if there is one. If there is no nominative NP before VP, the choice of features for Infl is free.

Suppose now that the lexical entry for an Infl element requires it to be a suffix, as specified in (180).

(180)   *-p/-i* (Nama):
         morphology = [x $\underline{}_{[3/M/s]}$]
         syntax = Infl
         interface: +LC

As a suffixal clitic, this lexeme could in principle either attach to a preceding word in order to satisfy the LC, or out of order as a suffix to the following word, in order to satisfy the CIC. As the examples above show, it satisfies the LC. Here, as in Santali, the CIC is literally irrelevant, since Infl is introduced with several sister phrases. The LC should, then, be the only important interface condition, making Nama clitics attach as a suffix to the preceding word, if there is one, and to the following word, otherwise. But the Nama Infl AL-WAYS attaches to a preceding word, and for that reason I have included an ad hoc interface stipulation in its lexical entry requiring it to obey the LC.

In the syntax of clauses not introduced by conjunctions, there would be nothing preceding Infl to support it morphologically. Therefore something must be moved into that position. Thus the topicalization rule will be effectively obligatory in main clauses, though not in subordinate clauses. Hagman (1977, 108) points out that the preposed constituent is in "the position of highest emphasis," although he also says that the "normal" word order has the subject initialized. I therefore assume that in Nama, as in more familiar languages such as German, subjects are default topics.

I turn next to a discussion of the morphology of nouns in Nama. As I stated, every Nama noun must bear a PGN suffix immediately following the stem. Assuming, as elsewhere (cf. (21) of chapter 2, and Sadock 1988b) that inflections and stems agree morphologically,[19] the inherent features of a noun stem and those of an inflectional affix will have to be nondistinct in a rule like (181).

(181) $N[-1] \rightarrow N[-0] + [PGN]$

Another feature of this language that we need to consider is a nominal suffix that Hagman calls the subordinative. Noun phrases of Nama generally have this suffix (phonologically -à) on the last word of the phrase, unless they are immediately followed by an element that shows their relation to the sentence. The only argument NPs that are not so marked are a preposed subject of a declarative clause, which is followed by the declarative particle ke, the objects of certain postpositions, and the first term of an "associative" phrase, which is followed by the associative element ti, that covers roughly the same semantic territory as the English genitive. Postposed subjects, subjects of interrogative and imperative/hortative clauses, objects, time adverbials, objects of certain postpositions, and predicate nominals all have the subordinative -à suffix (abbreviated SB in the glosses here.)

While other treatments are certainly possible and may turn out to be better justified, I will handle these case-marking facts by assuming that Nama has a syntactic rule (182) that adds surface case to NPs. I also assume that some, but not all postpositions assign an abstract case feature [OBL] to their objects. CASE is then realized as nothing in the presence of the abstract case features, [NOM] when immediately followed by ke, or [OBL] when immediately followed by a postposition (including the associative ti). Otherwise CASE is realized as -à. The lexical entries (183) and (184) will accomplish this, but bear in mind that more specific lexemes must be used where possible (Kiparsky 1973; 1982b).

(182) $NP \rightarrow NP$ CASE

(183)   Ø (Nama):
      syntax = CASE[NOM] / ____ke
                  CASE[OBL] / ____P

(184)   *à* (Nama):
         syntax = CASE
         morphology = $[_{x[-2]}X \text{\_\_\_}]$

Thus *à* is a (simple, final) clitic, and hence follows the inflectional PGN introduced by (181). A word of the form *N + à + PGN would be ungrammatical because *à* creates a morphological unit more complex than a stem, while the inflectional PGN must be added to a stem, as specified in (181).

In view of the role that they play in morphology, a minor correction needs to be made in the lexical specification of the PGN markers. An entry such as (180) above requires the PGN suffix to count as an element of the syntax, namely Infl, in which case it is a clitic that is attached to a preceding word for the reasons already mentioned. But PGN markers also function as nonsyntactic inflections of nouns, obligatory morphological elements of any independent nominal word. In such usages, they are not represented in the syntax at all, a fact that we can describe by parenthesizing the syntactic manifestation, as in (185). Where the affix does not express a syntactic category, but has reality only in the morphology, interface considerations become irrelevant, since there is no interface to constrain.

(185)   *-p/-i* (Nama):
         morphology = $[X \underset{[3/M/s]}{\text{\_\_\_}}]$
         syntax = (Infl)

When a constituent other than the subject is in initial position, there are two PGN markers with quite different functions.

(186)

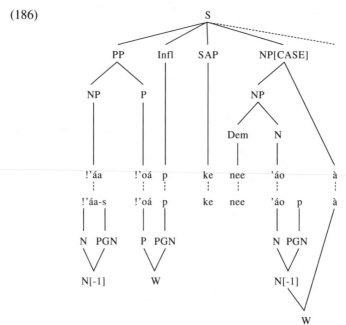

The suffix on the preposition *!'oá* is an expression of the syntactic element Infl, as its lexical entry optionally allows. As such, it is a clitic, and in the absence of marking to the contrary, it attaches to the preceding word in order to satisfy the strong Linearity Constraint, as we see here. The second PGN marker, on the unfronted subject *'áo*, has no connection to the syntax, again as its lexical specification makes possible. Here it counts as nominal inflection only, satisfying the wordhood requirement for nouns expressed by rule (181).

But when the subject is initial in the sentence, as in example (187), A SINGLE OCCURRENCE OF THE PGN MORPHEME CAN SIMULTANEOUSLY SATISFY BOTH THE SYNTACTIC REQUIREMENT OF THE CLAUSE AND THE MORPHOLOGICAL REQUIREMENT OF THE NOUN. It is a nominative PGN in the morphology, and hence can count as the nominative PGN in syntax, namely Infl.

(187)   nee 'áo-p   ke   !'áa-s   !'oá ra   !ũu

        this man-3/M/s DECL town-3/F/s to   PROG go
          'This man is going to the town.'

(188)

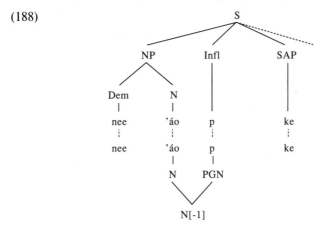

In this structure, the morpheme *-p* is an inflection when viewed from the morphological side of the diagram, and a clitic when both syntactic and morphological structure are considered. As a clitic, it must occur in the same linear order in both strings, which it can here, since the subject immediately precedes its position in syntax.

The duality of the PGN morpheme in Nama is neatly illustrated by what happens when an object occupies the initial-constituent position in the sentence. In the unmarked order, the subject is initial and is not marked with the subordinative *-a*, while the object follows the SAP, and is so marked.

(189)   'áo-p   ke   //'ĩp-à   hàí-p-à   kè   màa
        man-3/M/s SAP PRO-3/M/s-SB stick-3/M/s-SUB PAST give
        'The man gave him the stick.'

The three occurrences of the 3/M/s PGN in this sentence inflect each of the three nouns it contains, and additionally, the first counts as the syntactic Infl, as in diagram (188). When the object occurs initially, it is still marked with the subordinative, to show its status as object, the subject occurs after the SAP, and gains a subordinative suffix, as before.

(190)   hàí-p-à-p   ke 'áo-p-à   //'ĩ-p-à   kè   màa
        stick-3/M/s-SB-3/M/s SAP man-3/M/s-SB PRO-3/M/s-SB PAST give
        'The man gave him the stick.'

Notice that there are now FOUR PGNs in the sentence TWO OF THEM ON THE SAME WORD. The reason why there must be two PGNs in this word is that the first PGN feature is the object noun's agreement morpheme, and hence is not nominative, since the noun is not. But the syntactic Infl is always nominative, as required by (178), and cannot be associated with anything but a nominative PGN in morphology.

I will conclude this description of the Nama inflectional clitics with a discussion of the following example, in which a nondeclarative subject is in topic position. As rules (183) and (184) imply, the subject is marked with -*à*, since, though nominative, it does not precede the declarative particle. But there is only one PGN morpheme in this sentence, which counts both as the noun's inflection and the sentence's Infl.

(191)   //'ĩ-p-a[20]   //ań'-è   kè   ≠'uũ?

        PRO-3/M/s-SB meat-3/M/s/SB[21] PAST eat
        'Did he eat the meat?'

(192)

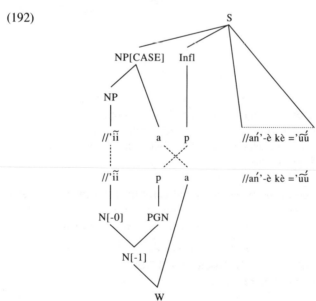

The autolexical diagram for this example must have crossing association lines even though both of the elements involved—the PGN marker and the subordinative marker—are simple suffixal clitics. The crossing of association lines is mandated here by the fact that if PGN is to count as the noun's inflection, it must occur next to the stem, but if it is also Infl in syntax, it follows the topic phrase, including its subordinative suffix. As was the case with other similar examples that we have encountered, this ordering clash is resolved in favor of the more stringent requirements of morphology.

5.6 N̄ → N, NP

A frequent instantiation of this rule is the marking of possession in natural language, as in (193).

(193)   Schloss der Königin von Dänemark
         'castle of the Queen of Denmark'

The N introduced by 5.6 is a member of an open lexical class, thus precluding realizations of this element as a clitic. Indeed I know of no clitic-like examples.

But the lexical N in this rule could be an incorporator, in which case it would show up in morphological association with the head noun of the modifying NP. It is possible that the noun will appear as an affix on the head, but this is not particularly likely, since the class of nouns is open ended. Much more likely is the possibility of there being NN compounds, where one is the N in 5.6, and the other the head of the NP in that rule. This would result in examples like the fictitious (194) as a counterpart to (193). The example is grammatical, but the prepositional phrase cannot be taken as an adjunct of the noun stem *Königin*.

(194)   Königinschloss von Dänemark

5.6.1 Hebrew Construct State

A language where this sort of incorporation is found is Hebrew. Nominal compounds in Hebrew are formed by placing the head noun in a special morphological guise called the construct state and following it by the modifying noun. The construct state is sometimes homophonous with the independent form of the noun, but is more often distinct:

(195)   bayit 'house'
         batim 'houses'

(196)   beyt-sefer 'school' (lit.: 'book house')
         batey-sefer 'schools'

Despite the morphological uniformity of the formation of compounds in Hebrew, Berman (1986) and Borer (1988) independently point out that they are of two radically different types with respect to their syntactic and semantic properties. One type is lexicalized and is opaque both semantically and syntactically. The other type, which is of interest here, displays many features pointing to the syntactic and semantic independence of the pieces of the compound. I shall summarize some of their arguments here.

First, Berman (1986) and Borer (1988) observe that the lexicalized forms have idiosyncratic meanings such that the compound does not necessarily denote a subset of what is denoted by the head noun alone. The productive forms, on the other hand, have predictable meanings such that the denotatum of the compound is always a thing of the kind denoted by the head N.

(197)   Lexicalized   Productive

         gan-yeladim   gan-peyrot
         garden children   garden fruit
         'kindergarten'   'fruit garden'

         gan-xayot   gan-'eden
         garden animals   garden Eden
         'zoo'   'garden of Eden'

         beyt-sefer   beyt-'ec
         house-book   house-wood
         'school'   'wooden house'

         shomer-mitzvot   shomer-mexoniyot
         guard-commandments   guard-automobiles
         'practicing Jew'   'automobile guard'

Berman and Borer also note that the number of the modifying element has an unpredictable effect on the meaning of the lexicalized compounds, but has its ordinary semantic effect in the case of the productive forms.

(198)   Lexicalized   Productive
         beyt-ha-sefer   shomer-ha-bayit
         house-the-book   guard-the-house
         'the school'   'the guard of the house'

         beyt-ha-sefarim   shomer-ha-batim
         house-the-books   guard-the-houses
         'the library'   'the guard of the houses'

On the syntactic side, the lexicalized compounds do not tolerate modification or conjunction of the modifying noun, whereas the productive forms do.

(199)   Lexicalized   Productive

         *gan-yeladim ve-xayot   shomer-batim u-mexoniyot
         garden-children and-animals   guard-houses and-cars
         not: 'kindergarten and zoo'   'guard of houses and cars'

         *gan-yeladim ktanim   shomer-mexoniyot gnuvot
         garden-children small   guard-cars stolen
         not: 'kindergarten for   'guard of stolen cars'
            small children'

Finally, the head noun in the lexicalized forms does not count as an antecedent for anaphoric processes, whereas the head noun of the productive forms can:

(200)   Lexicalized

         *shney batey-xolim   ve-'exad le-zkenim
          two   houses-sick.people and-one to-old.people

         Productive

         shney batey-ec   ve-'exad mi-plastik
         two   houses-wood and-one from-plastic
         'two wooden houses and one of plastic'

On the basis of this and other evidence, Borer suggests that morphology be made a parallel component to syntax so that the rule that forms compounds in the construct state, be allowed to operate both before and after deep structure. The essential feature of her theoretical innovation, namely that parts of a morphological structure can have independent reality in syntax, is directly formulable in the system advocated here. The facts concerning the productive construct state compounds that Borer and Berman have pointed to make sense in the present framework as an example of incorporation based on rule 5.6.

The construct state diverges somewhat from canonical incorporation as described in chapter 4, and tends toward cliticization as described in chapter 3. First, the construct state does not combine with a noun stem, but rather with a fully inflected noun, as shown in the examples above. Second, incorporation will typically fail to occur if the complement is conjoined, since the complement would not then have a unique head; but as example (199) shows, construct state nouns may incorporate only one of the heads of a conjunct, again behavior that is reminiscent of cliticization.

At any rate, it would seem appropriate that the transparent examples of construct state nouns such as *shomer* in (199) should be allowed to appear in the syntax even though they are bound up in the morphological structure.

The morphological component of Modern Hebrew will contain a rule forming N+N compounds, the first member of which is the head, and which is in the construct state, indicated here by the feature [CS], which is also a trigger for the morphophonological operation that returns the appropriate segmental form.

(201) $N[-0] \rightarrow N[-0, CS] + N[-1]$

Recall that in the default case, any feature of a lexeme in the morphology is a feature of it in the syntax, and vice versa (chapter 2, (21)). The sharing of the feature [CS] across the morphology-syntax boundary is important, since plain Ns in Hebrew take PP complements, not NP complements. Thus the syntax of Hebrew can contain a special rule combining construct-state nouns, i.e., those that are heads of NN compounds in the morphology, directly with NPs.

(202) $N[1] \rightarrow N[0, CS] + N[2]$

Taken together, these two rules sanction morphosyntactic diagrams such as the following, in which a noun with a certain morphosyntactic feature (and only such a noun) appears in a syntactic structure and in a noncongruent morphological structure. Note particularly that this bimodular structure conforms perfectly to the IP in that the elements of the complex morphological expression are a lexical head and the lexical head of its syntactic complement.

(203)

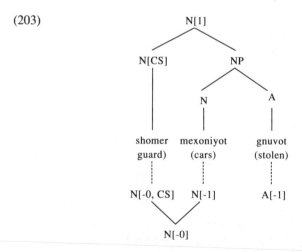

Now according to these rules, there is no need for a [CS] noun in the morphology to be found in a simultaneous syntactic structure. The complex noun stem that it forms can be the smallest node associated with a syntactic formative. On the other hand, construct state nouns only occur as members of larger morphological expressions. This asymmetry can be handled by supposing that syntactic nouns default to [−CS], a default that can only be overridden by the occurrence of the noun in a compound on the other side of the interface.

5.7 N̄ → A, N̄

Numerous languages contain morphological processes that produce modified nouns from noun stems, including, but by no means limited to diminutives, augmentatives, hypochoristics, and pejoratives. These are all prima facie candidates for adjectives that show up as morphology on the head of the phrase that they modify. Highly synthetic languages often contain a fairly impressive number of affixes with adjectival import and thus are likely to yield clear examples of incorporative versions of A in this rule, though I know of no persuasive case at present.

5.7.1 Spanish Diminutives

An interesting clitic-like example is the Spanish diminutive -ito/a in some of its uses.[22] Ordinarily, this suffix can perfectly well be treated as an ordinary N-to-N derivational suffix that increments just the meaning of the noun stem to which it applies, and therefore displays no bracketing mismatches with respect to other levels of representation.

However, as Varela (1986) has shown, this is not the case when it applies to the special Romance compounds formed from a verb and a plural noun, such as *tocadiscos* [record player] (*toca* 'play' + *discos* 'records') or *limpiabotas* 'bootblack' (*limpia* 'clean' + *botas* 'boots'). Note that the nominal element in these compounds is not the head, even though the complex expression is nominal, and the other element is a verb. If *botas* in *limpiabotas* were the head, then the compound should describe a type of boot, be feminine in gender, and be plural in number, none of which it is. Varela 1986 assumes that these compounds are headless in the morphology, which seems reasonable enough.

Despite the fact that the nominal in such Spanish compounds is not the head, they are diminutivized by attaching the regular derivational affix -ito/a to the noun stem. As in other uses of the diminutive suffix, the gender of the stem is transferred to the derived stem. Furthermore, the plural inflection of the second member of the compound is applied to the derived stem in the morphologically ordinary fashion, the result being that a small record player is *tocadisquitos*, and a small bootblack is *limpiabotitas*.

A structure that adequately represents the conflicted nature of a formation such as *limpiabotitas* 'little bootblack' is given in (204).

(204)

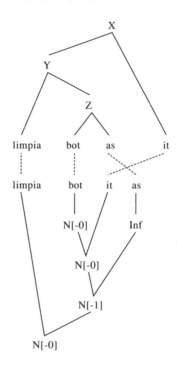

The bottom structure in (204) is morphology proper, where each subword piece is to be found in an appropriate structural position. But what is the top structure in this diagram? It is not syntax, as the categories involved are not phrases, and it is also not ordinary morphology, since that is what the lower structure represents. What the top structure in (204) represents is clearly the semantic organization of the morphemes in the lexical item *limpiabotitas*, something that Donka Farkas and I (Farkas and Sadock 1989) have dubbed "lexicosemantic structure." The form *botitas* that figures in the purely morphological organization is not a constituent in the semantics of the compound, since a *limpiabotitas* can polish any size boots, not just small ones.

Suppose the Spanish diminutive suffix has the following lexical representation:

(205)   *-it* (Spanish):
         morphology $= [_{N[-0]} \text{ N}[-0] \underline{\quad}]$
         syntax $=$ nil
         semantics $= M(F^n) = F^n$

The Spanish diminutive suffix is thus a lexicosemantic analog to a penultimate position clitic at the morphology-syntax interface, as the diagram in (204) shows.[23]

5.8 AP → A, NP

5.8.1 Sorbian Personal Adjectives

Consider the following rather surprising data discussed in Corbett 1987 as well as in Sadock 1985a. In Upper and Lower Sorbian, West Slavonic languages spoken in Lusatia in East Germany, there are adjective-forming suffixes that can be added to nouns denoting persons, forming from them adjectives with a meaning roughly equivalent to the adnominal genitive of the noun. These derived adjectives agree with the noun that they modify in just the way ordinary adjectives do:

(206)   (Upper Sorbian)
        žonina   drasta
        woman-ADJ-NOM/F/s dress-NOM/F/s
        'a woman's dress'

But remarkably, the noun from which the adjective is formed retains its referentiality, and can be modified, possessed, or subsequently referred to with personal pronouns:

(207)   (Upper Sorbian)
        star-eje   žon-in-a   drast-a
        old-GEN/F/s woman-ADJ-NOM/F/s dress-NOM/F/s
        'dress of an old woman'

(208)   (Upper Sorbian)
        moj-eho   bratr-ow-e   džéć-i
        my-GEN/M/s brother-ADJ-NOM/p child-NOM/p
        'my brother's children'

(209)   (Lower Sorbian)
        to   su nas-ogo   nan-ow-e   crejeje
        those are our-GEN/M/s father$_i$-ADJ-NOM/p shoes

        won jo je   zabyl
        he$_i$ is them forgotten
        'Those are our father$_i$'s shoes. He$_i$ has forgotten them.'

Note the agreement pattern in these examples. The derived adjective agrees with the noun that it modifies in case, gender, and number, but the modifier of the internal noun agrees with the internal noun in gender and number and is always in the genitive case. Syntactically, then, the incorporated noun forms a phrase with its modifier, while morphologically it is the root of an adjective. Suppose the Sorbian denominal adjective suffixes have the following lexical representations:

(210)   a. *-in*:
          morphology = [$_{A[-0]}$N[FEM]___]
          syntax = [$_{AP}$NP[GEN]___]
       b. *-ow*:
          morphology = [$_{A[-0]}$N[MASC]___]
          syntax = [$_{AP}$NP[GEN]___]

Then example (207) above could be analyzed in terms of the double tree below:

(211)

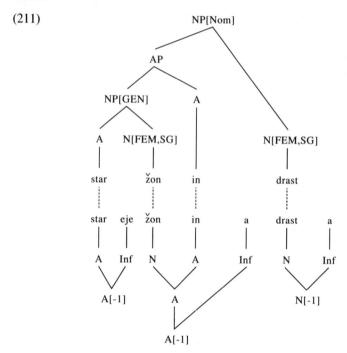

Both nouns are feminine singular, the whole NP is nominative (in this example), and the internal NP must be genitive because of the subcategorization requirements of the adjective-forming suffix *-in* and the general requirement that subcategorization requirements must be met at all levels in well-formed natural-language expressions. These features are distributed throughout the syntactic and morphological trees in the following manner: *drast* is nominative and NP dominating it is feminine and singular by the HFC. AP is nominative, feminine, singular by the CAP, and these features are all inherited by the adjective forming suffix *-in* by HFC. The noun stem *žon* and the NP that immediately dominates it must share the features genitive, feminine, and singular by the HFC, and so must the adjective stem *star*, by the CAP. The individual lexemes thus bear the following features in the morphological tree, matching those in the syntax according to the default association of categories across the morphology-syntax boundary (default principle in (21) of chapter 2).

(212)

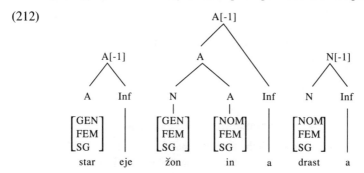

Note once again that these data conform perfectly to the IP. The autolexical element *-in* combines with a stem in the morphology which is the head of the phrase that it combines with in the syntax.

6

Autonomous Semantics

6.1 Semantic Representation

Of the many things for which the term "semantics" might be employed, I will use it only to refer to the kind of component sketched in chapter 2, section 1.2, a component that produces structures in which function-argument and variable-binder relations and their semantic scope are expressed. A single semantic component of this kind may contain too little, since it deals only with combinatorics and does not make any discriminations based on content, or it may contain too much, because it conflates quantification and function-argument structure, as is traditional in logic, but it will serve to advance the discussion.

In some conceptions of grammar, the semantic component interprets some level, or levels, of syntactic structure, making adjustments such that the result is arguably a representation in a disambiguated, interpreted, intensional language. In Montague grammar, GPSG, and the like, the construction of logical representations proceeds hand in hand with the construction of syntactic form, combining the meanings of expressions at the same time as their forms are combined syntactically. Both kinds of theories thus give a priority to syntactic structure that results in what seem to me to be unnecessary complications of the semantic machinery. In those views of the position of semantics within grammar, semantic representation is parasitic upon or coupled with the syntax, so in many cases special devices are required to "correct" the combinatorics that are found in the syntax.

In the present scheme, semantics is treated as a fully autonomous component, responsible only for the combinatoric regularities that have to do with the meanings of lexemes. In that the semantic component can be purged of those aspects of language that are properly seen as syntactic or morphological, it can perhaps be made much simpler than in other forms of grammar. For example, the logical scope of a semantic element can be directly specified without the need for it to be raised or lowered from some position in syntax, or stored (Cooper 1983) until more of the syntax is built up.

Adding a semantic component to the two that have been the focus of discussion to this point gives us two new interfaces, the semantics-syntax interface and the semantics-morphology interface, making it possible for discrepancies of structure to arise at these interfaces, just as they do at the syntax-morphology boundary. Of course there will be limits to the degree of discrepancy between autonomous semantic representations and other autonomous representations, just as there were in the case of syntax and morphology. There are strong (though preliminary) indications that these interfaces are constrained by analogs of the very same principles that were postulated on the basis of morphosyntactic interactions, certainly an intriguing and desirable result should it turn out to be true.

There will be some differences, of course. For example, the assumption that extrinsic ordering of elements does not characterize the semantic component mentioned in chapter 2 will certainly limit the role that constraints based on linear ordering play. But suppose we take the various interface constraints that were developed in chapters 3 and 4 and simply dispense with the identification of levels that was stipulated in their original formulations, thus fully generalizing the constraints to all modular interfaces. We would then have the following revised requirements on any pair of representations of a single linguistic expression:

(1)   Linearity Constraints
       a. Strong
          The associated elements of L_1 and L_2 representations must occur in the same linear order.
       b. Weak
          The associated elements of L_1 and L_2 representations must occur in the same linear order except where the L_2 requirements of lexemes make this impossible.

(2)   Constructional Integrity Constraints
       a. Strong
          If a lexeme combines with a phrase P at L_1 and with a host at L_2, then the L_2 host must be associated with the head of the L_1 phrase P.
       b. Weak
          If a lexeme combines with an expression P at L_1 and with a host at L_2, then the L_2 host must be associated with some element of the L_1 expression P.

(3)   General Intermodular Homomorphism Constraint[1]
       Let each of the strong homomorphism constraints count as two degrees of similarity, and let the weak homomorphism constraints count as one. The total degree of similarity between autonomous L_1 and L_2 representations must be at least two.

This complete generalization of the homomorphism constraints does not do exactly what the earlier formulation did at the syntax-morphology interface, for it fails to reflect the asymmetry between levels that was present there. Of the four homomorphism conditions, only the first was symmetrical. In the other three, L_1 had to be specifically syntax, and L_2 had to be morphology.

The intuitive reason for the lack of interchangeability of levels in these constraints has to do with the greater restrictiveness of one of the levels versus the other. The morphology, in particular, makes more stringent demands upon ultimate (i.e., phonetic) form than does the syntax as shown by the fact that syntactic requirements are sometimes relaxed because of morphological requirements, as when the Scandinavian definite article, discussed in chapter 5, section 1.1, appears after the head noun rather than at the beginning of the NP because of its morphological need to be a nominal suffix. (See also Baker 1988 and the references cited there.) Such cases are rather numerous, but I know of no convincing cases of the opposite kind, cases where, for example, what would be expected to be a suffix actually shows up as a prefix because of some syntactic exigency of the language.

Thus despite the egalitarian stance toward components of the grammar that has been adopted here, there is a sense in which the morphology is a more superficial level of representation than the syntax; morphological regularities are more transparently displayed in surface form than are syntactic regularities because whenever there is a direct conflict between a morphological and a syntactic requirement, the morphological requirement wins out.

In this sense too, semantics is not on a par with either morphology or syntax, both of which take precedence over semantically-driven features of form in cases of conflict. Of the three components, semantics makes the weakest demands, and plays the smallest role in deciding ultimate surface form, though this role is still considerable. There are a number of well-known semantic properties, such as scope of adverbs, that are rather poorly reflected in syntax because the syntax of a language requires expressions to occur in certain positions without (or nearly without) regard to their "logical" position. Semantic functors that are represented in morphology (as affixes, for example) are likewise positioned primarily according to the morphological, rather than the semantic demands of the language, because of the lesser stringency of the latter.

Yet another reflection of the asymmetry of components with regard to how transparently their features are mirrored in the overt form of language emerges in the divergent role that ordering plays in the several components. We rarely encounter free ordering of morphological elements, but free ordering is quite common in the syntax. Turning to semantics, it is possible (and hence desirable) to represent semantic relations in an order-free manner. Morphology is thus closer than syntax to the linear flow of information characteristic of surface form, and syntax is closer than semantics.

We thus arrive at the following hierarchy of strength of components, familiar from earlier grammatical work of several traditions:

(4)   Semantics $<$ Syntax $<$ Morphology

But there is no need to order the components, making the output of one the input to the next, in an effort to capture the unequal relations among them. In the present grammatical scheme we may include what is important about this hierarchy simply by identifying L_1 and L_2 in the generalized interface constraints as a weaker level, and a stronger level, respectively. Thus if the two levels with which we are concerned are morphology and syntax, as in the previous chapters, then L_1 is syntax and L_2 is morphology. But if one of the levels is semantics, then it must be L_1.

6.2 Semantic Incorporation

Can we find analogs to incorporation at the interfaces between semantics and either syntax or morphology? Diagrammatically, such a state of affairs would look like (5), where L_1 is semantics and L_2 is either syntax or morphology.

(5)

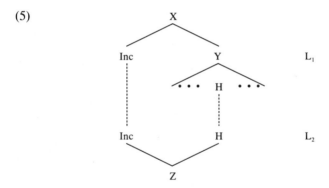

It appears that this diagram in fact describes some of the most common phenomena that have been analyzed as movement in the transformational literature—movement that is constrained by structural relationships like "government" or "command." The strong CIC is, after all, a requirement that elements that are amalgamated between levels stand in a governor-governed relation to one another at the less restrictive level, and this sort of relationship seems to constrain mismatched semantic elements as well as elements mismatched between other modular representations. Should discrepancies in structure between syntax and semantics turn out to be the appropriate way to handle certain phenomena that have traditionally been treated as movement, a rather vast and daunting reassessment of the syntactic literature would be called for. The following discussion must therefore be taken as programmatic and suggestive in the extreme, and not as anything approaching an exhaustive treatment to the possibilities and problems incidental to autonomous semantics.

Though the notion of headship is not well developed in semantics, it is reasonable to assume that it is to be determined according to the same criteria that are applied generally, the most important of which is the idea that the head determines the character of a complex expression in which it is found. Based on this criterion, functors should be taken to be semantic heads, and arguments should be semantic complements. Furthermore, quantifiers should be semantic heads in Q expressions.[2]

To take a typical example, consider the case of "raising-to-subject" verbs such as English *seem*, discussed briefly in chapter 2. It is reasonable to take this lexeme as a semantic operator that applies to a proposition and returns a proposition, i.e., as an O^{-1}, in the notation established in chapter 2, section 1.2. Thus it will appear in semantic trees such as the upper one in (6), a simplified semantic representation (minus variable binding expressions) for English sentences like *John seems to love Mary*. The lower tree is uncontroversially a simplified version of the surface syntactic structure of the relevant part of the sentence.

(6)

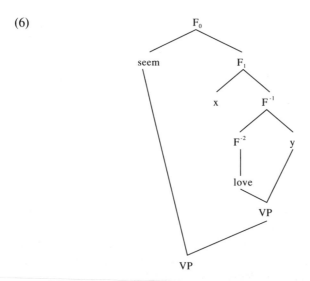

The figure in (6) conforms to the generalized strong CIC if predicates are the semantic heads of propositions, as seems reasonable. The F^{-1} expression is the semantic head of the proposition F_1, and we see that the syntactic association of *seem* with the VP *love(y)* is precisely in accord with the generalized strong CIC.[3]

Note that there is no movement of elements up or down between deeper and more superficial representations on this analysis. Rather we have discrepant configurations at two levels that fall within easily statable and quite general limitations on such discrepancies, just as we had in the case of incorporation in the morphosyntactic realm. The semantic and syntactic characteristics of this common sort of verb are strict analogs to incorporation between the syntactic and morphological planes.

A morphosyntactic incorporator incorporates because of the morphological requirement that it attach to a stem. A verb such as *seem* incorporates syntactosemantically because of an analogous syntactic requirement, namely its need to combine syntactically with VPs (of a certain form). It is, if you will, a syntactic prefix. In an autosemantic theory of syntax with interface constraints of the type developed here, the following simple lexical entry will suffice to determine the properties of the one use of English *seem*. Given the generalized strong CIC, nothing special needs to be said about which VP the lexeme will associate with in a complex sentence.

(7)   *seem*:
        syntax = $[_{VP[FIN]}$ _____ VP [to] (SF5)
        semantics = O^{-1}
        morphology = V^{-0}

Let us consider a somewhat different case that still conforms to the generalized CIC. It has been observed in several places in the literature that the word *right* can serve as a modifier of various sorts of adverbial expressions in English (Fraser 1976; Gazdar et al. 1985.) As modifier of prepositional phrases, the word *right* has several possibly distinct but clearly related uses, as we see in the following examples:

(8)   The memo is right on the desk.

(9)   Dan went right home without stopping at O'Rourke's.

(10)   The windows go right to the floor.

(11)   Liz feels right at home here.

(12)   I'll be right up there.

In (8), *right* means something like "precisely," in (9) something like "directly," in (10) something like "all the way," in (11) it means something like "completely," and in (12) something like "immediately," all of which are offered as separate meanings or submeanings in most dictionaries. (See, for example, *Webster's Ninth New Collegiate* (1983).)

Now it may well be the case that some of these understandings ought to be collapsed into more general readings, but at least two senses will have to remain, a temporal sense as in (12), and a locative sense as in all the rest. Part of the motivation for this claim is that *right* can contribute a genuine ambiguity. Example (13) can either be understood to mean that John left for home immediately after hearing the weather report, or that he took the most direct route home.

(13)   Because of the weather report, John went right home.

The temporal meaning demands a predicate with the appropriate aspectual properties. In particular, it cannot occur with statives since the notion of beginning immediately is inappropriate with predicates describing states. Thus (14) is unambiguously locative:

(14)   The letter is right in your mailbox.

On the other side of the coin, the locative sense of *right* demands a relatively specific location to modify, and since none is found in (15), only the temporal sense survives.

(15)   Dan went right out.

Therefore, if neither the meaning of the locative expression nor the aspect of the predicate is appropriate to either of the senses of *right*, it cannot be used at all:

(16)   *Dan is right out.

Compare:

(17)   Dan is right outside.

(18)   Dan will be right out.

We may conclude that the aspect of the verb phrase is crucial to the temporal use of *right*, and that it is a semantic modifier of the verb phrase on this reading.

Though the locative and temporal understandings of adverbial *right* clearly emerge as two distinct senses, they share a syntactic peculiarity: they must immediately precede, and presumably be in syntactic construction with, a prepositional phrase or other adverbial of the same syntactic character. The surprising thing is that even in its temporal sense of "immediately," *right* demands an overt adverbial of some kind:

(19)   John went right out the door.

(20)   John went out the door immediately.

(21)   *John departed right.

(22)   John departed immediately.

When there is no otherwise motivated adverbial, the adverbial *away* (here without its usual significance) can be found holding open the required syntactic slot for *right*.[4]

As some of the examples above show, and as (23) and (24) confirm, particles are sufficient to support *right* in either sense, thus confirming their
analysis as "intransitive prepositions" (Jackendoff 1977).

(23)   Dan came right down.

(24)   I'll look it right up.

What I suggest is that *right* has two lexical representations that share a syntactic subentry but differ in their semantics. On one reading, *right* is a
semantic function from verb phrase modifiers to verb phrase modifiers, that is,
from the kinds of meanings that adverbs of place typically display, to the same
kinds of meanings. On the other reading it is a semantic function from verb-
phrase-type meanings to verb-phrase-type meanings. In either case, though,
right takes a locative expression as a syntactic complement, whether or not
this has a locative meaning, or indeed, any meaning at all.

When *right* is a semantic function from verb-phrase modifiers to verb-
phrase modifiers, there is no mismatch between its position in syntax and its
position in semantic structure; its syntactic complement is its semantic argument. But as a semantic function of verb-phrase meanings themselves, it is
unusual; it borrows its syntax from the other (historically prior?) meaning. In
such usages, it occurs mismatched between semantics and syntax as illustrated
in (25). This sense of the word will have to have a more complex lexical entry
than the other, viz. (26), in which the unpredictable syntax is made explicit.

(25)

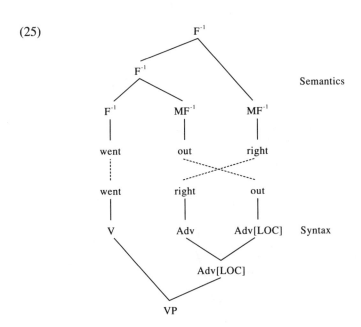

(26)   *right* (temporal):
        syntax = [$_{ADV}$ ——— ADV[LOC]]^5
        semantics = MF^{-1} ('immediately')
        morphology = Adv^{-1}

The difference between the *seem* and *right* (on its temporal reading) is that the former takes VPs as syntactic complements, whereas the latter, (somewhat unusually) combines with adverbials. Still in all, the syntactosemantic position of *right* in (25) is in conformity with the generalized IP, since semantic modifiers are functions and hence heads.

6.2.1 Morphosemantic Incorporation

Lexemes expressing intransitive operator notions (particularly those with such indispensable meanings as tense, aspect, and modality) are often reflected as morphology, rather than as roots or independent words. In such a case, the lexeme will regularly appear as verbal morphology, indeed, morphology on the highest verb of the clause that corresponds to the semantic complement of the operator. In Greenlandic, for example, a derivational affix *-gunar(poq)* expresses a similar notion to English *seem*, giving rise to semantics-morphology mismatches such as that in example (27), diagrammed in (28).

(27)   Kaali-p Amaalia   asa-gunar-paa.
        Karl-ERG Amaalia (ABS) love-appear-INDIC/3s
        'Karl seems to love Amaalia.'

(28)

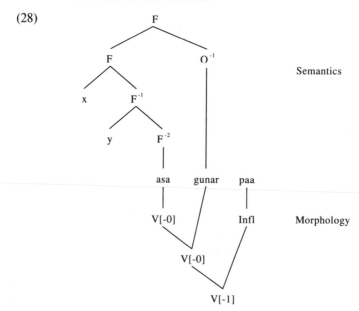

This diagram is surely in keeping with the generalized IP; the morphological host *asa-* 'love' is the lexical head in semantic structure of the semantic complement of the operator *-gunar-* 'seem'.

It is not immediately clear, however, that this is a case of direct semantics-to-morphology incorporation, for the syntax of the sentence might directly map the semantics, making this an example of morphosyntactic "verb incorporation," as Baker (1988) has termed it. The question is an empirical one the answer to which depends upon whether or not the suffix behaves *syntactically* like a complement-taking verb, or whether all the evidence for a more complex structure than what is found on the surface is essentially semantic in nature.

In chapter 5, the Kirundi future-tense morpheme *-zoo* (as opposed to the other tense morphemes that fill the same slot in the Kirundi verb's morphology) was analyzed as taking a syntactic complement. The language provided indisputable evidence for an infinitive in the complement of *-zoo*, and since infinitives are syntactic, not semantic, objects, it was fair to conclude that we were dealing there with a morphosyntactic mismatch. However, in the case of the Greenlandic suffix in question, the only evidence I am aware of that motivates a complex structure associated with (27) comes from observations concerning the scope of logical elements, and is thus semantic.

For example, sentence (29) can only be read with a specific understanding of the subject nominal, whereas in (30), with the suffix *-gunar(poq)*, the nominal can be taken as specific or nonspecific. This fact can be accounted for in the manner familiar from the literature on predicate logic in terms of variability of the scope of the quantifying expression *inuit pingasut*. It either includes or is within the scope of the operator *-gunar(poq)*. Since there is no operator in (29), however, there is no possibility of varying the scope of the quantifying expression.

(29)   Inuit   pingasut toqu-pput.
         people three   die-INDIC/3p
         'Three people died.'

(30)   Inuit   pingasut toqu-gunar-put.
         people three   die-seem-INDIC/3p
         'Three people seem to have died.'

From the point of view of syntax, however, there is no way to distinguish a sentence containing verbs bearing this suffix from sentences with underived verbs.[6] The obvious conclusion is that the Greenlandic suffix presents a case of incorporation at the semantics-morphology interface, in accordance with the generalized CIC, and determined by a lexical entry such as (31).

(31)   *-gunar* 'seem' (West Greenlandic):
         semantics = O^{-1}
         morphology = $[_{V[-0]} V[-0]$ _____$]$
         syntax = nil

There is one more feature of this lexeme that needs to be made explicit, namely the fact that the syntax of the derived verb is always identical to that of the semantically subordinate verb. This can be made formal by including in the morphological field an indication that the rule feature borne by the derived verb is the same as that of the stem to which the affix is attached. Recall that features pass freely across the morphology-syntax boundary according to (21) of chapter 2, so the rule feature specified in this field will automatically be a syntactic feature as well.

(32)   morphology = $[_{V[-0,SF\alpha]} \, V[-0,SF\alpha] \underline{\quad\quad}]$

Morphological causatives deserve a similar treatment in many cases. Suppose we were to treat a causative morpheme, such as Japanese *-sase* in a sentence like (33), as semantically analogous to an independent causative verb and as a morphological affix—two things that somehow need to be said in any grammar of Japanese.

(33)   Taroo wa Hanako o   aruk-ase-ta.
          T.   TOP H.   ACC walk-cause-PAST
          'Taroo made Hanako walk.'

(34)   (s)ase (Japanese);
          syntax = nil
          morphology = $[_{V[-0]} \, V[-0] \underline{\quad\quad}]$
          semantics = O^{-2}

The morphosemantic description of (33) will then be (35), where once again, the IP correctly allows the association of the higher predicate with the semantic head of its complement.

(35)

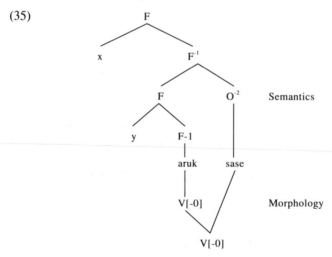

The specification "syntax = nil" in (34) ensures that the morphologically complex verb *aruk-ase* will be an atom in the syntax, so (33) will be mono-clausal, and there will be no mismatch between syntax and morphology. Assuming for the sake of discussion that Japanese has VPs whose form is determined by rules like (36)–(39), the syntax and morphology of (33) will be (40).

(36)   S → NP[NOM] VP

(37)   VP → V[SF2]

(38)   VP → NP[ACC] V[SF3]

(39)   VP → NP[DAT] NP[ACC] V[SF4]

(40)

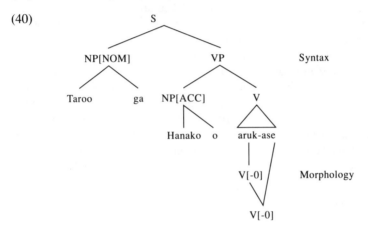

Because verbs formed with *-sase* are not analyzed in the syntax, they will behave syntactically as ordinary underived verbs in the language. Indeed, the syntax of (33) is exactly that of a simple transitive verb like *tabe* 'eat' in (41), and the syntax of the causative verb in (42) is exactly that of a ditransitive verb such as *ut-* 'sell' in (43).

(41)   Taroo ga   sakana o   tabe-ta
        T.   NOM fish   ACC eat-PAST
        'Taroo ate the fish.'

(42)   Taroo ga   Hanako ni   sakana o   tabe-sase-ta
        T.   NOM H.   DAT fish   ACC eat-cause-PAST
        'Taroo made Hanako eat the fish.'

(43)   Taroo ga   Hanako ni   sakana o   ut-ta
        T.   NOM H.   DAT fish   ACC sell-PAST
        'Taroo sold Hanako the fish.'

While there are certainly strong tendencies for causative verbs to have predictable syntax that depends upon the valence of the verb they combine with in
the morphology, I will not try to formulate any general principles here, as that
is a task that goes well beyond the aims of this work.[7] The facts themselves
can be stated (if not explained) in the present case in a fashion analogous to
what was done in the case of the intransitive operator in (32). To get the facts
right, it is sufficient to indicate what rule feature the derived causative verb
will have, as a function of the rule feature of the stem the causative morpheme
applies to. The full morphological field for Japanese -*sase* could, for example,
be something like (44), where N refers to the rule number in (36)–(39).

(44)   morphology $= [_{V[-0,SF\alpha+1]}\ V[-0,SF\alpha]\ \underline{\quad\quad}]$

Thus the basic properties of this sort of causative are straightforwardly
handled by assigning the causative morpheme a semantic and morphological
role, but no direct place in the syntax at all.

Suppose, however, that a verbal derivational affix that is understood as a
semantic operator DID have independent status in the syntax. Such a morpheme would have quite different properties from Japanese -*sase*. In particular, it would produce unique surface patterns in which all syntactic features of
the two clauses in its syntactic frame were preserved, with the exception of
there being a single, morphologically complex verb. For example, if both
clauses contained nominative-case subjects, the surface pattern would contain
TWO nominatives, but only one morphological verb, as shown in the following
diagram.

(45)

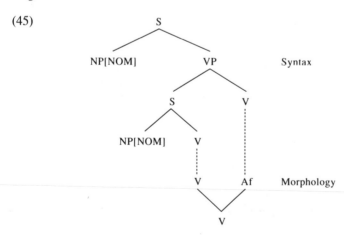

The only examples like this that I know of occur with certain postinflectional (i.e., clitic-like) affixes in Eskimo languages. The following, from

Woodbury and Sadock 1986, is an illustration of the phenomenon from Central Alaskan Yup'ik. Sentences in this language never have two absolutives outside of this particular construction.

(46)   Liisaq-una   tai-gu-ur-tuq
        Lisa(ABS)-this.one(ABS) come-INDIC/3s-say-INDIC/3s"
        'Lisa said this one is coming.'

To round out this discussion of the properties of semantic operators, consider the case of those auxiliary-like verbs that have been analyzed in the literature as examples of "restructuring." Such analyses respond to the intuition (or demonstration) that a complement-taking verb and the verb of its complement comprise a constituent at some level. The question is, what level? It has been identified as a sort of auxiliary syntactic level (e.g., Zubizaretta 1985; Haegeman and van Riemsdijeck 1986), as a morphological level (Farkas and Sadock 1989), and even as LF (Baker 1988).

Here I will consider the possibility that the restructured level is, at least in some instances, merely surface syntax. For a Spanish verb such as *hacer*, which gives evidence of a bracketing paradox inasmuch as it allows clitics from a semantically lower verb to occur before it, as in (47), the idea would be that the auxiliary incorporates verbs syntactically, rather than verb phrases. Though in semantic structure it occurs in representations like (48), it is to be found (optionally) in syntactic structures like (49), a behavior that can be accommodated straightforwardly by assuming that it combines syntactically with verbs to form verbs, as set forth in the lexical entry (50).

(47)   Juan lo   hiço llorar.
        Juan 3s/M made cry
        'Juan made him cry.'

(48)

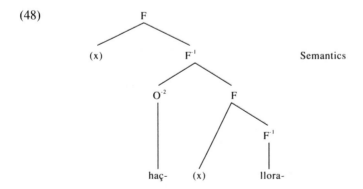

(49)

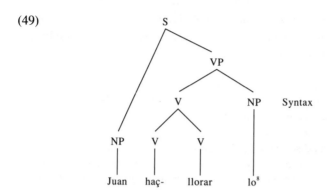

(50)   *hac-* (Spanish):
        semantics = O^{-2}
        syntax = $[_{V[SF\alpha+1]} \underline{\quad\quad} V[INF, SR\alpha]]$
        morphology = $V[-0]$

Just as in the case of the Japanese causative suffix discussed above, the Spanish verb creates a constituent with subcategorization properties that are a function of the subcategorization properties of the item to which it is ad-joined. The difference between the two cases is that in Japanese the level at which the causative is incorporated is morphology, whereas in Spanish, it is syntax.

Let us now return briefly to the topic of noun incorporation. The canonical bimodular structure for an example of this phenomenon will be as in (51).

(51)

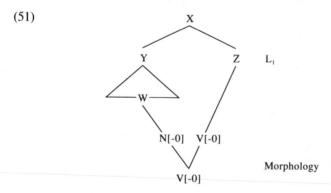

In chapters 3 and 4, I provided evidence that L_1 in the above diagram some-times had to be identified with ordinary syntax. But now we see that another possibility is that the level at which the nominal and verbal lexemes are sepa-rate could conceivably be semantics. If that were the case, then the syntax of the corresponding sentence would contain only a simple, unanalyzed verb, and thus would have to match in every way the syntax of underived verbs in the language.

Thus, as Tony Woodbury (p.c.) has pointed out to me, there are three quite different sets of behaviors of morphological verbs containing a noun stem, depending on whether the noun stem has reality in the syntax, the syntax and semantics, or neither.

What I mean by semantic reality here, as elsewhere in this work, is that the lexeme occupies a position in the combinatoric tree that represents the meaning of an expression. Thus *baby* in the notorious English compound *babysit* is not semantically real in this sense, since one can babysit a plant, a dog, or a senior citizen; there is no semantic baby in *babysitting*.[9] Of course babysitting is not the same thing as sitting, so there is a semantic effect that is achieved in the formation of the compound, but it is not one that should be stated by assigning *baby* to an argument position in semantics.

If the incorporated noun is semantically real in the favored sense, there are two possibilities as to its value. Either it has the meaning of a whole argument phrase, including some quantifier (such as an indefinite or generic quantifier), and the predicate restricting this quantifier, or it represents just the restricting predicate. If the incorporated noun is an entire argument in the semantics, then it should be incompatible with the expression of an argument of that kind in any fashion. It should not allow external phrases that quantify or modify the understood argument, since those functions are already present in semantic form.

As far as I can tell, this is exactly the behavior of the included stem in English synthetic compounds like *bread baker*. (See Bloomfield 1933; Levi 1978; Roeper and Siegel 1978; Selkirk 1982; and the references in these works.) A bread baker really bakes bread, so the idea of making generic bread the argument of the semantic predicate that *bake* stands for is entirely sensible. Doing so in fact explains the frequently observed fact that an argument position is used up by the modifying noun: *a bread baker of rye/many loaves*. That the incorporated noun represents the semantic argument, rather than the syntactic object is also borne out by the fact that idiomatic objects (which are indubitable syntactic entities) fail to show up in synthetic compounds: *mint-maker*, *bucket kicker*, *gun jumper*, etc., etc. Note also that proper nouns can be the first element of synthetic compounds, as in *Tribune readers*, *Nixon lovers*, and so on. Proper nouns are semantic arguments, a fact that is compatible with the idea that synthetic compounds include semantic arguments.

Suppose that the incorporated noun represents the semantic predicate in an argument expression, rather than the whole argument. In that case, an incorporated nominal should be compatible with the external expression of additional elements of the argument, e.g., modifiers and quantifiers, but not with full external NPs with no semantic room in them for a predicate. In particular, it should not be possible to duplicate the incorporated noun in an external phrase without semantic redundancy. If, furthermore, the incorporated noun plays no role in the syntax, then the external argument will always have to be a possible syntactic NP in the language. It seems to me that this constellation of properties closely models one kind of noun incorporation in Iroquoian (Mithun 1984; H. Woodbury 1975).

Finally, there is the syntactically real type of noun incorporation that we find in Eskimo, Gta?, and perhaps Southern Tiwa, the hallmark of which is that external arguments are not always well formed NPs, but sometimes fragments of NPs. I assume that whenever an incorporated nominal is represented in the syntax as a noun, it is also represented in the semantics as a predicate, a general cross-modular feature of the syntax-semantics interface. A syntactically real incorporated nominal will thus have the meaning of free nominal of the same kind.

Complicating this picture is the possibility that several of these types will occur in the same language. Nothing in the present theory rules out such a possibility. In her discussion of noun incorporation in a number of languages, Mithun (1984) argues that Iroquoian languages present several varieties of noun incorporation. I suggest that they can be understood as differing from one another as to whether the incorporated nominal is represented in the semantics, and if so, how and whether or not it is represented in the syntax.

6.3 Semantic Clitics

Let us consider next whether there are analogs to cliticization at the semantics-syntax interface. Cliticization differs fundamentally from incorporation in that it is limited by linear order rather than headship. At first sight, then, it would appear that there could be no semantic clitics, since semantic representations, according to my assumptions, are unordered.

Here we need to think a little more carefully about what it means for a level to be unordered. Of the several construals of the notion that are possible, the one that is most in keeping with the framework of grammar adopted here is the idea that no external ordering statements (LP rules) are allowed. A syntax of semantic representations is thus a phrase-structure grammar in the ID-LP format of Gazdar et al. 1985, where there are no LP rules whatsoever. A rule such as (52) thus implies that all of the trees in (53) are admissible substructures of semantic representation.

(52) $A \rightarrow x, y, z$

(53)

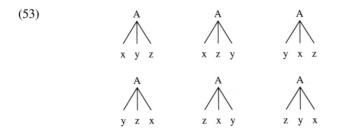

Such a system does impose some ordering restrictions in and of itself because it demands that sister expressions be contiguous. For example, the grammar consisting of the two rules below admits four possible orders of the three terminal elements it introduces, the two orders in which the sisters z and y are interrupted being impossible.

(54)   A → x, B
         B → y, z

(55)   x y z
         x z y
         y z x
         z y x
     *y x z
     *z x y

In contradistinction to semantics, the phrase-structure grammar of syntactic representation is (or can be) subject to language-particular linear-precedence restrictions, such that only some of the possible orders of sister nodes are allowed. In a language like English, most ordering is rigidly constrained. Now since the default association between corresponding elements at different levels accords with the strong LC, the only semantic structures that can actually be found in multimodular representations of well-formed expressions of English will display much the same linear order as their syntactic counterparts. Thus while the semantics of both English and Japanese would allow structures with either of the orderings of semantic elements in (56), only the first of these is ever found associated with a well-formed syntactic structure in English, and only the second is found in Japanese.

(56)   a.   John-is-in-school
         b.   John-school-in-is

Since semantic structure is partly ordered in these two ways, it is, in fact, sensible to consider the possibility of semantic clitics. Just as in the case of semantic incorporation, there are two interfaces at which such a phenomenon could arise, namely between semantics and morphology, or between semantics and syntax.

6.3.1 Morphosemantic Clitics

Dixon (1980, 284) mentions a class of sentence-modifying clitics in Australian languages:

> [A] clitic is not a separate word inasmuch as it cannot bear major stress and must be attached to the end of an inflected word.
> We can distinguish two types of clitic. One set will always be added to the first word of a sentence, whatever it is. These items generally qualify the complete sentence; they can indicate that it is certainly true, possibly true, or that the sentence reports what the speaker was told by someone else, and so on.

As an illustration, Dixon offers the Dyirbal interrogative clitic *-ma*, which occurs after the first word of a sentence, regardless of what that word is. All of the following mean 'Is the man taking a long time to come?'.

(57)   bayi-**ma**   yara wundi+nyu bani+nyu
        CL.1-INTER man slowly-PRES come-PRES

(58)   yara-**ma**   wundi+nyu bayi bani+nyu
        man-INTER slowly-PRES CL.1 come-PRES

(59)   wundi+nyu-**ma**   bayi yara bani+nyu
        slowly-PRES-INTER CL.1 man come-PRES

Indicators of illocutionary force quite commonly turn up sentence initially (as in Welsh), sentence finally (as in Hidatsa, Japanese, and Korean), or after the first word of the sentence, as illustrated by Dixon's Dyirbal examples above, and in Philippine languages. These are, of course, exactly the positions in which we would find simple initial, simple final, and second-position clitics as described in chapter 3. Therefore, one possible treatment would be to make such items sentence adverbials in syntax that attach morphologically to full words which will thus be positioned according to the various interface principles that have been developed here.

However, it is not clear that such entities as interrogative clitics ought to be located in the syntax at all, but rather in semantics, or perhaps in a separate illocutionary component of the kind under investigation by William Eilfort. In Japanese, for example, there are no independent elements in the language with the positional privileges that would be required; Japanese is a rigidly verb-final language, and this otherwise valid principle would have to be violated by an element that followed the verb in the syntax. If Japanese speech-act clitics were located in the semantics (or illocutionary module), their clitic-like distri-

bution could be accommodated without losing sight of a basic feature of the
syntax of the language.

6.3.2 Syntactosemantic Clitics

Consider a semantic functor and its semantic argument expression. The default association between the semantic and syntactic structures ought to
preserve constituency, as is the case, say, with sentence adverbials in English.

(60)

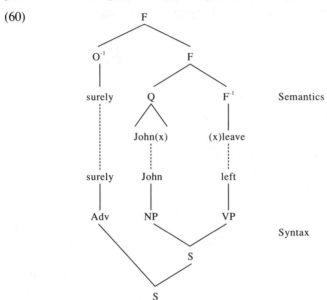

Now if the semantic functor behaved as a (simple phrase-initial) clitic, it
would be associated syntactically not with the entire phrase that corresponds
to its semantic argument, but with a peripheral syntactic constituent of that
phrase. Perhaps there are such cases, but in the absence of morphological attachment, it is hard to imagine what evidence would place it in this constituency rather than in its default position in syntax.

Suppose, though, that the semantic functor violated the strong Linearity
Condition. Then it would show up *after* the first syntactic constituent, that is
to say, in Wackernagel's position (Wackernagel 1892). In fact it is quite frequently the case that a semantic functor whose argument is a proposition turns
up as a separate word in this position (i.e., as a "particle," cf. Zwicky 1985).

Thus in Tagalog, as described by Schachter (1985, 53–54), a class of particles occurs after the first word of the sentence, i.e., in the same position as
the Dyirbal clitics. There can be several of these in a row, and it is not clear
that they are morphologically, or even phonologically, dependent.

(61)   Hindi **pa man lamang tuloy**   **siya** nakakapagalmusal.
         NEG   yet even just   as.a.result he   can.have.breakfast
         'As a result, he hasn't even been able to have breakfast yet.'

A semantic entity that attaches in the fashion of a clitic to the end of a syntactic constituent may be positioned after the first word, since a word is
(usually!) a syntactic constituent, but it is not limited to that position. There
are several well-known cases of sentence particles occurring after the first
major constituent, rather than the first word, and some where either position is
allowed.

In Serbo-Croatian, for example, a clitic cluster appears after the first
stressed word, as in (62), or after the first major constituent, as in (63) (see
Browne 1974).

(62)   Taj-mi-je   pesnik napisao knjigu.
         that-me-PAST poet   wrote   book
         'That poet wrote me a book.'

(63)   Taj pesnik-mi-je napisao knjigu.
         that poet-me-PAST wrote   book
         'That poet wrote me a book.'

If we assume that there is a level of structure in which the clitics appear
outside the rest of the clause, then they behave as second-position clitics with
respect to that level of structure and syntax. It is not unreasonable to take the
level of structure where clitics appear outside the rest of the clausal material as
semantics, since the clitics include only auxiliary verbs, topical personal pronouns, and one speech-act particle, all of which are elements with wide semantic scope.[10] Suppose the syntactic character of the clitics is that they must
follow some syntactic constituent. Given that they are initial at one level of
structure, their appearance after the first syntactic constituent makes them
analogs of those morphosyntactic clitics that appear only after the first word.

But regardless of position, the Serbo-Croatian clitic cluster is phonologically dependent upon the word that immediately precedes it. Thus the clitics
attach as second-position particles between semantics and syntax, and as
simple final clitics between syntax and morphology, as can be seen by com-
paring the three structures for an example like (63).

(64)   a. Semantics

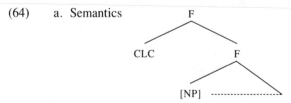

b. Syntax

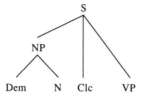

c. Morphology

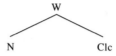

Such behavior would be captured by a lexical entry for the clitic-cluster itself along the following lines:

(65)   ClC (Serbo-Croatian):
        syntax = [$_{XP}$ XP ____]
        morphology = [$_{X[-2]}$ X[-1] ____]
        semantics = O^{-1}

The clitic cluster is itself morphologically complex. As Browne 1974 shows, there is a fixed template order of elements within it, which we can state in the present framework as a morphological rule. Here I give only a partial treatment of the facts. For the details, the reader is referred to Browne 1974.

(66)   (Serbo-Croatian morphology)
        ClC → (I)(II)(III)(IV)

The description is completed by supplying lexical entries for the clitics in question.

(67)   *mi* (Serbo-Croatian):
        syntax = NP[DAT]
        semantics = Q ("me")
        morphology = II

(68)   *je* (Serbo-Croatian):
        syntax = [$_{VP}$ ____ VP[LFORM]]]
        semantics = O^{-1} (PAST)
        morphology = IV

The clitics themselves thus form a second, cross-cutting set of structural discrepancies partially independent of those formed by the clitic cluster itself. I leave it to the reader to contemplate this exquisite intricacy.

6.3.3 Anticipatory Clitics

The final class of misplaced semantic elements that we might expect would include those with the properties of anticipatory clitics, attached syntactically to a preceding syntactic element outside of their own semantic argument. Since such an item would violate the weak version of the Constructional Integrity Constraint, it would have to obey the strong form of the Linearity Constraint, and occur in the same order in both semantic and syntactic representation. It would, in other words, be an example of "vacuous movement," since its aberrant attachment could not be reflected in linear order lest its total discrepancy be too great.

This immediately suggests a treatment of that most infamous putative example of vacuous movement, raising to object in English. If we consider the pair of structures in (69) and (70), familiar from early transformational grammar as the deep and surface structure of (71), we see that the relationship between the position of the subject of the lower clause in the two trees is quite analogous to the position of an anticipatory clitic between syntactic and morphological form.

(69)

(70)

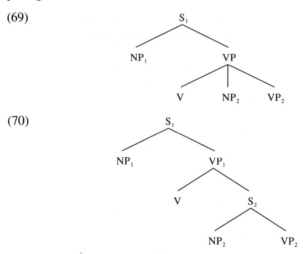

(71)   John knows Nancy to be intelligent.

Here the structure topologically similar to (70) would have to be identified with semantics, since there is only one level of syntax proper in the present theory. Of course such a treatment raises any number of difficult questions, but it is at least an intriguing fact that the assumption of autonomous semantic and syntactic representations makes such a treatment available in principle.

7

Extensions of the Method

The examples discussed so far have all been of a very circumscribed type. They concerned only mismatches in the structural position of atomic, lexical-level morphemes at the interfaces between morphological, syntactic, and semantic representations. The general idea that lexical entries can have rather different properties in various dimensions of representation can be extended from these relatively simple cases in several imaginable ways. In this rather speculative chapter, I briefly touch on some of these possible extensions.

In section 1, I relax the informal requirement that lexemes that participate in clitic-like or incorporative mismatches are internally unstructured in each of the components in which they are represented. In section 2, the restriction that such lexemes represent the smallest building blocks in each component is relinquished, and finally, in section 3, the idea that there are more than three autonomous dimensions of representation is briefly pursued.

As with any complex system, there is a trade-off between descriptive power and empirical content. The greater the number of degrees of analytical freedom, the less predictive the system becomes, to the point where anything can be described, perhaps even in several different ways. Still, the expansion of the analytical weapons in the automodular arsenal seems well worth investigation, especially as the original restrictions were more the product of the history of the idea than based on any theoretical or methodological principles.

7.1 Complex Lexical Items

The lexemes that have so far been used to illustrate the utility of viewing the several components of grammar as autonomous have all been atoms with respect to the components in which they have non-null representations. While they may combine with other expressions to form more complex expressions in one component or another, they themselves have had no internal structure at any level of representation.

As has been observed elsewhere (see especially Beard 1977; Dowty 1979; Sadock 1984), however, the fact that an expression is listed in the lexicon is by no means an indication of its atomicity. A natural language expression must be listed in the lexicon if its properties in any component are not predictable. This is invariably the case for morphemes traditionally defined as "the smallest meaningful units" (e.g., Bloch and Trager 1942, 54); since they are by definition not composed of meaningful elements, no combinatoric rules predict their meanings, and they must therefore be listed. But it is also the case that a complex expression whose meaning is not a predictable function of the meaning of its parts, or whose phonology is not predictable from the phonology of the parts, and so on, must have these properties registered in the list we call the lexicon.

There is nothing controversial in the claim that lexical items sometimes have internal structure. The original argument in favor of lexicalism (Chomsky 1970), for example, was based upon the fact that nominalizations, such as English *commencement*, while morphologically complex, have unpredictable meanings. A lexical item such as this can be naturally represented in the present theory with a morphological description that provides information concerning the internal structure of the expression, in addition to information concerning how the whole expression behaves vis-à-vis the combinatoric rules of the several modules. The lexical entry for *commencement* might be something like the following, where the morphological field shows two internal lexemes, "commence" and "ment," but the expression is an atom in the other two components. By convention, the name of a lexeme in a particular field in the lexical entry of another is to be taken as the corresponding field of the named lexical entry. In (1), "commence" and "ment" in the morphological field are the morphological fields of the lexemes so identified. Since *ment* is a deverbal nominalizer, it is unnecessary to indicate in the lexical entry for *commencement* that the complex stem is a noun.

(1)   *commencement*:
         morphology = [[commence] ment]
         syntax = N[0]
         semantics = F^{-1} 'graduation'

It is intuitively clear that a lexical item such as this is internally complex in the morphology, so that a lexical specification like (1) is appropriate. Often, however, it is not just reasonable but necessary to have some way of representing this complexity in order to avoid the redundant specification in the lexicon of morphologically general facts. For example, Dutch has a perfectly productive diminutive suffix *-((e)t)je* that forms neuter nouns that invariably pluralize with *-s*. The suffix is also found in numerous lexicalized forms that have unpredictable meanings (*lepeltje* 'teaspoon' < *lepel* 'spoon'; *kastje* 'locker' < *kast* 'cupboard'.) Some diminutives must also be listed because of unpredictable phonology. It is not clear that there is any rule that will predict whether a noun that has a short vowel in the singular and a long vowel in the plural will have a short or a long vowel in the diminutive: *schip* 'ship', *sche-*

pen 'ships', *scheepje* 'little ship'; but *stad* 'city', *steden* 'cities', *stadje* 'little city'. Another incompletely predictable fact has to do with whether the diminutive morpheme is realized as *-etje*, *-tje*, or *-je*. Except for stems that end in a liquid or nasal, the ordinary suffix is *-je*. If a stem ending in a liquid or nasal has a long vowel, it regularly gets the ending *-tje*, and otherwise *-etje*.

But there are exceptions. Thus *weg* 'road', *wegen* 'roads', *weggetje* 'little road', and *vlag* 'flag', *vlagen* 'flags', *vlaggetje* 'little flag'. Compare the regular *dag* 'day', *dagen* 'days', *dagje* 'little day'.

Whether or not a particular diminutive must be listed because of semantic or phonological irregularity, the fact that it contains the diminutive suffix must somehow be formally recognized in any adequate grammar of Dutch, because such forms will invariably be neuter (*het lepeltje*, *het stadje*, *het weggetje*) and will regularly pluralize with *-s* (*lepeltjes*, *stadjes*, *weggetjes*), two aspects of morphosyntactic behavior that are not accidental, but follow from the properties of the diminutive suffix.

Let us assume that the diminutive morpheme in Dutch has the following lexical entry, where [+S] is a declension-class feature that stipulates the form of the plural.

(2)   *etje* (Dutch):
        syntax = nil
        morphology = [$_{\text{N[0, +S, NEUT]}}$ N[0] ____]
        semantics = F^{-1} 'little'

Then a partially irregular form like *weggetje* might receive a lexical specification that includes only the nonredundant information, namely the phonological form and the morphemic composition, all other information being derivable from the combinatoric properties of the lexemes and transmodular default specifications.

(3)   *weggetje* (Dutch):
        syntax = (default)
        morphology = weg + etje
        semantics = [[weg]etje]

We need not stipulate that *weggetje* is a neuter gender noun stem in the morphology that pluralizes with *-s*, since that follows from its containing the morpheme *((e)t)je*, in its morphological field, a morpheme that forms noun stems with just these properties. Nor is it necessary to specify that *weggetje* is a neuter N[0] in the syntax, because of the general, intermodular default—(21) of chapter 2—that allows morphosyntactic features such as [N], [NEUT], and [+S] to penetrate the morphology-syntax interface. Similarly, the meaning of this lexeme is predictable from the meaning of its parts, and need not be separately mentioned here.

In general, a hierarchical theory of the arrangement of grammatical components supplemented with a bracketing erasure principle, or the like, will allow for complex expressions at a lower level of structure to correspond to atoms at a higher level, as in the morphosyntactic examples just discussed. But unless the bracketing erasure principle is relaxed, such theories will disallow complexity at a lower level from remaining at the next level of representation, and under no circumstances do such theories provide a mechanism whereby atoms at a lower level are associated with complex expressions at a higher level.

The present theory, because of its lack of hierarchiality, imposes no such asymmetries. Just as there are lexical items with complex morphology and atomic syntax, the present theory allows for there to be lexical items with complex morphology and complex syntax, or monomorphemes that correspond to complex syntactic expressions. Such cases exist and have always been problematic for hierarchical theories of the traditional kind. The remainder of this section will be devoted to a discussion of a sampling of such examples.

7.1.1 Portmanteaus

The term "portmanteau" was first used by Hockett (1947) to describe the behavior of French *au*, which, he argued, had to be seen as a single morph (because it is a single phoneme) that nevertheless represented a sequence of the two morphemes *à* and *le*. Hockett correctly noted several advantages in this analysis, including the elimination of a morpheme with otherwise unattested behavior, i.e., one that took N-bars directly into prepositional phrases, and the provision of an account of the defective distribution of *à*, which occurs before *la* but not before *le*, vis-à-vis the majority of the other prepositions in the language, which occur in both positions. Despite the disarming simplicity and intuitive appeal of Hockett's analysis, it is not one that could comfortably be maintained in theories with a strictly hierarchical relation between morphology and syntax. Several attempts have been made to deny the syntactic complexity of *au* and to attribute it to a fresh category that otherwise does not occur, except in *du*, *des*, and *aux*, or to posit new mechanisms of grammar to account for it, as is done, for example in Moortgat (1985), Schmerling (1983), and Steedman (1987).

Lacking hierarchiality, the present theory is able to incorporate Hockett's analysis straightforwardly. There is nothing to prevent the lexical items *au*, *du*, etc., from having the internal syntactic structure shown in the upper tree in (4), while counting as a single, unanalyzable morpheme, as in the lower tree.[1]

(4)

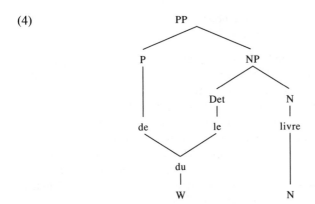

Suppose we treat *au*, *du*, and so forth, as lexical items that have internal syntactic structure, but no internal morphological structure, as stated in the following entry, where "de" is the name of the lexeme in (6), and "le" is the name of the lexeme in (7).[2]

(5)   *du* (French):
       syntax = de, le
       morphology = [$_W$de+le]

(6)   *de* (French):
       syntax = [$_{PP}$ ____ NP]
       morphology = P
       semantics = F^{-2}

(7)   *le* (French):
       syntax = [$_{NP}$ ____ N[1]]
       morphology = Det[MASC, SG]
       semantics = Q^{-1}

This lexical entry for *du* allows for it to lexicalize syntactic and morphological trees such as (4), but does not in and of itself impose any further interface constraints. However, we must consider whether any of the interface constraints will be applicable in this case, and if so how. In particular, will *au*, *du*, etc., pattern as if they contained clitics, or as if they contained incorporators?

Examples such as those in (8), from Grevisse 1980, clearly show that *du* behaves as if it were made up of the syntactic elements *de* and *le* joined according to the CP. In these examples, *le* is in no sense the head of the object of *de* in syntactic structure. In (8a) it is the determiner of one conjunct, and in (8b), it is the determiner of the subject NP in the title of a play. The joined lexemes are merely adjacent, as in cliticization.

(8)   a. l'auteur du "Rouge et le noire"
         b. l'auteur du "Roi s'amuse"

The lexical entry in example (5) is sufficient to guarantee this result, since it does not require that *de* and *le* be a lexical head and the head of its syntactic complement. Therefore the strong CIC may be violated, and the process will be governed by at least the weak LC, so as not to violate (3) of chapter 6, making the two lexemes mentioned in (5) necessarily adjacent in syntax.

I turn next to a vexing example from English. Zwicky and Pullum (1983) addressed the question of the correct treatment of English negative contractions like *can't*, *won't*, *shouldn't*, and so on. They presented incontrovertible evidence, including the following, to the effect that these are lexical items:

1. They are sometimes phonologically unpredictable (*won't*).
2. They are sometimes semantically unpredictable. Thus *can't* means "not possible S," and never "possible not S," whereas *mustn't* means "necessary not S," and never "not necessary S."
3. There is no productive rule joining *n't* to auxiliaries, and therefore there are some missing forms (e.g., **amn't*).

But in the strictly hierarchical theory these authors assumed, the lexical nature of the contracted forms implied that the negative morpheme is either derivational or inflectional. Since it cannot be derivational because it occurs outside inflection (cf., *doesn't*, *didn't*, etc.), it had to be inflectional, given their view of the organization of grammar. Their idea was that negative contractions are inflectional alternatives to free words, much as the comparative suffix *-er* is an inflectional alternative to the free word *more*.

While there is no room for doubt concerning the lexical status of the contracted negative forms, I find Zwicky and Pullum's idea that such forms are inflectional pure and simple rather implausible. Their own analogy to comparatives in English is instructive in this regard. It is true, as they point out, that in the standard language the free comparative word and comparative morphology on the adjective are mutually exclusive options. Nonstandardly (and in children's speech), though, both can appear, the inflectional morphology then being a kind of agreement:

(9)   %She's more prettier than I thought.

As far as I know, neither children nor adult speakers of nonstandard forms of English ever use contracted forms as a sort of agreement with an overt negative. Example (10) never occurs with the meaning "I can't see it," even in styles of English in which so-called double negatives, like (11) are acceptable.

(10)   I can't not see it.

(11)   I can't hardly see it.

The complete mutual exclusivity of the contracted and uncontracted form would be explained, of course, if the contracted negative element were actually the syntactic negative.

A second source of worry concerning the inflectional theory of negative contractions has to do with their shape. Such a paradigm as *isn't, aren't, wasn't, weren't* clearly shows that there is inflectional morphology inside of these lexical items. On Zwicky and Pullum's theory, this would require an otherwise unattested and typologically odd rule of English morphology that added inflection to an already inflected form, in the manner of an agglutinative language. This unwarranted complication of English morphology would be avoided if the contracted forms were analyzed as inflected verbs plus the negative adverb.

By allowing lexemes to have internal structure in one or more dimensions it is possible to say in this case that the lexeme *hasn't*, for example, counts as a word in the morphology, but nevertheless corresponds to two words in the syntax, just as it was possible to say that for the French *du*. For the English word *hasn't*, we could postulate a lexical entry such as the following, which is quite parallel to the French portmanteau discussed above. Unlike *du*, however, *hasn't* is claimed to be a morphological verb with all the features of its component verb *hasn't*. The reason for this will be explained shortly.

(12)   *hasn't*:
        syntax = [have [not [. . .]]]
        morphology = [$_{[\alpha F]}$ has [αF]+not]
        semantics = default

The relevant component lexemes in this lexical entry would be as in (13) and (14). The lexical entry in (13) is for those speakers who treat *has* as a syntactic auxiliary, regardless of whether it has main-verb semantics (F^{-2}), or auxiliary semantics (O^{-1}). The entry for *not* indicates that it forms verb phrases with the same featural composition as the nonfinite verb phrase it takes as a complement, though it itself is not a morphological verb. Though its own features thus differ from those of the category it forms, it is nevertheless to be considered as the head of its phrase, because it does determine the character of the whole VP.[3]

(13)   *has*:
        syntax = V[PERS 3, NUM SG, AUX]
        morphology = V[−1]
        semantics = F^{-2} or O^{-1}

(14)   *not*:
        syntax = [$_{V[\alpha F]}$____V[1, −FIN, αF]]
        morphology = Adv^{-1}
        semantics = O^{-1}

An important difference between the French example and this English form is that the lexical entry for *hasn't* mentions the bracketing of the lexeme-internal syntactic structure. This bracketing makes *not* the head of the complement of *has*, given the syntactic properties of *not* mentioned in its lexical entry. Thus *hasn't* is, in effect, a lexical example of incorporation, rather than cliticization, at least as far as the interface constraints are concerned, so that linear adjacency of *has* and *not* is neither necessary nor sufficient for the contracted form to be sanctioned. Therefore examples with *hasn't* parallel to the French (8b) are quite impossible. **He hasn't "As a Stranger"* isn't even a remotely possible alternative to *He has "Not as a Stranger."* More interestingly, the contracted negative element must be the head of the whole complement of *has*, not just of a first conjunct. Thus (15a) is quite grammatical, while (15b) is ungrammatical, where the bracketing indicates the syntactic organization of the sentences.

(15)   a.   Jan has[n't [eaten a bite or slept a wink]]
         b.   *Jan has[[[n't eaten a bite] and [not slept a wink]]

If *haven't* is taken as involving lexicalized incorporation, then a mundane but theoretically puzzling fact that has necessitated various ad hoc analytical adjustments is explained, namely the fact that negative contractions appear in the position of fronted auxiliaries, though uncontracted sequences of auxiliary and negative are forbidden there: *Haven't you left?* but **Have not you left?* In the grammatical form, the negative element is in its ordinary position in syntax, heading the VP, but it is combined with the auxiliary in morphology, as required by the lexical entry (16). The free negative can never be fronted because the rule for interrogatives puts only auxiliary verbs in sentence-initial position (see Gazdar et al. 1985)

(16)

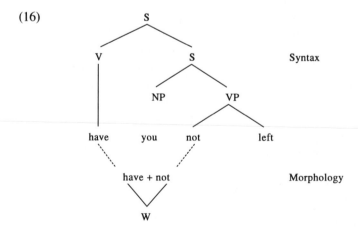

The direction of incorporation is handled by the stipulation that *haven't* is a verb (with the same features as *have*), so by (59) of chapter 4, the morphological complex will appear where its verbal member would, as desired.

7.1.2 Idioms

A common type of phrasal idiom, exemplified by *kick the bucket*, is intuitively simple semantically but nevertheless shows some evidence of its morphosyntactic complexity. Thus the verb in this idiom has all the inflectional forms of the verb *kick* used with its ordinary meaning, and the NP is modifiable by a few adjectives (*proverbial*, *ol'*). As is well known, however, the idiom is not found in the full range of syntactic frames that a nonidiomatic expression of the same apparent form is (Fraser 1970; Newmeyer 1972; Quang 1971).

The framework of autolexical syntax suggests an obvious way of handling such an expression: the idiom itself would be a lexical entry with internal structure at the syntactic level exactly like that of a nonlexical phrase like *slap the wall*, but no internal structure in the semantics, where it would be combinatorically indistinguishable from atomic predicates like *die*. I believe that Newmeyer's (1972) early suggestion that the flexibilities of idioms can be partly predicted from their meanings could be easily modeled in this way, but as the job of doing so is a very big one, I merely point out its possibility here.

7.2 Higher Categories

The majority of lexemes discussed so far in this book have been affixes or exemplars of the stem category in the morphology. We expect morphological stems to correspond to 0-bar categories in the syntax by (21) of chapter 2, and we expect them to represent semantic atoms by the default correlation that was called Sapir's Rule, (145) of chapter 5. Run-of-the-mill common nouns like *dog*, verbs like *vanish* and *see*, and adjectives like *good* and *fond*, all fit this trimodular pattern.

But as defaults, (21) of chapter 2 and (145) of chapter 5 can be overridden, and the associations they predict are not always in effect. In particular, it is quite common to find lexemes that are not exemplars of an atomic category in one or the other module, but rather of categories that are ordinarily compositional constructs in that module. There are lexemes like *so* in English that, on one reading, count as clauses in the syntax (*Bill thinks so too*), and on another reading as VPs (*I would never do so*), but are nevertheless internally unanalyzed in one or more modules. Far and away the most common sort of lexeme that counts as a member of an ordinarily complex category is what is usually called a pronoun. It will be useful to examine them in more detail.

An ordinary personal pronoun is a lexeme that counts as an NP in the syntax, and as an argument binder (Q), complete with a definite quantifier and a restricting expression, in the semantics. (Compare Postal's (1966) elaborate transformational treatment for deriving pronouns from semantic structures similar to the ones postulated here.)

(17)   typical personal pronouns:
       syntax = N[2]
       semantics = $[_Q \text{DEF}[_F F^{-n}(x)]]$

One of the most important dimensions of variation within this restricted range of expressions has to do with whether the lexeme bears morphosyntactic case. Latin *mihi*, for instance, is lexically marked as [DAT] and can therefore be found in syntax only where dative NPs can be found, for example as the complement of verbs and adjectives that govern the dative. Assuming that it is a lexical property of certain semantically transitive verbs and adjectives in Latin that they take dative complements in the syntax, as in (18) and (19), then the entry in (20) will suffice to distribute *mihi* correctly in the syntax, when it is construed with such governing lexemes. The morphological field in (20) indicates that *mihi* is a full word. It cannot be inflected, but is, as it were, pre-inflected.

(18)   *satisfece(re)* (Latin):
       syntax = $[_{V[-1]} \underline{\quad\quad} N[2,\text{DAT}]]$
       morphology = V[$-$0]
       semantics = F^{-2} ('satisfy')

(19)   *utili(s)* (Latin):
       syntax = $[_{A[-1]} \underline{\quad\quad} N[2,\text{DAT}]]$
       semantics = F^{-2} ('useful')

(20)   *mihi* (Latin):
       syntax = N[2, DAT]
       morphology = N[$-$1]
       semantics = $[_Q \text{DEF}[_F \text{SPEAKER}(x)]]$

The second important parameter according to which pronouns in natural languages vary regards the nature of their semantic content, i.e., what the restricting notion in the lexical entries above has to do with. The simplest of these to capture in the present system are stable real-world properties of the referent like sex, shape, humanness, animateness, the cardinality of a set, and so forth. Thus English *she* means (roughly) 'the one female (x).' Indexical properties, that is, properties that are not stable but must be referred to the speech situation, are also frequently used in the semantics of pronominal reference. Every language makes some distinctions along these lines, the most frequently encountered being reference to participants versus nonparticipants, and among participants, reference to the speaker, or the absence thereof. Other indexical restrictions on the variable quantified by pronominal forms have to do with the position of the referent relative to participants, its visibility, tactile availability, etc. Metalinguistic indices to the linguistic context are also employed, so that a referent might be restricted to something that has been explicitly mentioned, or to something which could be described with a noun of a certain grammatical (rather than real-world) gender. All of these categories can also be mixed in the pronominal systems of natural languages.

The final syntactosemantic dimension of contrast among pronouns within and across languages involves their binding properties. A discussion of these facts lies well outside the aims of the present work, necessitating, as it does, a rather thorough account of the semantics and syntax of binding.

There is a considerably expanded range of variability when the morphological properties of pronominals is included. For example, it seems that in some cases, in some languages, person and number inflection on verbs seems to "count as" a pronoun in both the syntax and semantics, a view that can also be found in traditional grammatical discussions (see for example Kroeber 1909). This insight can be modeled straightforwardly in an autolexical scheme, since it is possible in this theory for a lexeme to be represented in the syntax and the semantics in ways analogous to the lexemes above, while counting as an affix in the morphology (Sadock 1986b). Verb inflection commonly defines paradigms according to exactly the same features, or some subset of the features that categorize pronouns. Inflection can supplant, and be mutually exclusive with, external pronominal arguments, and it can have essentially the same discourse-referential semantics as a pronoun. All of these facts are directly accounted for if the lexemes in question are syntactically and semantically indistinguishable from lexemes like English pronouns, but are morphologically affixes or morphological operations.

Now since representation in any of the three components is independent, there is in principle a family of eight separate sorts of pronominal-like elements that we may expect to show up in the grammars of natural languages. They are differentiated from one another according to whether the lexeme is represented in a manner typical of pronouns in one or more of the components of the grammar. These classes are displayed in the following chart, where a "+" in the row marked Semantics means that the element functions as a quantifier restricted in a way that pronouns often are; a "+" in the row marked Syntax indicates that the element in question functions as a syntactic NP; and a "+" in the Morphology row means that the element is represented as a morphological noun stem, or an inflected noun. A "−" value for morphology will then indicate a lexeme that is realized as an affix or morphological process of some kind. I will restrict my attention to verbal morphology here, for reasons that will shortly become obvious.

Figure 7.1

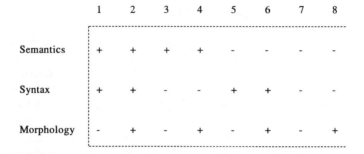

	1	2	3	4	5	6	7	8
Semantics	+	+	+	+	-	-	-	-
Syntax	+	+	-	-	+	+	-	-
Morphology	-	+	-	+	-	+	-	+

Class 2 contains the least-marked exemplars. This is the class of ordinary, nonemphatic, free pronouns in non-pro-drop languages, such as we find in the following syntactic paradigm of Danish, a language that lacks subject-verb agreement entirely:

(21)   Jeg er her.   'I am here.'
        Du er her.   'You are here.'
        Han er her.   'He is here.'
        Vi er her.   'We are here.'
        I er her.   'You (pl) are here.'
        De er her.   'They are here.'

The mirror image class is 7, which consists of lexemes that are not represented at all in the semantics or the syntax, and have representations in the morphology as inflections on verbs. This is the class of true agreement affixes or processes. Since by assumption they are not represented semantically, such morphemes convey no information in and of themselves, and since they are not represented in the syntax, they cannot count as filling obligatory syntactic positions, though they might redundantly replicate (part of) the semantic content of some other syntactic element or elements. The fully-featured inflections of Icelandic verbs, which nonetheless must occur with overt subjects are likely exemplars of this class. Though the information borne by the pronouns is largely redundant in this language, the pronoun is obligatory in all cases.

(22)   Ég er hérna.   'I am here.'
        Þú ert hérna.   'You are here.'
        Hann er hérna.   'He is here.'
        Við erum hérna.   'We are here.'
        Þið eruð hérna.   'You (P) are here.'
        Þeir eru hérna.   'They are here.'

Class 3 includes elements that have a semantic reality, are not syntactic NPs, and appear as verbal morphology. Within the family we are considering here, namely discourse-referential items, there would seem to be such things.

For example, number inflection on English verbs often disagrees with the formal number of the subject, supplying its own independent semantics:

(23)   Manchester are ahead by two goals.

(24)   Ham and eggs tastes good.

Rather than giving the NP subject some elaborate meaning (e.g., "the members of the team from Manchester," "the dish consisting of ham and eggs"), it would seem preferable to let the inflection itself, the actual linguistic bearer of the information, be responsible for the nuances here. After all, it is in the inflection that we find the difference, not in the NP. But semantically contentful inflection in English has no influence on the external syntax. It never displaces an external subject and therefore the inflection should receive no independent representation in the syntax.

Class 6, consisting of morphological stems or free words that are represented as NPs in the syntax, but have no semantic value, is the mirror image of class 3. Here belong obligatory syntactic dummies fulfilling syntactic roles, but with no apparent interpretation. Since the syntax of English requires subjects regardless of whether the semantics does, and since no bound morphemes of English count as syntactic subjects, English requires subject pronouns belonging to class 6, and indeed, it has them. English expletive *it*, for example, might receive the following lexical representation:

(25)   phonology $=$ /it/
         morphology $=$ N[-1]
         syntax $=$ N[2, 3SG]
         semantics $=$ nil

What of class 4 lexemes, meaningful independent pronoun-like elements that lack a syntactic role? Here we have to ask what the element is doing in the expression in the first place. Morphemes with a purely formal function in the morphology are possible, and so are independent words that fulfill some function in the syntax. But neither of these characteristics could explain the occurrence of a class 4 lexeme, which is an independent form, hence not required for morphological completeness, and syntactically empty, hence incapable of playing some indispensable role in the syntax. The answer is that it must be sanctioned by some other component, such as the discourse-functional component that was mentioned in connection with West Flemish cliticization above, and which will be taken up briefly again below. It must, in other words, be a topic pronoun, replicating the reference of some filled syntactic position.

Class 8, then, should be unattested. Pronominals that have no content cannot be topics, since that notion requires meaning, as shown by the fact that dummy pronouns may not be topicalized: *It, it's raining*; *It I hate that there is so much pollution*. Lexemes with the characteristics of class 8 have, as it were, committed intermodular suicide.

7.2.1 Agreement as NP

I turn at last to classes 1 and 5, containing elements that are formatives in the syntax, and affixes or processes in the morphology. As such, they are predicted to have certain properties on the basis of the homomorphism constraints and other principles constraining associations between these two levels. Depending on whether such an element attaches morphologically to a stem or to a potentially free word, it will be an incorporator or a clitic, respectively. If it is an incorporator, it will necessarily attach to the lexical head of the phrase that it takes as a sister in the syntax, and if a clitic, it will attach to the nearest word of its syntactic complement, or to the word immediately to its left, depending on the language. In languages that conform strictly to Greenberg's (1966) type III, there is no difference between the nearest word in the syntactic complement, the word immediately to the left of a syntactically vital element, and the lexical head of the syntactic complement. As mentioned earlier, the distinction between incorporation and cliticization is diminished or disappears entirely in such languages. Furthermore, since all homomorphism and intermodular default association principles are satisfied by suffixation of a head element, such languages often show a profound tendency toward the morphologization of pieces of syntax.

At any rate, consider the case of an element which counts as a noun phrase in the syntax, and is realized as morphology on a verb stem. That is, suppose it has a lexical entry like (26):

(26)   /. . ./:
        morphology $= [_{V[-1]}V[-0], \underline{\quad}]$
        syntax $=$ NP[2]

Since this hypothetical element is specified as attaching to a stem, it should be an incorporator. As such it should follow the strong CIC and combine morphologically with the head of the phrase it combines with in the syntax. If this lexical NP is a clausal subject, this will be the verb of the clause, since that is the head of the VP that it combines with. If it is a direct object, then it will also be able to combine with the verb, since that is the sole element (hence head) in the phrase that it combines with. For descriptive purposes, the two cases can be kept apart by distinguishing the incorporating pronouns as nominative and accusative, and distributing these features appropriately in the syntax by means of rules like (27) and (28).

(27)   S → NP[NOM] VP

(28)   VP → VP[ACC]

Let us consider an incorporating nominative pronoun a little further. Since it counts as a subject NP in the syntax, and sanctions autolexical diagrams like (29), it cannot occur with an overt subject.

(29)

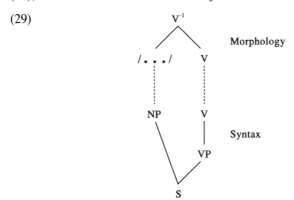

A language containing lexical items like the one represented by (26) would have to eschew person inflection on verbs exactly where there is an overt subject, and display such inflection exactly where there is no overt subject. Breton, described by Anderson (1982) and Stump (1984), is just such a language.

(30)   Levrioù a   lenn-an
        books PRT read-1s
        'I read books.'

(31)   Me a   lenn levrioù
        I   PRT read books
        'I read books.'

(32)   *Me a   lenn-an levrioù
         I   PRT read-1s books

(33)   Levrioù a   lenn-ont
        books PRT read-3p
        'They read books.'

(34)   Ar vugale   a   lenn levrioù
        the children PRT read books
        'The children read books.'

(35)   *Ar vugale   a   lenn-ont levrioù
         the children PRT read-3p books

The verbal inflection in Breton IS the subject in the syntax on this view. To quote Anderson (1982, 580–81):

> [T]he morphological material which represents agreement in Breton is an element which has an independent function in the syntax. . . . It is impossible to avoid the conclusion, then, that in Breton an element of morphological structure (verbal agreement for person and number) is referred to by syntactic principles.

In the present framework this observation is captured straightforwardly by giving the agreement morphemes of Breton lexical representations that make them syntactic formatives despite the fact that they are not stems or free words. Furthermore, the semantics of the agreement suffixes are just the same as those of the free pronouns with which they alternate and are in complementary distribution. The full lexical representation of the Breton first-person affix would then include a semantic statement that is shared with the semantic subpart of the entry for the corresponding independent pronoun:

(36) *an* (Breton first-person marker):
  morphology = $[_{V[-1]}$ V$[-0]$ ____]
  syntax = N[2, NOM] (i.e., $[_S$ VP, ____])
  semantics = $[_Q$ DEF$[_F$ SPEAKER(x)]]

(37) *me* 'I' (Breton):
  morphology = N$[-1]$
  syntax = N[2, NOM]
  semantics = $[_Q$ DEF$[_F$ SPEAKER(x)]]

To account for the data in (30)–(35), there is one more thing one needs to say, namely that Breton verb inflection for person and number is optional, i.e., that the language has a morphological rule like (38). If Breton inflection were obligatory, and if the agreement element always counted as a subject in the syntax, then Breton would never have overt subjects.

(38) V$[-1]$ → V$[-0]$

An alternative treatment that is consistent with what I know of Breton would be to assume obligatory inflection, but provide the Breton lexicon with a phonologically and syntactically null agreement morpheme. Because of its lack of syntactic reality, this morpheme would always have to be chosen in the presence of a subject and could never be chosen in the absence of one, or syntactic ill-formedness would result. This is perhaps the more attractive theory, since the form of the verb in (32) and (33) is homophonous with the third-person singular form:[4]

(39) Levrioù a   lenn.
  books PRT read-3s
  'He/she reads books.'

On this analysis the lexical representation of the third-person singular morpheme would be as in (40), where the syntactic and semantic fields of the entry are either both present or both absent.

(40)   Ø (Breton 3s inflection):
        morphology = [$_{V[-1, 3SG]}$ V[-0] ____]
        $\begin{pmatrix} \text{syntax} = \text{N[2, NOM]} \\ \text{semantics} = [_Q \text{ DEF}[_F \text{ NONPART(x)]]} \end{pmatrix}$

In describing the complementarity of inflection and subject pronouns in Breton this way, there turns out to be no need to postulate, as Stump does, a language-particular principle to the effect that "AGR must have a null governee" (Stump 1984), nor is there a need to assume a transformation moving a subject pronoun into a verb, as Anderson (1982) does. General principles of the interface between syntax and morphology, established on the basis of other phenomena in other languages, along with universal principles of each of these components are sufficient to get these results with a minimum of language-specific descriptive apparatus. The agreement affixes of Breton are simply examples of the first class of hypothetical lexemes in figure 7.1 above.

Breton is unusual in having what appears to be optional inflection on the verb, but it is not unparalleled. According to the description of the Bantu language Chichewa provided by Bresnan and Mchombo (1986), the object prefixes in this Bantu language work just like the subject inflection in Breton. The object suffix is optional for transitive verbs and is mutually exclusive with an explicit ordinary direct object. If a transitive verb has an object prefix and there is a NP co-referent with the object in the same sentence, it must be interpreted as a topic and shows grammatical behavior distinct from that of a genuine direct object. (See Bresnan and Mchombo 1986 for details.)

(41)   njúchi zi-na-lúm-á   alenje
        bees   SM-PAST-bite-INDIC hunters
        'The bees bit the hunters.'

(42)   njúchi zi-ná-wá-lúm-á   alenje
        bees   SM-PAST-OM-bite-INDIC hunters
        'The bees bit them, the hunters.'
        (*'The bees bit the hunters.')

Assuming that Chichewa has a morphological rule along the lines of (43), and syntactic rules along the lines of (44a and b), and that the Bantu class 10 object prefix is an autolexical element with obligatory syntax as specified in (45), this pattern emerges without the need for any further stipulation. Note

particularly the great similarity between the lexical representation of this
Bantu object prefix and the Breton subject suffix in (36).

(43)   V[−1] → Pref[NOM]+Tns+(Pref[ACC])+V+Mood

(44)   a. S → NP[NOM] VP
         b. VP → V (NP[ACC])

(45)   *wa* (Chichewa class 10 object marker):
         morphology = [$_{Pref}$ ACC, CLASS 10]
         syntax = N[2, ACC]
         semantics = [$_Q$ DEF[$_F$ NONPART (x)]]

Most languages that have personal inflections on verbs require them for
morphological completeness on every verb form. Breton and Chichewa are
unusual in having optional inflectional elements in the verb. Suppose a language with obligatory inflection had only autolexical affixes like *an* in Breton.
Since the obligatory inflection would count as the subject in such a language,
one simply could not say anything quite like "The boys are reading a book."
One would first have to mention the boys and then refer to them through the
inflection, something like "There are some boys and they-read a book," or
focus or topicalize the subject in every sentence in which a subject was desired, saying something on the order of "As for the boys, they-read a book."

The unhandiness of expression of such a system is enough to suggest that a
language like this would be very rare, if one could be found at all. It is not
impossible in principle, but is highly unlikely given the natural forces of par-
simony operating in language. All languages I know of in which verbs must
be inflected for categories of their arguments have found a way of shortening
the clumsy locutions that would result from having inflection with unavoidable syntactic reality.

In Irish, there is a default inflection that does not count as an NP (cf.
note 4). But the most common resolution of this problem is for the language to
have one inflectional form that is only optionally the realization of a syntactic
category. Thus the first- and second-person inflections in Spanish clearly can
count as subjects in that they may occur by themselves with no external subject in the sentence, and are inconsistent with ordinary subject pronouns.
They can occur only with focal or topical pronouns, as shown in the Spanish
examples below.

(46)   Bailas   tangos.
         dance-2s tangos.
         'You dance tangos.'

(47)   Tú   bailas   tangos.
         you dance-2s tangos
         '**You** dance tangos.'

(48)   *Tu bailas   tangos.
         'You dance-2s tangos'

But the third-person Spanish verb inflection can perfectly easily coexist with a real, nontopical, nonfocal, full NP subject:

(49)   Entró   un perro.
         enter-PAST/3s a   dog
         'A dog came in.'

So Spanish third-person verb inflections must be considered only **optionally** autolexical, a situation with parallels in other cases unrelated to agreement (see Sadock 1986b).

Furthermore, examples of "disagreement" (see Schroten 1981) like (50) show that the semantic function of the suffix is independent of whether or not it has syntax.

(50)   Los norteamericanos so-mos sus   amigos.
         The North.Americans be-1p   your friends
         'We North Americans are your friends.'

Thus the lexical representation of the first-person plural suffix would be something like the following:

(51)   *mos* (Spanish 1p agreement):
         morphology $= [_{V-1}$ V, ____]
         (syntax $=$ N[2, NOM])
         semantics $= [_Q$ DEF$[_F$ (SPEAKER & OTHER)[x]]]

Both the subject NP and the nonsyntactic version of the agreement suffix contribute to the meaning of the sentence in (50). The set referred to must be the set of North Americans (from the meaning of the subject NP) and must include the speaker (from the meaning of the verbal inflection). The semantics turn out to be just the same as those of the English phrase *we North Americans*, though the syntax is different.

Furthermore, no complication of the syntax issues from assuming optional syntactic relevance for the agreement affixes of languages like Spanish. The entry with the syntactic statement intact can only be found in autolexical diagrams like (52), else the syntactic lexical requirement will not be met. The entry lacking the syntactic subentry can occur in verb phrases, but must occur in sentences with external subjects or the general requirement that sentences have subjects will not be met.

(52)

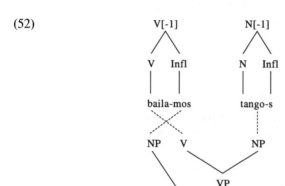

But the semantic field, as well as the syntactic field of at least the third-person singular Spanish inflections must also be optional, for there are cases where it would otherwise contradict the sense of the sentence:

(53)   Esta   gente   habla   bien.
        this-F/s people(F/s) speak-3s well
        'These people speak nicely.'

On the favored interpretation of this sentence, the individual members of the group referred to by *esta gente* speak nicely. If the singular verb form always meant reference to a single entity, then the sentence presumably could not mean this, but only that they speak well as a group, or something of the sort. Therefore, the third-person singular inflection should be represented autocomponentially along the following lines:

(54)   *a* (Spanish 3s inflection):
        morphology = [$_{V[-1]}$ V[−0], ____]
        (syntax = N[2, NOM])
        (semantics = [$_Q$ DEF[$_F$ NONPART(x)]])

If we assume that the independent pronouns of Spanish always have semantic relevance (surely the null hypothesis), then this explains the well-known fact that expletive pronouns do not occur in this language, only expletive agreements, as it were. In that (54) allows third-person singular inflection in Spanish to have a syntactic representation but no semantic representation, it is the only element in the language that can be found in those syntactically required positions in sentences that are not associated with semantic arguments.

Consider a sentence such as *Parece que Juan salió*. The verb *parecer* is semantically a function from meanings of propositions to meanings of propositions, i.e., an O^{-1}, in the notation employed here. Syntactically, it takes a complement clause with complementizer *que*. Assuming that the basic phrase-structure rule of the syntax of Spanish is (55), then the sentence *Parece que Juan salió* would have the morphological, syntactic, and semantic analyses represented in the triple structure (56), where the bracketing of the string represents the morphology, the upper tree represents the syntax, and the notation under the morphemes represents their semantic values. All three of these structures are well formed; the association of elements of the morphology and the syntax conforms to the interface principles, in particular to strong CIC, and therefore the sentence is well formed.

(55)   S → NP VP

(56)

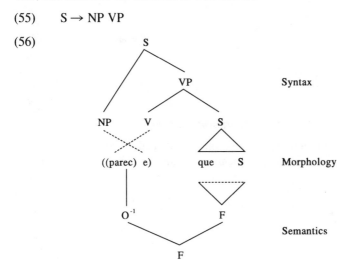

But consider the ill-formed example (57).

(57)   *El parece que Juan salió.

We have already seen that the verbal affix is only optionally a NP in the syntax of Spanish, and since the pronoun *el* is always of syntactic relevance, it must be the subject in this example. The sentence is therefore syntactically and morphologically· fine. The problem is in the semantics. *El* is obligatorily a referential expression. But it must combine with the meaning of *parece que Juan salió*, which is itself a saturated proposition with respect to semantics. There is therefore a category error in the semantics, and the sentence is ill formed.

(58)

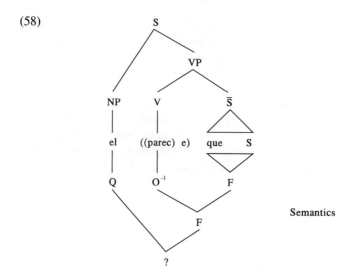

7.2.2 *Other Incorporated Pronominals*

Subject and object pronoun incorporation were treated in the section above as involving syntactic and morphological representations like (59) and (60) respectively. In both diagrams, H(P) is V(P).

(59)

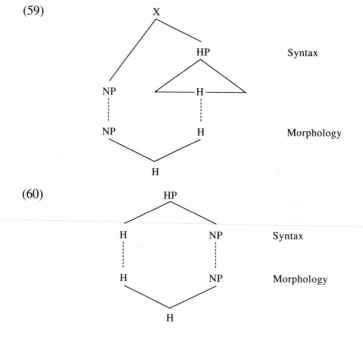

There is no theoretical reason to restrict the identification of H in such diagrams to V, and indeed, it is extremely common for other categories to show up here.

It is quite common to find NP objects of prepositions that must obligatorily incorporate the preposition, yielding a bimodular structure exactly analogous to the object incorporation in (60), but with H = P. There are "inflected" prepositions like this in numerous languages, including Turkish, Celtic, Hungarian, and Semitic. Note that these inflected prepositions can be obligatorily autolexical, as the following Hebrew paradigm shows. The occurrence of personal inflection on the preposition is strictly complementary to the appearance of an unincorporated NP argument, one or the other, but not both, being found in prepositional phrases. As in the example of Chichewa object incorporation, the personal morphological element is the syntactic object of the preposition.

(61)   ecl-o
       near-3s
       'near him'

(62)   ecel Uri
       near U.
       'near Uri'

(63)   *ecel hu/oto
       near he/him

(64)   *ecl-o   Uri
       near-3s U.

Besides subject incorporation, pronominals are also found as the NP in structures like (59), where H(P) is N(P), turning up as possessive inflection on the head noun of a possessed phrase. Arabic provides one of innumerable examples of this. Head nouns of possessed phrases can be inflected for the categories referring to the possessor, but such inflection is mutually exclusive with the appearance of an external possessor phrase:

(65)   baytu-hu   (al-jamiilu)
       house-3sM (DET-beautiful)
       'his (beautiful) house'

(66)   baytu Zayd-in
       house Zayd-gen
       'Zayd's house'

(67)   *baytu-hu   Zayd-in
       house-3sM Zayd-gen

(68)   *baytu huwa
       house 3sM

7.3 Additional Modules

Besides the three components that have been adopted in this book, it is clear that the grammar must somehow include a phonology. An important attempt to integrate a phonological component into an automodular grammar is the work of Shobhana Chelliah (1989) on Manipuri, a language that presents several interesting discrepancies of morphological, semantic, and phonological structure.

But what about the rather conservative choice of components that has been made here? Are there too many components? Too few? Are they the appropriate ones? At least this much is clear: besides the rather traditional triumvirate, there is a fourth source of structured representations, namely the lexicon. In that the lexicon must contain complex items—semantically irregular morphological items, phrasal idioms, complex semantic categories like pronouns, and the like—the lexicon can specify constituency that does not appear anywhere else in the grammar. This constituency is of use in explaining otherwise paradoxical bracketing facts that cannot be relegated to any of the productive components.

Willem de Reuse (1988), for example, has pointed out that bracketing paradoxes within Siberian Yupik Eskimo words are conveniently explained by recognizing the existence of lexicalized pairs of derivational suffixes in addition to the productive, recursive right-branching derivational principle of this language. To take a similar example from West Greenlandic, consider the sequence of affixes *-u+galuaq*, which forms noun stems from noun stems N, meaning 'former/dead N.' The parts of this lexicalized sequence are the copular suffix *-u* 'to be N,' and the verb-to-verb affix *-galuaq* 'to V in vain.' It is clear that *-u+galuaq* is lexicalized both because of its unpredictable meaning and because *-galuaq* does not otherwise occur as a nominalizer. Nevertheless, the sequence *-u+galuaq* can be interrupted by productive verb-to-verb suffixes, as in *palasi-u-sima-galuaq* 'one who has been a priest,' with *-sima* 'to have Ved.' The discrepant structure is displayed in (69), where the lower bracketing is lexicosemantic structure.

(69)

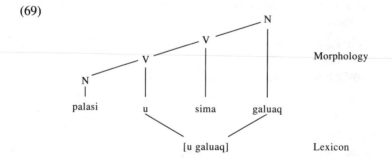

Donka Farkas and I (Farkas and Sadock 1989) have also made extensive use of this level of organization in our account of the complex distribution of preverbs in Hungarian. The lexicon is not, however, the functional equivalent of the other components, since, as opposed to the morphology, it is not endowed with generative power, and so characterizes only a finite, though large, number of expressions, most of which are atomic, but some of which are structured.

Returning to the question of the number and nature of the productive components, one possibility is that the ones I have employed are too coarse, including in some cases information that should actually be separated into two or more autonomous modules. Consider the sort of semantic structures I have been using, courtesy of Russell, Carnap, and Quine. These contain two sorts of intertwined information: function-argument information and quantifier-variable information. While it is absolutely traditional in logical studies to put these two kinds of information into a single structure, it is not clear that there is anything of a grammatical nature that compels us to do so. Perhaps there should really be two components here, one responsible for function-argument structure and the other for variable binding. In the course of writing this book, I have often found it convenient to suppress quantifiers so as to isolate function-argument structure, as the reader might have noticed. The cost of making such a maneuver formal is that if we separate the two kinds of information, something must be done to reconstruct the notion of scope that is so handily represented in the traditional semantic structures. We will need to say that somehow, a quantifier can have scope over either predicate in "Nancy wants to marry a Norwegian," just as either quantifier may have scope over the other in "Everybody loves somebody." I will not pursue this suggestion here.

Besides the possibility that there is too much information in traditional logical structures, it is also imaginable (some might say obvious) that there is too little. One of the many things the theory in its current state does not do is make any discriminations on the basis of semantic content, dealing, as it does, exclusively with the combinatorics of the semantic elements. As far as the present theory is concerned, intransitive agentive predicates like *sing*, "unaccusatives" like *roll*, and "undatives" (if I may call them that) like *be hungry*, are indistinguishable in semantic structure, all falling under the rather general rubric of one-place predicates. Now it might be the case, as has frequently been suggested, that classes based not upon semantic configuration, but upon semantic content differentiae like these, need to find a place in linguistic description. The question is, then, where to insert such information in an autolexical model. One idea is that semantic structures are to be enriched by features relating to content. We could distinguish one-place predicates by means of features such as [AGT] (agentive), [THM] (thematic), and [EXP] (experiential), for example. Then these features relating to semantic import

could be used in connecting the semantics to different syntactic or morphological realizations without denying their combinatoric similarity. Eric
Schiller (1989) has suggested that it is arguments, rather than predicates, that
should be distinguished featurally, in a manner reminiscent of early case
grammar (Fillmore 1968).

Alternatively, abstract predicates of doing, undergoing, and experiencing
might be added in a fashion reminiscent of generative semantics. *John is hungry* would then be analyzed as "John(x) [(experiences ((x) hungers)) (x)]" or
something like that.

As a third possibility, an autonomous level of thematic organization, as in
the work of Lapointe (1987) and Faarlund (1989), might be the appropriate
method of capturing generalizations that depend upon semantic content. It is
certainly harmonic with the general style of analysis that has been adopted
here. Numerous questions arise concerning the number of thematic roles, the
structural relationships that obtain in the autonomous module where they are
located, and the interface principles that are at play in relating this dimension
to others. In his implementation of the idea, Faarlund (1989) assumes a very
simple array of theta roles, indeed only three: Agent, Locus, and Theme.
These are arranged into propositions and ordered in a fixed way within each
proposition. A sentence such as *Sue made Max eat the vegetables* would have
a representation along the lines of (70) on the thematic role tier:

(70)

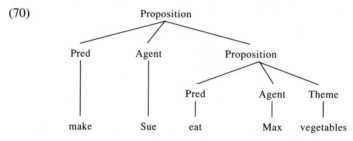

Another component that may have considerable utility in accounting for linguistic fact is an illocutionary module, presently under investigation by
William Eilfort (1989). Eilfort argues that the encoded speech-act potential
that natural language sentences include is not correctly handled pragmatically
or semantically. Given that sentence type is registered in terms of word order,
intonation, morphology, and lexical matter, he suggests that the basic distinctions as to encoded force be handled on an autonomous level of representation. This level of organization will also be home to adverbials that modify the
speech act, rather than the proposition (e.g., words like *please*) and might
also be useful in accounting for "misplaced epithets" such as we find in emo-
tionally charged imperatives like *Get off my damn foot*.[5]

Finally, it has been suggested by Smessaert (1988) that discourse-
functional information, encompassing notions like topic, comment, and

focus, forms a dimension of informational organization orthogonal to syntax and semantics. This idea has also been taken up in recent work by Ligang Li (1989) and Zixin Jiang (1989). As students of these matters (Firbas 1966 and the references there) have pointed out, discourse-functional notions find their expression in natural language in word order (as in Slavic), derivational morphology (as in Philippine languages), particles (as in Japanese and Korean), stress (as in English), and even (if Atlas and Levinson (1981) are right) in the semantic representations of cleft and pseudo-cleft sentences. One of the strongest reasons for setting up an autonomous level of organization is, after all, the fact that the information it encodes can surface in the forms that are the responsibility of various other components.

The other principal argument for an autonomous module is the demonstration that discontinuities of structure at a single level can be exchanged for discrepancies between continuous structures at two levels, as is done in the locus classicus of automodular phenomena, noun incorporation. Topicalization, in the form of constituent fronting, produces discontinuities, so it might well be a perfect case for reanalysis in automodular terms.

What would an automodular grammar of the topic-comment component of a language like Czech, which is said to place topics before comments, look like? In and of itself, it would not be a particularly intricate system, perhaps consisting only of the rules in (71)–(73), or perhaps only the first one of them:

(71)   U = Top Com

(72)   Top = Top Com

(73)   Com = Top Com

Now since the simple structures that are the province of a component like this must be associated with both syntactic and semantic representation, it looks possible to explain some of the well-known interactions between discourse-functional notions and syntax or semantics. For example, the fact that subjects tend to be default topics is just what we would expect in a language where subjects are the default-initial constituents of sentences. The normal situation would correspond to a bimodular state of affairs in which there is no conflict whatsoever between the autonomous representations:

(74)

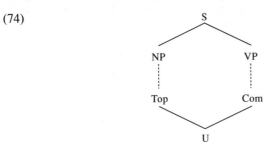

Discrepancies would arise when there is a conflict between the demands of one component and those of another, as when, for example, the syntax would regularly place the verbal object after the verb, but as a topic, the discourse-functional model would make it the initial constituent in the utterance. Assuming that the ordering requirements of the discourse-functional system are more stringent than those of the syntax, the effect will be to dislocate a syntactic constituent without actually moving it.

(75)

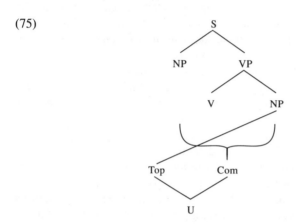

It is not at all clear that a workable account of unbounded movement could ever be couched in such terms, but it is at least intriguing (as Donka Farkas (p.c.) has also observed) that the major sources of unbounded movement—relativization, interrogation, and topicalization—all have clear discourse-pragmatic functions. For example, in languages where one can tell by other means what a clausal topic is, the relativized position is regularly the topic in a relative clause. See Schachter and Otanes (1972) for Tagalog, and Na (1986) for Korean.

Perhaps more interestingly, some of the effects of topic-comment structure on preferred or required semantic scope begin to make sense in a theory with an autonomous discourse-functional component. As has often been observed, there is a tendency to interpret quantifiers as having scope from higher to lower mapped onto linear order from left to right. If a nonstandard syntactic order occurs, this association is virtually unbreakable.

In a familiar pair like (76) and (77), there is a clear tendency to interpret the first logical element as having scope over the second, so as to interpret (76) to mean "The president visited few cities," and (77) as approximately equivalent to "Many cities were skipped by the president." Sentence (76) can also easily have the other scopal interpretation, in which case it might be continued ". . . including Keokuk, Peoria, Davenport, and Boise." The unnatural reading for (77), the one with the negation outside the scope of the quantifier, is more difficult to get, but it is clearly available, as shown by such examples as *All the money wasn't spent* (= "Some of the money remains") (see Carden 1973).

(76)   The president didn't visit many cities.

(77)   Many cities were not visited by the president.

Now (78), an example with a constituent in the position determined by discourse-functional, rather than syntactic principles, is tricky, since for many speakers (as pointed out by Prince (1978)) it represents at least two different discourse-functional patterns, only one of which is topicalization in the sense intended here. It can be used to contradict a statement to the effect that the president visited many cities, in which case it is equivalent to (76), perhaps with contrastive stress on *many*. In this case, it helps to read the sentence with a Yiddish accent, and to accompany the production of the sentence with "a distal presentation of the right hand," as Prince so aptly put it. But in the form usable by most speakers of English (Queen's English, as opposed to Brooklyn English),[6] it cannot, so far as I can tell, be construed to mean that the president visited only a few cities.

(78)   Many cities, the president didn't visit.

If we consider what a trimodular structure for each of the three sentences would be, these data begin to be understandable. The question I am interested in is whether the topic-comment organization of the sentence agrees or disagrees with the (ordinary) syntax, and whether it agrees or disagrees with the semantics. The point I would like to make is that in the case of (76), there is no disagreement at either interface on either scopal interpretation, while in the case of (77), there is a structural mismatch at one interface on the disfavored interpretation and none on the favored interpretation, and in (78) there is a disagreement at both interfaces with the impossible scope of quantifiers, and at one interface with the only available reading.

If the initial element (the topic) is also the subject of the sentence, then there is no disagreement between topic-comment structure and syntax. If an element other than the subject appears initially, as in (78), there is a mismatch between this pair of representations. It is a little less obvious how to compare the discourse functional structure with semantic structure. Since there is no intrinsic ordering of elements in logical representations, we must rather seek structural resemblance in the notion of scope, which in tree terms is equivalent to asymmetric c-command, as in the following definition that holds for representations of all kinds that take the form of trees.

(79)   A is **in the scope of** B iff
         B c-commands A, and
         A does not c-command B

For the purposes of this definition, c-command can be taken as the simple structural relation proposed by Reinhart (1983).

(80)   A **c-commands** B iff
        the first branching node dominating
        A also dominates B

On the assumption that all the structure that is present in a simple topic-comment form is merely that given by (71), then anything within the comment is in the scope of the topic, and there are no other scopal distinctions. In (76), neither the negation nor the quantifier is in the scope of the other on the discourse-functional plane, since both are within the comment. In both (77) and (78), the negation is discourse-functionally inside the scope of the quantifier. In semantics, more scope distinctions are made, since there is considerably more structure there.

We thus arrive at the following analysis of the three examples above for the two semantic scopes.

(81)

Example	Semantic Scope	T-C/Syntax	T-C/Semantics
(76)	N > Q(favored)	agree	—
	Q > N(disfavored)	agree	—
(77)	Q > N(favored)	agree	agree
	N > Q(disfavored)	agree	disagree
(78)	Q > N(favored)	disagree	agree
	N > Q(impossible)	disagree	disagree

This suggests a global homomorhpism condition to the effect that mismatches at more than one modular interface are disallowed. Much more work would be needed to flesh out this suggestion and see how generally it applies, but at least in the present case, this intuitively plausible constraint gives the right results.

Attractive as this result might be, there is a serious danger posed by the multiplication of components that the foregoing discussion depended upon. Part of the attraction of Autolexical analysis is that it allows for the explanation of complex grammatical phenomena in terms of relatively simple components that have an indispensable role to play in virtually any theory of grammar. In the best cases, all we need to do is to describe the basic features of each of the autonomous, independently motivated modules, and let natural constraints on their association do the rest.

But as we multiply the number of autonomous levels, their a priori character is gradually reduced, and each begins to look not so much like a module as like a construction. How many components can we postulate before we end up with a separate component for each phenomenon? Relational grammar went through a baroque phase where the few standard and mutually compatible grammatical relations with which it started (subject, object, etc.) were supplemented with such relations as "Topic," for fronted constituents, and "Overweight" for postponed heavy constituents. This proliferation of relations weakened the foundational notion of grammatical relation and considerably lessened the appeal of the theory.

I cannot predict how many components will ultimately be needed in a full deployment of the autolexical idea, but I can suggest that a spirit of realism serve as a guide. Any postulated component should be of a kind that one might want in a full description of the basic facts of language, regardless of the way in which the modules are related to one another. Thus I am fairly comfortable when it comes to suggesting a discourse-functional plane of organization, because that strikes me as something that one might want anyway. Levels that are entirely abstract, say those that display nonsemantic coindexing relations, or abstract entities such as traces, or that are said to reflect directly the inscrutable structure of cognition, probably should be avoided.

Appendix: Abbreviations

Agreement Glosses

Person	Number	Gender
1	s	M
2	p	F
3	d(ual)	N
4		

Other Glosses

ADJ	adjectivalizer	INC	inclusive
ABL	ablative case	INDIC	indicative mood
ABS	absolutive case	INF	infinitive
ACC	accusative case	INST	instrumental case
AGR	agreement	INTER	interrogative mood
ALL	allative case	LOC	locative case
AOR	aorist tense	NEG	negative
AUX	auxilliary	NOM	nominalizer *or*
CL	clitic		nominative case
CONTEMP	contemporative mood	OM	object marker
DAT	dative case	PASS	passive voice
DECL	declarative marker	PAST	past tense
DEF	definite marker	PRE	prefix
DEM	demonstrative	PRES	present tense
DET	determiner	PRO	pronoun
DIST	distributive	PROG	progressive
ERG	ergative case	PRT	particle
FUT	future tense	SB	subordinative suffix (Nama)
GEN	genitive case	SF	syntactic rule
GOAL	goal	SM	subject marker
HP	head phrase	TOP	topic
INAN	inanimate		

Category Labels

A	adjective	P	pre- *or* postposition,
Adv	adverb		preposition *or* phrase
Af	affix	PGN	person/gender/number

AP	adjective phrase	PP	pre- *or* postpositional phrase
Art	article	Pred	predicate
Asp	aspect marker	Pref	prefix
Cl	clitic	Q	restricted quantifier
ClC	clitic cluster	Q^{-1}	quantifier
Com	comment	RC	relative clause
Comp	complementizer	S	sentence
Con	conjunction	SAP	speech-act particle
CP	complementizer phrase	Subj	subject
Def	definite quantifier	Tns	tense
Dem	demonstrative	Top	topic
Det	determiner	TP	topicalized sentence *or* topic phrase
F	formula *or* function		
F^{-n}	function of n variables	U	utterance
H	phrasal head	u	variable over strings
HP	phrase with H as head	V	verb
I	head of IP	VP	verb phrase
Inc	incorporating category	W	morphological word
Inf	infinitive marker	w	variable over strings
Infl	inflection	X	variable over categories
IP	Infl phrase	x	individual variable
L	lexeme	X^{-n}	variable over morphological categories
MX	semantic modifier of X		
$\bar{N}$	phrasal head of NP	XP	variable over phrasal categories
N	noun		
NP	noun phrase	Y	variable over categories
O	operator	y	variable over strings
O^{-n}	n-place operator	ZP	variable over phrasal categories

−n convention
X^{-0} = X-stem
X^{-1} = inflected X word
X^{-2} = super X word

Features

(These occur in square brackets [ ].)

ABS	absolutive case	LOC	locative case
ACC	accusative case	MASC	masculine
ANIM	animate	N	nominal
AUX	auxiliary	NEUT	neuter
BSE	base verb form	NOM	nominative case
CL	clitic	NONPART	nonparticipant
CS	construct state	NUM	number
DAT	dative case	OBJ	object

DEF	definite	OBL	oblique
ERG	ergative case	PERS	person
F	variable over feature names	PL	plural
FEM	feminine	PPL	past participle
FIN	finite	PRES	present tense
G	variable over feature names	R	relational
GEN	genitive case	+S	declension class
GEND	gender		(Dutch)
GN	gender/number	SFα	syntactic rule
INDIC	indicative mood		feature
INF	infinitive	SG	singular
LFORM	verb with suffix [l] (Serbo-	SUBJ	subject
	Croation)	TNS	tense
		VFORM	verb form

Other Abbreviations Used in the Text

α	⎰variables over	LF	logical form
β	⎱feature values	LFC	logical form component
ALS	autolexical syntax	LFG	lexical functional grammar
AP	adjective phrase	LP	linear precedence
CAP	Control Agreement	MF	semantic modifier of F
	Principle	MS	morphological structure
CIC	Constructional Integrity	p.c.	personal correspondence
	Constraint	PF	phonological form
CP	Cliticization Principle	PFC	phonological form
FEM	feminine		component
GB	Government-Binding	PIE	Proto-Indo-European
	theory	Pl	plural
GPSG	Generalized Phrase	SOV	subject-object-verb word
	Structure Grammar		order
H	phrasal head	SS	surface structure
HFC	Head Feature	T-Marker	transformation marker
	Convention	VSO	verb-subject-object word
ID	immediate dominance		order
Imp	imperative	WFF	well-formed formula
IP	Incorporation Principle		
LC	Linearity Constraint		

special symbols
< derived from, also less than, depending on context
* ungrammatical expression
% grammatical for some speakers

Notes

Chapter 1

1. The theoretical models of tagmemics (Pike and Pike 1982) and stratificational grammar (Lamb 1966), rough contemporaries of early transformational grammar, are in some ways closer to the model proposed in this book than orthodox generative grammar is. In the modern context, one can find parallels to some of the basic tenets of my view in the work of Alec Marantz (1984) and in the theory of lexical-functional grammar, developed by Joan Bresnan and her co-workers (Bresnan 1982). The present view is sufficiently different from all of these models that I will not make explicit comparisons with them here.

2. Strictly speaking, the components listed as LFC and PFC do not specify semantic and phonological content, but rather syntactic representations suitable for interpretation by two other strictly hierarchical components.

3. Chomsky (1981) finds that the effort to REDUCE redundancy in grammatical description has proved fruitful, while admitting that for essentially biological reasons, redundancy might turn out to characterize actual linguistic systems.

> Biological systems—and the language faculty is surely one—often exhibit redundancy and other forms of complexity for quite intelligible reasons, relating both to functional utility and evolutionary accident. To the extent that this proves true of the faculty of language, then the correct theory of U[niversal] G[rammar] simply is not in itself an intellectually interesting theory, however empirically successful it may be. (Chomsky 1981, 14)

Needless to say, I do not share Chomsky's opinion as to what is and is not intellectually interesting.

4. Children do not learn the syntax in isolation, but simultaneously learn the other dimensions of analysis relevant to a full mastery of the language. In all of the lengthy discussions of learnability that have peppered the recent linguistic literature, one question that does not seem to have been taken up is whether a single formal phase of language structure, such as syntax, is learnable at all. Children do not learn syntax in a vacuum, after all, but receive their data contextualized in such a way as to provide clues as to both the pragmatic and semantic value of the form. At the same time, the form provides clues as to situational and truth-conditional import.

Chapter 2

1. The diagram here follows a drawing kindly provided by Elisa Steinberg.

2. Beginning with two basic categories "0" for propositions and "1" for entity expressions, as Cresswell (1973) does, the following would be the categorial representa-

tions of the various mnemonics used in the text where these correspond to lexical items:

$$F^{-1} = <0,1> \qquad \text{(rule LF1)}$$
$$F^{-2} = <0, 1, 1> \qquad \text{(rule LF2)}$$
$$O^{-1} = <<0,1>, 0> \qquad \text{(rule LF4)}$$
$$O^{-2} = <<0,1>, 1, 0> \qquad \text{(rule LF5)}$$
$$Q = <0, 0, 0> \qquad \text{(rule LF8)}$$

3. We may, for example, wish to enrich semantic representations for natural language expressions by dividing the purely combinatoric classes F^{-1}, F^{-2}, etc., into semantically significant subclasses (as Eric Schiller suggests in ongoing work), distinguishing, for example, between agentive, and nonagentive predicates of all kinds. On the other hand, we may want to encode such semantic distinctions, to the extent that they are needed to express grammatical generalizations, as thematic role relations in the semantics per se (Lapointe 1987), or in an entirely separate subcomponent (Faarlund 1989). See chapter 7, section 3.

4. The Saussurian sign is bipartite, including both a formal and a denotational aspect. Here the formal facet of the lexeme is divided into at least a morphological and a syntactic part, making the sign in this theory at least tripartite.

5. This assumes that the word *dog* (as opposed to the stem) bears a phonologically null singular affix. The existence of singular-plural pairs like *index/indices* and *radius/radii* lends support to this assumption. Alternatively, one could postulate a general rule for English and other lightly-inflected languages promoting any stem to the status of word.

6. I use the traditional term "particle" for stems that are morphologically inert, taking neither inflections nor participating in derivational morphology. Particles in this sense might well be classifiable as syntactic nouns, verbs, and so on, a possibility that is simple to convey in the present framework, which radically separates morphological and syntactic behavior. See Zwicky 1985 for a rather different discussion of the status of particles in grammar.

7. The feature [to] borne by *to* will be inherited through the HFC to the VP of which *to* is the head. This is the only lexical item that bears that feature, so the complement of a verb that is introduced by SF5 will have to be headed by *to*.

8. By saying that *to* has the syntax of a complement-taking verb, we capture all of the syntactic generalizations listed in Pullum 1982. But by saying that it has the morphology of a preposition, we automatically predict that it will have none of the inflectional forms of a typical complement-taking verb, a fact that needs to be stipulated by Pullum. Though *to* is homophonous with, and historically derived from a preposition, it might better be treated as acategorial in the morphology (though not the syntax) of Modern English. I will not pursue this issue here.

9. Actually, given the semantic representations implied by LF1–LF7, both these sentences should be ambiguous. In addition to the well-formed formula in (17), both can also be assigned structure (i) by these rules. This result is not obviously incorrect, as indicated by the perceptible ambiguity of scope in sentences like *Three students seem to be absent.*

(i)

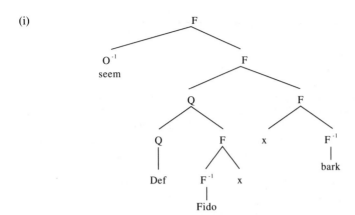

10. While this is treated as a brute fact at the moment, regularities among lexical entries can be captured by redundancy rules over lexical entries of the sort that have frequently been proposed (Jackendoff 1975). In the present case, for example, we might say that the clausal object is basic and that the existence of the infinitival complement can be predicted from it. The required lexical redundancy rule might look something like the following:

(LR1)   If there is a lexeme with syntax = [SF7] and semantics = O^{-1}, then there is another lexeme otherwise identical but with syntax = [SF5].

11. Note how this recapitulates some of the work and spirit of the "Theta Criterion" of GB, or the combination of the principles of Functional Uniqueness, Completeness, and Coherence in LFG. There is no need to stipulate any such principle or principles in the present framework because the semantic theory has an explicit syntax. It is no more necessary to impose external well-formedness conditions to the effect that predicates must take the appropriate number of arguments and that arguments must be arguments of predicates in any well-formed semantic structure than it is to impose external constraints on the syntax itself to the effect that NPs must go in syntactic trees only where they go and that everywhere there is a required NP we find one. The rules of the component imply these results. Similarly, the surface phrase-structure grammar does some of the essential work of the Case Filter by putting noun phrases in only those places where noun phrases are found.

12. The morphological expression in (20c) is actually a string of two separate outputs of M1–M4. If one wanted, the morphological words could be combined into a single structure by supplementing the rules of the morphology with the rule MS → W*. Such a rule makes the claim that there is no interesting morphological constituency above the level of the word, which may or may not turn out to be true.

13. It is the tense information that this inflectional ending bears that makes it a sentential operator in the semantics. If this suffix were "pure agreement," it would presumably have no semantic value.

14. Though most features play a role in only one module, there is no harm in

making this convention perfectly general, so that in principle, any features may be used by any module.

15. A better treatment would supply a lexical rule that would derive the entry in L15 from the ordinary adjective whose default values make its syntax and morphology correspond.

16. If the vocabulary of C_1 and C_2 were the same, then this result would be obtained simply by intersecting the two languages. I have described a much more elaborate interface here because it corresponds to the grammatical system developed in this book and because it has interesting applications to real phenomena. The association scheme employed here matches structures to structures, something that simple intersection does not do.

17. There is considerable disagreement as to the correct surface structure for these clauses. See Manaster-Ramer 1987 for a discussion of some of this debate. However, as the matching system described here regards only the linear order of elements, it is consistent with any phrase structure that may turn out to have independent justification.

As suggested to me by Arnold Zwicky and others, the structure in (39) is not really appropriate for what we would ordinarily call syntax, since it does not provide the government relations required, inter alia, for case assignment. We might take (39) to be a morphophonological form in which a sort of verb compounding is found. (See Woodbury 1989 for a development of the idea of such a level of structure.)

Chapter 3

1. The fact that the clitic is a suffix to the preceding word, and not to the first word of its complement, derives from the fact that all English cliticization is leftward. There are languages in which clitics do attach as suffixes to the word that follows them in the syntax, and thus are not in the same linear position in the syntactic and morphological trees. See the discussion of Latin *-que* surrounding example (58).

2. This quotation continues, "or (if the notion of head is needed for some languages) immediately to the left or right of X[0]." We may guess that at least some of the cases of attraction to the head that Kaisse (again following Zwicky) allows for are really incorporations, to be discussed in detail below. As instances of incorporation, they should be expected to involve the head, rather than the periphery. The rest are likely to be of an intermediate kind, having some of the properties of incorporation and some of the properties of cliticization. Several of these will be discussed in chapter 5.

3. This high degree of selectivity is part of the reason that Zwicky and Pullum (1983) conclude that the negative suffix on *can't*, *won't*, etc., is an inflection. The present theory does not distinguish absolutely between clitics and other morphological categories, since the multimodular constellation of properties that characterizes the typical members of these classes do not necessarily go together in the autonomous theory that I am assuming. See chapter 7, section 1.1.

4. I am grateful to Ivan Sag for assistance in formulating and naming this constraint.

5. This term is used very differently by S. Anderson (1987) and Zwicky (1977).

6. The definitive accent of Tongan may not be the clearest example of a simple,

suffixal, phrase-final clitic, but I choose it because of its parallelism to the three cases already discussed. It is arguably a definite marker.

7. Kaisse (1985) says that it is a second-position clitic, but she did not present any convincing examples. According to Kostas Kazazis (p.c.), the clitic appears absolutely normally in the position indicated in (81). It is abnormal, or perhaps ungrammatical in spoken Athenian when it appears on the first adjective as in (82).

8. Whether it is necessary to make this an absolute constraint on the system is unclear to me. If, for example, prefixes are simply rarer than suffixes, and mismatched lexemes are simply rarer than those whose structural positions in two autonomous representations are compatible, then these three types will simply be so uncommon that our limited data may not happen to contain any examples.

Pursuing this line of reasoning, there ought to be differences among the three types. The two impossible phrase-final clitics, for example, could be predicted to be rarer than the one phrase-initial type for which no good examples exist. This is because phrase-final function words are most likely to occur in a strict verb-final type language (Greenberg's type III). Such languages will strongly tend toward suffixation, a fact that while not observed as a special universal in Greenberg's work, can be reconstructed from his data. Thus for a language to have a phrase-final function word and realize this as a disharmonic prefix should be highly unusual.

Chapter 4

1. A rather frequent exception is where the empty position is understood as referring generically to human beings, e.g., German *Alle sind nach Hause gegangen*, Hebrew *Kulam halxu habayta*, Greenlandic *Tamarmik angerlapput*, all of which mean 'Everyone went home.' English (and other languages) also provide examples like *The poor went down with the ship*, etc.

2. Taken from Bugge et al. (1960, 122).

3. Adapted from Nielsen (1965, 33).

4. The symbol "&" represents a low front vowel, "N" a velar nasal, and "ʔ" a glottal stop.

5. In the modern language, verbs of naming can also take the name in the absolutive, following the verb, alternating with a preverbal instrumental form. In the older language, the instrumental was required regardless of the position of the name.

(i)   Taanna   taaneqartarpoq Kaali.
        that (ABS) is.called   Karl (ABS)
        'That one is called Karl.'

(ii)   Taanna   Kaali-mik taaneqartarpoq.
        that(ABS) Karl-INST is.called
        'That one is called Karl.'

6. My researches in Eskimo Point and Rankin Inlet, N.W.T., confirmed that this construction exists in Inuktitut with the same restrictions as in West Greenlandic.

7. In chapters 6 and 7 these constraints will be extended so as to apply to other modular interfaces.

8. The modifier or the argument may also appear after the verb, but with the same stylistic effect in both cases.

9. The claim here is that forms such as *házról* 'house-from' are morphological nouns. This is quite compatible in the present autonomous system of grammar with the analysis of a phrase like *egy fehér házról* 'from a white house' as a prepositional phrase in the syntax, exactly the same structurally as *egy fehér ház mellett* 'beside a white house.' The suffix *-rÓl* can, in other words, be a nominal inflectional suffix in the morphology at the same time that it is an adposition in the syntax. See chapter 5, section 4.2 for further details.

Chapter 5

1. The discussion that follows has benefited greatly from conversations with Howard Aronson, Bill Darden, and Milan Panic in addition to the help that Victor Friedman has given me.

2. There are several complications here which I will neglect. One is that the finite forms of *have* and *be* have clitic counterparts regardless of which rule they are introduced by. While this would seem to be an exception to the rule according to which only closed-class lexemes can be clitics, I think it is not, for even when these verbs take NP complements, they are members of the small class of verbs (which we can label [+AUX]) that can (1) host contracted negatives, (2) invert, and (3) form tag questions. Note that there are two dialects with regard to whether *have* followed by NP behaves like an auxiliary. For those speakers who say *I haven't a car*, treating the verb as [+AUX], there is a clitic form: *I've a car*. Those who, like the author, must say *I don't have a car* can only say *I have a car*, since the verb for them is not a member of the closed class of [+AUX] verbs.

3. I am indebted to Donka Farkas and George Fowler for helpful discussions of the facts of Hungarian.

4. The demonstrative has the allomorph *e* before consonants.

5. Vowels written in capital letters represent harmonizing archiphonemes.

6. The polite second person forms are exceptions.

(i)   *ön mellett* 'beside you (polite)'

The polite second-person form *ön* behaves here like a noun rather than pronoun, behavior that shows up in other ways as well.

7. The polite second person forms are again exceptional; with them, the suffixes resurface as harmonizing affixes:

(i)   *önben* 'in you (polite)'

8. Only their behavior with respect to prepositions is mentioned here for expository purposes. This description is too specific. The personal suffixes also count as possessor NPs and as arguments of verbs, and while this generalization can be made in the present framework, it is irrelevant to the discussion at hand.

9. I list the adposition with a full vowel assuming that the relevant features will be overridden by the automatic phonological rules of vowel harmony when the form occurs as a suffix.

10. Actually, the morphology of Hungarian is not really sufficient to make it clear that it really is stems rather than inflected words that the adpositional suffixes attach to. In fact, forms like *házambán* '*in my house*' (cf. *házam* 'my house') look like counterexamples to the claim. But the agglutinative character of Hungarian morphology often makes it difficult to distinguish between stems and full words on morphological grounds alone. Thus the plural of a noun is formed from phonological material which when used alone expresses the singular; the accusative is formed from a stem which could also be used independently as a nominative, and so on. Since (123) shows the suffixal adpositions to behave entirely in the manner expected of a morpheme distributed according to the IP, I will assume that they are added to stems.

11. I neglect here the role in the syntax of the object NP, which is reflected in this example only as verbal morphology. Should it turn out (as Graczyk has, in fact, argued) that such items have syntactic reality, the upper tree in (131) would have to be modified. In this connection see also chapter 7, section 2.1.

12. I am indebted to Lauri Karttunen for bringing this example to my attention.

13. This fact is handled in the Barriers framework by the postulation of a special Head Movement Constraint that is quite reminiscent of the IP of the present theory.

14. This must be the category of particles.

15. One-to-many associations may turn out to be the appropriate mechanism to account for multiple negation in languages like Spanish, Russian, and English dialects, or for the spreading of adverbials in Yiddish examples like (i):

(i)   Der doktor geyt arayn in hoyz arayn.
        the doctor goes into   in house into.
        'The doctor goes into the house.'

In such cases it is not unreasonable to associate a single semantic entity with multiple syntactic entities.

16. I am grateful to Roy Hagman for the assistance he provided in checking this section of the manuscript.

17. The position of the auxiliary here is explained by the fact that both sentence initial and sentence final auxiliaries are considered awkward.

18. The 3/M/s PGN marker (here -*i*, since the stem ends in a consonant) and the SB marker, to be discussed below, coalesce to -*a*.

19. Strictly speaking, features inherent in the stem must not conflict with features inherent in the affix. If the stem is inherently feminine, a masculine PGN suffix will be disallowed, but if the stem is neutral with regard to gender (i.e., *kxòe-* 'human being'), masculine or feminine suffixes may be used freely: *kxòep* 'man', *kxòes* 'woman', *kxòekxà* 'two men', etc.

20. The low tone on the subordinative suffix is raised to mid for intonational reasons in this question.

21. The -*è* here represents both the -*i* allomorph of the PGN suffix and the subordinative -*à*.

22. The discussion in this section has benefited much from suggestions and comments by Alexander Caskey and Elisa Steinberg.

23. This suffix also has interesting properties at the phonology-morphology boundary, as pointed out to me by Elisa Steinberg. Under certain circumstances it is clearly

interposed before the last syllable of a full word, rather than being added to a stem to form a stem. The diminutive of *azúcar* 'sugar' is *azuquítar*, and the diminutive of the proper name *Oscar* is the expected *Oscarcito* when the base is stressed on the final syllable, but is *Osquítar*, if the name is stressed on the first syllable. Between morphology and phonology, then, the diminutive suffix also looks like the analog of a penultimate-position clitic.

Chapter 6

1. This statement is related to the notion that there is a quite general tendency for representations from various modules to coincide. What (3) does is places a limit on how much two such representations may deviate from one another.

2. This latter fact makes it possible to maintain the traditional notion that NPs are $\bar{\text{N}}$ headed in the syntax. The arguments for determiner heads (Abney 1987) might be construed as semantic, at which level the correspondent to the determiner will be a head.

A problematic case is the question of headship between a quantifying expression and the open formula containing the variable that it binds. This is a difficult problem that I will not be able to address here.

3. Connecting semantic headship with eventual surface form in this way provides a method of deciding in the unclear cases which is the semantic functor and which the argument, a choice that is not particularly well motivated on internal semantic grounds only. Montague, for example saw certain formal advantages in taking subjects to be functions, and predicates to be arguments, rather than the reverse. But if subjects are functors, and therefore heads, and if heads can be the hosts of incorporators, then we should expect that when prepositional modifiers show up syntactically or morphologically associated with some element of the proposition, at least in some cases that element ought to be the subject. While it is not unimaginable that some language might have an auxiliary adjective as an equivalent to other languages' auxiliary verbs, such that one says "The future weather changes" for our *The weather will change*, such languages are surely extremely rare compared with those in which the adverbial is expressed as an auxiliary verb. Thus there is independent reason to doubt Montague's unorthodox analysis.

4. Bill Darden independently discovered this way of looking at *right away*.

5. The feature [LOC] here is a syntactic feature, not a semantic one. Thus the particle *up* counts as a syntactic locative even when it does not have a locative meaning, as in *I'll look it up*, and in that use will still support the temporal adverbial *right: I'll look it right up*.

6. It is claimed in Woodbury and Sadock 1986 that there is one distinction between clauses containing affixes of the type of *-gunar* and others, namely that they do not form exterior passives and antipassives. Even though the derived stem *asagunar-* is transitive, as shown by (i), it does not have a passive form of its own.

(i)   *Amaalia Kaali-mit asa-gunar-neqar-poq
        A.   K.-ABL   love-seem-PASS-INDIC/3s

Passives and antipassives are possible for such sentences, but the passive or antipassive morpheme must (with a very few exceptions) immediately follow the underived verb stem:

(ii)   Amaalia Kaali-mit asa-neqar-unar-poq
          A.   K.-ABL   love-PASS-seem-INDIC/3s
          Amaalia seems to be loved by Karl.

In Woodbury and Sadock 1986 this was taken as evidence of the syntactic spe-
cialness of verbs derived with this class of suffix. In the present context, however, it is
not at all clear that the cited facts need to be handled by reference to syntax, rather than
by direct reference to semantics and morphology.

7. Generally speaking, causatives of intransitives will look like simple transitives
and causatives of transitives like simple ditransitives, whatever their form happens to
be. There is sufficient variability, however, that a brute force treatment like that given
below might well be correct as a synchronic description.

8. I assume that the clitic is syntactically an independent NP. In the morphology it
would be attached as a prefix to a finite verb, and a suffix to a nonfinite verb.

9. As Eric Schiller pointed out to me, there may well be a metaphorical baby in
babysitting. The babysittee must be relatively helpless, feeble, or the like. For this
reason, it sounds odd to say that one is babysitting a house. Special verbs *housesitting*,
apartment sitting, etc., exist to describe such enterprises.

10. It is at least as reasonable to consider the level of structure where the clitic cluster occurs outside of the clause to be the level of discourse-functional organization
briefly discussed below in chapter 7, section 3. For one thing, I have assumed that
semantics itself is freely ordered, but for the treatment sketched here to work, the clitic
cluster must be not just higher than, but before the rest of the clausal content. However, if low informational content of the items that are realized as enclitics forces them
into initial position at some level, then the LC will assure that they are initial in semantic structure as well, and the account given here holds firm.

Chapter 7

1. The tree in (4) is adapted from one found in an unpublished paper by Steven
Lapointe (Lapointe 1984). This note was written some time before the publication of
my paper (1985a) and foreshadowed much of the analysis I will defend.

Another foreshadowing of the approach taken in my 1985 paper and subsequent
work including the present book is Mohanan (1983).

2. Heretofore I have used these lexeme names in the dual function of indices to the
lexical entries and indications of phonological content, but it is now necessary to separate the two functions. A more careful representation of lexical content will require a
fourth field for phonological content, but as I will not be much concerned with phonology, I will continue to suppress the phonological field where it is not relevant.

3. There would be no harm in saying that the features of the subordinate VP are also
features of *not*, thus making it an official as well as a de facto head.

4. Furthermore, other Celtic languages have explicit affixes in all forms of the verb,
whether or not these count as the subject in the syntax. Consider the following typical
paradigm of Irish (from McCloskey and Hale 1984):

          cuirfinn (*me)   'I would put'
          cuirfeá (*tú)   'you would put'

cuirfeadh *(sé)	'he would put'
cuirfeadh *(sí)	'she would put'
cuirfimis (*sinn)	'we would put'
cuirfeadh *(sibh)	'you (p) would put'
cuirfeadh *(siad)	'they would put'

From this paradigm it appears that the suffix -*feadh* is merely morphological and does not count as the subject NP, therefore obligatorily appearing with one. The other suffixes in the paradigm always count as NPs and therefore are ungrammatical with an overt subject.

5. Similar observations have been made by Mark Liberman in an unpublished paper on Vietnamese, and by Elinor Ochs in a paper presented to the Workshop on Language Acquisition at the University of Chicago in 1988.

6. This joke is Jim McCawley's.

References

Abney, Steven Paul. 1987. "The English Noun Phrase in Its Sentential Aspect."
Ph.D. diss., M.I.T.

Allen, Barbara J., Donna B. Gardiner, and Donald G. Frantz. 1984. "Noun Incorporation in Southern Tiwa," *IJAL* 50:292–311.

Anderson, Paul K. 1979. "Word Order Typology and Prepositions in Old Indic." In
Bela Brogyani, ed., *Studies in Diachronic, Synchronic, and Typological Linguistics*. Amsterdam: John Benjamins.

Anderson, Stephen R. 1982. "Where's Morphology?" *Linguistic Inquiry* 13:
571–612.

———. 1984. "Kwakwala Syntax and the Government-Binding Theory." In Cook
and Gerdts, eds. (1984), 21–76.

———. 1987. "Clitics Are Phrasal Affixes." Paper delivered at the Inflectional Morphology and Syntax Conference, University of North Carolina, February 21.

Anderson, Stephen R., and Sandra Chung. 1977. "On Grammatical Relations and
Clause Structure in Verb-Initial Languages." In Cole and Sadock, eds. (1977),
1–25.

Atlas, Jay David, and Stephen Levinson. 1981. "*It-* Clefts, Informativeness, and
Logical Form: Radical Pragmatics (Revised Standard Version)." In Peter Cole, ed.,
Radical Pragmatics, 1–62. New York: Academic Press.

Baker, Mark C. 1988. *Incorporation: A Theory of Grammatical Function Changing*.
Chicago: University of Chicago Press.

Barwise, Jon, and Robin Cooper. 1981. "Generalized Quantifiers and Natural Language." *Linguistics and Philosophy* 4:159–219.

Beard, Robert. 1977. "On the Extent and Nature of Irregularity in the Lexicon." *Lin-
gua* 42:305–41.

Berman, Ruth A. 1986. "Between Syntax and the Lexicon: Noun Compounding in
Hebrew." Talk presented at Linguistics Group Meeting, University of California,
Berkeley, February 11, 1986.

Bever, Thomas G. 1975. "Functional Explanations Require Independently Motivated
Functional Theories." In Robin E. Grossman, L. James San, and Timothy Vance,
eds., *Papers from the Parasession on Functionalism*. Chicago: Chicago Linguistic
Society.

Bissantz, Annette. 1983. "The Syntactic Conditions on *Be* Reduction in GPSG." In
Richardson, Marks, and Chuckerman, eds. (1983), 28–37.

Bloch, Bernard, and George L. Trager. 1942. *Outline of Linguistic Analysis*. Linguistic Society of America. Baltimore: Waverly Press.

Bloomfield, Leonard. 1933. *Language*. New York: Holt, Rinehart & Winston; reprint Chicago: University of Chicago Press, 1984.

Bodding, P.O. 1929. *Materials for Santali Grammar*. Vol. 2, *Mostly Morphology*. Benagaria, India: Santal Mission Press.

Borer, Hagit, ed. 1986. *Syntax and Semantics*. Vol. 19, *The Syntax of Pronominal Clitics*. New York: Academic Press.

———. 1988. "On the Morphological Parallelism between Compounds and Constructs." In G. Booij and J. V. Marle, eds., *Yearbook of Morphology*. Dordrecht: Foris.

Borgida, Alexander T. 1983. "Some Formal Results about Stratificational Grammars and Their Relevance to Linguistics." *Mathematical Systems Theory* 16:29–56.

Bresnan, Joan, ed. 1982. *The Mental Representation of Grammatical Relations*. Cambridge: MIT Press.

Bresnan, Joan, and Sam Mchombo. 1986. "Grammatical and Anaphoric Agreement." In *CLS 22 Parasession*, 278–97. Chicago: Chicago Linguistic Society.

Browne, Wayles. 1974. "On the Problem of Enclitic Placement in Serbo-Croation." In Richard D. Brecht and Catherine V. Chvany, eds., *Slavic Transformational Syntax*, 36–52. Michigan Slavic Materials no. 10. Ann Arbor: University of Michigan.

Buchholz, Oda, and Wilfried Fiedler. 1987. *Albanische Grammatik*. Leipzig: VEB Verlag Enzyklopedie, 64–65. (1.2.1).

Bugge, Aage, Kristoffer Lynge, A. D. Fuglsang-Damgaard, and Frederik Nielsen. 1960. *Dansk-Grønlandsk Ordbog*. Copenhagen: Ministeriet for Grønland.

Capell, A. 1976. "Rapporteur's Introduction and Summary." In Dixon, ed. (1976), section 78, 615–24.

Carden, Guy. 1973. *English Quantifiers*. Tokyo: Taishukan.

Carlson, Greg N. 1983. "Marking Constituents." In F. Heny and B. Richards, eds., *Linguistic Categories: Auxiliaries and Related Puzzles*, vol. 1, 69–98. Dordrecht: D. Reidel.

Chafe, Wallace L. 1970. *A Semantically Based Sketch of Onandaga*. IJAL Memoir 25.

Chelliah, Shobhana. 1989. "An Autolexical Account of the Lexical Rule of Voicing Assimilation in Manipuri." Paper presented at the Workshop on Autolexical Syntax, University of Chicago, April 16.

Chomsky, Noam. 1957. *Syntactic Structures*. The Hague: Mouton.

———. 1965. *Aspects of the Theory of Syntax*. Cambridge: MIT Press.

———. 1970. "Remarks on Nominalizations." In Jacobs and Rosenbaum, eds., *Readings in English Transformational Grammar*, 184–221. Reprinted in Chomsky, *Studies on Semantics in Generative Grammar*, 11–61. The Hague: Mouton, 1972.

———. 1977. *Language and Responsibility*. New York: Pantheon.

———. 1981. *Lectures on Government and Binding*. Dordrecht: Foris Publications.

———. 1986. *Barriers*. Cambridge: MIT Press.

Cole, Peter, ed. 1978. *Syntax and Semantics*. Vol. 9, *Pragmatics*. New York: Academic Press.

Cole, Peter, and Jerrold M. Sadock, eds. 1977. *Syntax and Semantics*. Vol. 8, *Grammatical Relations*. New York: Academic Press.

Cook, Eung-Do, and Donna B. Gerdts, eds. 1984. *Syntax and Semantics*. Vol. 16, *The Syntax of Native American Languages*. New York: Academic Press.

Cooper, Robin. 1983. *Quantification and Syntactic Theory*. Dordrecht: D. Reidel.

Corbett, Greville D. 1983. *Hierarchies, Targets, and Controllers: Agreement Patterns in Slavic*. London: Croom Helm; University Park: Pennsylvania State University Press.

————. 1987. "The Morphology/Syntax Interface." *Language* 63:299–345.

Cresswell, M. J. 1973. *Logics and Languages*. London: Methuen.

Culy, Christopher. 1985. "The Complexity of the Vocabulary of Bambara." *Linguistics and Philosophy* 8:345–52.

de Reuse, Willem. 1988. "The Morphology/Semantics Interface: An Autolexical Treatment of Eskimo Verbal Affix Order." *CLS* 24:112–25.

Di Sciullo, Anna Maria, and Edwin Williams. 1987. *On the Definition of Word*. Cambridge: MIT Press.

Dixon, R. M. W., ed. 1976. *Grammatical Categories in Australian Languages*. Linguistic Series no. 22, Australian Institute of Aboriginal Studies, Canberra. New Jersey: Humanities Press.

————. 1980. *The Languages of Australia*. Cambridge: Cambridge University Press.

Dowty, David R. 1979. *Word Meaning and Montague Grammar*. Dordrecht: D. Reidel.

————. 1982. "Grammatical Relations and Montague Grammar." In Pauline Jacobson and Geoffrey K. Pullum, eds., *The Nature of Syntactic Representation*, 79–130. Dordrecht: D. Reidel.

Einarsson, Stefán. 1949. *Icelandic: Grammar, Texts, Glossary*. Baltimore: Johns Hopkins Press.

Eilfort, William. 1989. "The Illocutionary Module." Paper presented at the Workshop on Autolexical Syntax, University of Chicago, April 16.

Faarlund, Jan Terje. 1989. "Autostructural Analysis." Paper presented at the Workshop on Autolexical Syntax, University of Chicago, April 16.

Farkas, Donka F., and Jerrold M. Sadock. 1989. "Preverb Climbing in Hungarian." *Language* 65:318–38.

Fiengo, Robert. 1980. *Surface Structure: The Interface of Autonomous Components*. Cambridge: Harvard University Press.

Fillmore, Charles J. 1968. "The Case for Case." In Emmon Bach and Robert Harms, eds., *Universals in Linguistic Theory*. New York: Holt, Rinehart, & Winston.

Firbas, Jan. 1966. "On Defining the Theme in Functional Sentence Analysis." In Josef Vachek, ed., *Travaux Linguistiques de Prague*, 267–80. University, Alabama: University of Alabama Press.

Fodor, Jerry A. 1983. *The Modularity of Mind*. Cambridge: M.I.T. Press.

Fortescue, Michael. 1984. *West Greenlandic*. London: Croom Helm.

Fraser, Bruce. 1970. "Idioms within a Transformational Grammar." *Foundations of Language* 6:22–42.

————. 1976. *The Verb-Particle Combination in English*. New York: Academic Press.

Gardenfors, Peter, ed. 1987. *Generalized Quantifiers: Linguistic and Logical Approaches*. Dordrecht: D. Reidel.

Gazdar, Gerald. 1979. *Pragmatics: Implicature, Presupposition, and Logical Form*. New York: Academic Press.

Gazdar, Gerald, Ewan Klein, Geoffrey Pullum, and Ivan Sag. 1985. *Generalized Phrase Structure Grammar*. Cambridge: Harvard University Press.

Goldsmith, John. 1976. "An Overview of Autosegmental Phonology." *Linguistic Analysis* 2:23–68.

Graczyk, Randolph. 1989. "Postpositional Phrase Incorporation in Crow." Paper presented at the Siouan Languages Conference, Morley, Alberta, Canada, June 2–3.

Gregory, R. L. 1963. "The Brain as an Engineering Problem." In W. H. Thorpe and O. L. Zangwill, eds., *Current Problems in Animal Behavior*, 307–30. Cambridge: Cambridge University Press.

Greenberg, Joseph H. 1957. *Essays in Linguistics*. Chicago: University of Chicago Press.

———. 1966a. "Some Universals of Grammar with Particular Reference to the Order of Meaningful Elements." In Greenberg, ed. (1966b), 73–113.

———, ed. 1966b. *Universals of Language*. 2d ed. Cambridge: MIT Press.

Grevisse, Maurice. 1980. *Le bon usage: Grammaire francaise avec des remarques sur la langue francaise d'aujourd'hui*. Paris: Duculot.

Haegeman, Liliane, and Henk van Riemsdijk. 1986. "Verb Projection Raising, Scope, and the Typology of Rules Affecting Verbs." *Linguistic Inquiry* 17:417–66.

Hagman, Roy S. 1977. *Nama Hottentot Grammar*. Bloomington: Research Center for Language and Semiotic Studies, Indiana University.

Hammond, Michael, and Michael Noonan, eds. 1988. *Theoretical Morphology: Approaches in Modern Linguistics*. New York: Academic Press.

Harada, H. I. 1976. "Honorifics." In Masayoshi Shibatani, ed., *Syntax and Semantics*, vol. 5, *Japanese Generative Grammar*, 499–561. New York: Academic Press.

Harrington, J. P. 1910. "An Introductory Paper on the Tiwa Language, Dialect of Taos, New Mexico." *American Anthropologist* 12:11–48.

Harris, Zellig. 1951. *Methods in Structural Linguistics*. Chicago: University of Chicago Press.

Hewitt, J. 1903. "Iroquoian Cosmology." *21st Annual Report of the Bureau of American Ethnology*, Washington, D.C.

Hockett, Charles F. 1942. "A System of Descriptive Phonology." *Language* 18:3–21. Reprinted in Joos, ed. (1957), 97–108.

———. 1947. "Problems of Morphemic Analysis." *Language* 23:321–43. Reprinted in Joos, ed. (1957), 229–42.

Hoeksema, Jacob. 1984. *Categorial Morphology*. Groningen: Van Denderen.

Hoppenbrouwers, G. A. J., P. A. M. Seuren, and A. J. M. M. Weijters, eds. 1985. "Meaning and the Lexicon." In proceedings of the Second International Colloquium on the Interdisciplinary Study of the Semantics of Natural Language, held at Cleves, Germany, August 30–September 2, 1983. Dordrecht: Foris.

Hopper, Paul J., and Sandra A. Thompson. 1984. "The Discourse Basis for Lexical Categories in Universal Grammar." *Language* 60:703–52.

Hudson, Joyce. 1976. "Walmadjari." In Dixon, ed. (1976), section 82, 653–66.

Humboldt, Wilhelm von. 1836. *Über die Verschiedenheit des menschlichen Sprachbaues und ihren Einfluss auf die geistige Entwicklung des Menschengeschlechts*. Translated by Peter Heath as *On Language: The Diversity of Human Language-Structure and Its Influence on the Mental Development of Mankind*, with an introduction by Hans Aarsleff. Cambridge: Cambridge University Press, 1988.

Jackendoff, Ray S. 1975. "Morphological and Semantic Regularities in the Lexicon." *Language* 51:639–71.

———. 1977. *X' Syntax: A Study of Phrase Structure, Linguistic Inquiry Monograph Two*. Cambridge: MIT Press.

Jacobs, Roderick, and Peter S. Rosenbaum, eds. 1971. *Readings in English Transformational Grammar*, 166–83. Boston: Ginn.

Jensen, John T., and Margaret Stong-Jensen, 1984. "Morphology Is in the Lexicon!" *LI* 15:474–98.

Jiang, Zixin. 1989. "The Necessity of an Omnipresent Lexicon in Chinese Grammar." Paper presented at the Workshop on Autolexical Syntax, University of Chicago, April 16.

Joos, Martin, ed. 1957. *Readings in Linguistics I: The Development of Descriptive Linguistics in America 1925–56*, 97–108. Chicago: University of Chicago Press.

Kaisse, Ellen M. 1983. "The Syntax of Auxiliary Reduction in English." *Language* 59:93–122.

———. 1985. *Connected Speech: The Interaction of Syntax and Phonology*. New York: Academic Press.

Karlsson, Fred. 1983. *Finnish Grammar*. Translated by Andrew Chesterman. Porvoo: Werner Söderström Osakeyhtiö.

Keenan, Edward. 1976. "Towards a Universal Definition of 'Subject'." In Charles Li, ed., *Subject and Topic*, 303–33. New York: Academic Press.

Kiparsky, Paul. 1973. "Elsewhere' in Phonology." In Stephen R. Anderson and Paul Kiparsky, eds., *A Festschrift for Morris Halle*, 93–106. New York: Holt, Rinehart & Winston.

———. 1982a. "Lexical Morphology and Phonology." In *Linguistic Society of Korea*, ed., *Linguistics in the Morning Calm*, 3–91. Seoul: Hanshin.

———. 1982b. "Word-Formation and the Lexicon." In F. Ingemann, ed., *Proceedings of the 1982 Mid-America Linguistics Conference*. Lawrence: University of Kansas.

Klavans, Judith L. 1980. "Some Problems in a Theory of Clitics." Ph.D. diss., University College, London.

———. 1983. "The Morphology of Cliticization." In Richardson, Marks, and Chuckerman, eds. (1983), 103–21.

———. 1985. "The Independence of Syntax and Phonology in Cliticization." *Language* 61:95–120.

Koneski, Blaze. 1967. *Gramatika na Makedonskiot Literaturen Jazik*. Skopje: Kultura.

Kroeber, A. L. 1909. "Noun Incorporation in American Languages." In *Verhandlungen der XVI. amerikanisten Kongress*, 568–76. Vienna.

———. 1911. "Incorporation as a Linguistic Process." *American Anthropologist* 13:577–84.

Lakoff, George. 1971. "On Generative Semantics." In Danny D. Steinberg and Leon A. Jacobovits, eds., *Semantics: An Interdisciplinary Reader in Philosophy, Linguistics and Psychology*, 232–96. Cambridge: Cambridge University Press.

———. 1972. "The Arbitrary Basis of Transformational Grammar." *Language* 48:76–87.

Lamb, Sydney M. 1966. *Outline of Stratificational Grammar*, rev. ed. Washington, D.C.: Georgetown University Press.

Langacker, Ronald W. 1987. "Nouns and Verbs." *Language* 63:53–94.

Lapointe, Steven G. 1980. "A Theory of Grammatical Agreement." Ph.D. diss., University of Massachusetts, Amherst.

———. 1984. "An Autosegmental Approach to the Problem of *du*." Typescript.

———. 1987. "Some Extensions of the Autolexical Approach to Structural Mismatches." In Geoffrey J. Huck and Almerindo E. Ojeda, eds., *Syntax and Semantics*, vol. 20, *Discontinuous Constituency*, 152–84. Orlando, Florida: Academic Press.

———. 1988. "Distinguishing Types of Morphosyntactic Cooccurrences: Mismatch Resolution, Agreement, Government." In Diane Brentari, Gary Larson, and Lynn MacLeod, eds., *CLS 24, Part Two: Parasession on Agreement in Grammatical Theory*, 181–201. Chicago: Chicago Linguistic Society.

Lees, Robert B. 1957. Review of Noam Comsky, *Syntactic Structures*. *Language* 33:375–408.

Levi, Judith N. 1978. *The Syntax and Semantics of Complex Nominals*. New York: Academic Press.

Li, Ligang. 1989. "*Ba*-construction in Mandarin Chinese: An Autolexical Approach." Paper presented at the Workshop on Autolexical Syntax, University of Chicago, April 16.

Lockwood, David G. 1972. *Introduction to Stratificational Linguistics*. New York: Harcourt Brace Jovanovich.

Lunt, Horace G. 1952. *Grammar of the Macedonian Literary Language*. Skopje.

McCarthy, John J. 1981. "A Prosodic Theory of Nonconcatenative Morphology." *LI* 12:373–418.

McCawley, James D. 1967. "Meaning and the Description of Languages." *Kotoba no Uchu*, vol. 2, nos. 9, 10, and 11. Tokyo: TEC Co. Reprinted in McCawley (1973), 99–120.

———. 1968a. "Lexical Insertion in a Transformational Grammar without Deep Structure." *CLS* 4:71–80. Reprinted in McCawley (1973), 155–66.

———. 1968b. "Concerning the Base Component of a Transformational Grammar." *Foundations of Language* 4:243–69. Reprinted in McCawley (1973), 35–58.

———. 1968c. "The Role of Semantics in a Grammar." In Emmon Bach and Robert T. Harms, eds., *Universals in Linguistic Theory*, 124–69. New York: Holt Rinehart & Winston; reprinted in McCawley (1973), 59–98.

———. 1973. *Grammar and Meaning: Papers on Syntactic and Semantic Topics*. Tokyo: Taishukan.

———. 1978. "Conversational Implicature and the Lexicon." In Peter Cole, ed. (1978), 245–59.

———. 1981. *Everything That Linguists Have Always Wanted to Know about Logic, but Were Ashamed to Ask*. Chicago: University of Chicago Press.

———. 1988. *The Syntactic Phenomena of English*, vols. 1 and 2. Chicago: University of Chicago Press.

McCloskey, James, and Kenneth Hale. 1984. "On the Syntax of Person-Number Inflection in Modern Irish." *Natural Language and Linguistic Theory* 1:487–534.

Manaster-Ramer, Alexis. 1987. "Dutch as a Formal Language." *Linguistics and Philosophy* 10:221–46.

Marantz, Alec. 1984. *On the Nature of Grammatical Relations*. Cambridge: MIT Press.

————. 1988. "Clitics, Morphological Merger, and the Mapping to Phonological Structure." In Hammond and Noonan, eds. (1988), 253–70.

Mithun, Marianne. 1984. "The Evolution of Noun Incorporation." *Language* 60:847–93.

Mohanan, K. P. 1983. "Mismatches." Paper presented at the Workshop on Lexical Phonology and Morphology, Stanford, February–March.

————. 1986. *The Theory of Lexical Phonology*. Dordrecht: D. Reidel.

Montague, Richard. 1970. "English as a Formal Language." In B. Visenti et al., eds., *Linguaggi nella Società et nella Tecnica*. Milan: Edizioni di Comunità; Reprinted in Thomason, ed. (1974), 188–221.

Moortgat, Michael. 1985. "Functional Composition and Complement Inheritance." In Hoppenbrouwers, Sueran, and Wiejters, et al., eds., (1985).

Morgan, J. L. 1972. "Verb Agreement as a Rule of English." *CLS* 8:278–86.

Na, Younghee. 1986. "Syntactic and Semantic Interaction in Korean: Theme, Topic, and Relative Clause." Ph.D. diss., University of Chicago.

Nevis, Joel A. 1985. *"Finnish Particle Clitics and General Clitic Theory."* Ph.D. diss., Ohio State University, Columbus.

Newmeyer, Frederick J. 1972. "The Insertion of Idioms." *CLS* 8:294–302.

————. 1980. *Linguistic Theory in America: The First Quarter Century of Transformational Generative Grammar*. New York: Academic Press.

Nida, Eugene A. 1976. *Morphology: The Descriptive Analysis of Words*. 2d ed. Ann Arbor: University of Michigan Press.

Nielsen, Frederick, trans. 1965. H. C. Andersen, *Oqaluttualiat Oqaluppalaallu*. Godthaab: Det Gronlandske Forlag.

Ochoa Peralta, Angela. 1984. *El Idioma Huasteco de Xiloxuchil, Veracruz*. Códoba, Mexico: Instituto nacional de Antropología e Historia.

Olsen, Inooraq. 1980. *Silarssuaq Angmarmat*. Odense: Det Gronlandske Forlag.

Payne, Doris L. 1986. "Derivation, 'Internal Syntax', and External Syntax in Yagua. Preliminary version. Typescript, University of Oregon.

Pike, Kenneth L. and Evelyn G. Pike. 1982. *Grammatical Analysis*. 2d ed. Arlington, Texas: Summer Institute of Linguistics.

Poser, William. 1985. "Cliticization to NP and Lexical Phonology." *Proceedings of the Fourth West Coast Conference on Formal Linguistics*. Stanford Linguistics Association, Department of Linguistics, Stanford University, Stanford, CA.

Postal, Paul M. 1966. "On So-Called 'Pronouns' in English." In F. Dineen, ed., *The 19th Monograph on Languages and Linguistics*. Washington, D.C.: Georgetown University Press. Reprinted in David A. Reibel and Sanford A. Schane, eds., *Modern Studies in English: Readings in Transformational Grammar*, 201–24. Englewood Cliffs, N.J.: Prentice-Hall, 1969.

————. 1969. "Anaphoric Islands." *CLS* 5:205–39.

Pranka, Paula M. 1983. "Syntax and Word Formation." Ph.D. diss., MIT.

Prince, Ellen F. 1978. "A Comparison of *Wh*-Clefts and *It*-Clefts in Discourse." *Language* 54:883–906.

Pullum, Geoffrey K. 1982. "Syncategorematicity and English Infinitival To". *Glossa* 16:181–215.

Quang Phuc Dong. 1971. "The Applicability of Transformations to Idioms." In *Papers from the Seventh Regional Meeting*, 198–205. Chicago: Chicago Linguistic Society.

Ramamurti, G. V. 1931. *A Manual of the So:ra: (or Savara) Language*. Madras: Government Press.

Reinhart, Tanya. 1983. *Anaphora and Semantic Interpretation*. Chicago: University of Chicago Press.

Richardson, John F., Mitchell Marks, and Amy Chukerman, eds. 1983. *Papers from the Parasession on the Interplay of Phonology, Morphology, and Syntax*. Chicago: Chicago Linguistic Society.

Rischel, Jorgen. 1971. "Some Characteristics of Noun Phrases in West Greenlandic." *Acta Linguistica Hafniensia* 12:213–45.

———. 1972. "Derivation as a Syntactic Process in Greenlandic." In Ferenc Kiefer, ed., *Derivational Processes*, 60–73. KVAL PM Ref. No. 729. Stockholm.

Roeper, Thomas, and Muffy E. A. Siegel. 1978. "A Lexical Transformation for Verbal Compounds." *LI* 9:148–73.

Rosen, Sara Thomas. 1989. "Two Types of Noun Incorporation." *Language* 65:294–317.

Rosenbaum, Peter. 1967. *The Grammar of English Predicate Complement Constructions*. Cambridge: MIT Press.

Ross, John Robert. 1970. "On Declarative Sentences." In Roderick A. Jacobs and Peter S. Rosenbaum, eds., *Readings in English Transformational Grammar*, 222–77. Waltham, Mass.: Ginn & Company.

Sadock, Jerrold M. 1980. "Noun Incorporation in Greenlandic: A Case of Syntactic Word-Formation." *Language* 57:300–319.

———. 1983. "The Necessary Overlapping of Grammatical Components." In J. F. Richardson, M. Marks, and A. Chukerman, eds., *Papers from the Parasession on the Interplay of Phonology, Morphology, and Syntax*, 198–221. Chicago: Chicago Linguistic Society.

———. 1984. "The Polyredundant Lexicon." In David Testen, Veena Mishra, and Joseph Drogo, eds., *Papers from the Parasession on Lexical Semantics*, 250–69. Chicago: Chicago Linguistic Society.

———. 1985a. "Autolexical Syntax: A Theory of Noun Incorporation and Similar Phenomena." *Natural Language and Linguistic Theory* 3:379–440.

———. 1985b. "The Southern Tiwa Incorporability Hierarchy." *IJAL* 51:568–72.

———. 1986a. "Some Notes on Noun Incorporation." *Language* 62:19–31.

———. 1986b. "An Autolexical View of Pronouns, Anaphora, and Agreement. *University of Chicago Working Papers in Linguistics*, vol. 2, 143–64. Chicago: Department of Linguistics, University of Chicago.

———. 1988a. "The West Greenlandic Clitic Cline." Paper presented at the Sixth Inuit Studies Conference, Copenhagen.

———. 1988b, "A Multi-Modular View of Agreement." *CLS 24 Parasession*: 258–77.

Sag, Ivan, and Carl Pollard. 1987. *Head-Driven Phrase Structure Grammar: An Informal Synopsis*. CSLI Report no. CSLI-87-79. Stanford: Center for the Study of Language and Information.

Sapir, Edward. 1910. "Yana Texts: Together with Yana Myths Collected by Roland B. Dixon." *University of California Publications in American Archeology and Ethnology*, vol. 9, 1–235.

———. 1911. "The Problem of Noun Incorporation in American Languages," *American Anthropologist* 13:250–82.

———. [1921] 1949. *Language: An Introduction to the Study of Speech*. New York: Harcourt, Brace, & World.

Saussure, Ferdinand de. 1959. *Course in General Linguistics*, ed. by Charles Bally and Albert Sechehaye in collaboration with Albert Riedlinger, trans. with an introduction and notes by Wade Baskin. New York: McGraw-Hill.

Schachter, Paul. 1977. "Reference-Related and Role-Related Properties of Subjects." In Cole and Sadock, eds., (1977), 279–306.

———. 1984. "Auxiliary Reduction: An Argument for GPSG." *LI* 15:514–23.

———. 1985. "Parts-of-Speech Systems." In Timothy Shopen, ed., *Language Typology and Syntactic Description*, vol. 1, *Clause Structure*, 3–61. Cambridge: Cambridge University Press.

Schachter, Paul, and Fe T. Otanes. 1972. *Tagalog Reference Grammar*. Berkeley: University of California Press.

Schiller, Eric. 1989. "The Case for Autolexical Case." Paper presented at the Workshop on Autolexical Syntax, University of Chicago, April 16.

Schmerling, Susan F. 1983. "Montague Morphophonemics." In *CLS 19 Parasession*, 222–38. Chicago: Chicago Linguistic Society.

Schroten, Jan. 1981. "Subject Deletion or Subject Formation: Evidence from Spanish." *Linguistic Analysis* 7:121–70.

Selkirk, Elisabeth O. 1982. *The Syntax of Words*. Linguistic Inquiry Monograph Series. Cambridge: MIT Press.

Shibatani, Masayoshi, and Taro Kageyama. 1988. "Word Formation in a Modular Theory of Grammar." *Language* 64:451–84.

Shieber, Stuart M. 1985. "Evidence Against the Context-Freeness of Natural Language." *Linguistics and Philosophy* 8:333–44.

Smessaert, Hans. 1988. *An Autolexical Syntax Approach to Pronominal Cliticization in West Flemish*. Master's thesis, University of Chicago.

Spencer, Andrew. 1984. "Towards a Unified Theory of Inflectional Morphology." Typescript. Central School of Speech and Drama, London.

Steedman, Mark. 1987. "Combinatory Grammars and Parasitic Gaps." *Natural Language and Linguistic Theory* 5:403–40.

Stump, Gregory T. 1984. "Agreement vs. Incorporation in Breton." *Natural Language and Linguistic Theory* 2:289–348.

Sugioka, Yoko. 1984. "Interaction of Derivational Morphology and Syntax in Japanese and English." Ph.D. diss., University of Chicago.

Thomason, Richmond, ed. 1974. *Formal Philosophy: Selected Papers of Richard Montague*. New Haven: Yale University Press.

Varela, S. 1986. "Inflectional and Diminutive Affixation inside Spanish Noun-Compounds." Paper presented at the Milwaukee Morphology Meeting: Fifteenth Annual Linguistics Symposium of the University of Wisconsin, Milwaukee.

Wackernagel, Jakob. 1892. "Uber ein Gesetz der indogermanischen Wortstellung." *Indogermanische Forschungen* 1:333–436.

Webster's Ninth New Collegiate Dictionary. 1983. Springfield, Mass.: Merriam-Webster.

Wells, Rulon S. 1947. "Immediate Constituents." *Language* 23:81–117. Reprinted in Joos, ed. (1957), 186–207.

Whitney, William D. 1870. *A Compendious German Grammar*. Boston: Holt & Williams.

Williams, Edwin. 1981. "On the Notions 'Lexically Related' and 'Head of a Word'." *LI* 12:245–74.

Wimsatt, William C. 1974. "Complexity and Organization." In Kenneth F. Schaffner and Robert S. Cohen, eds., *Boston Studies in the Philosophy of Science*, vol. 8, 67–86, Dordrecht: D. Reidel.

Woodbury, Anthony C. 1989. "On Restricting the Role of Morphology in Autolexical Syntax." Paper presented at the Workshop on Autolexical Syntax, University of Chicago, April 16.

Woodbury, Anthony C., and Jerrold M. Sadock. 1986. "Affixal Verbs in Syntax: A Reply to Grimshaw and Mester." *Natural Language and Linguistic Theory* 4:229–44.

Woodbury, H. 1975. "Onondaga Noun Incorporation, Some Notes on the Interdependence of Syntax and Semantics." *IJAL* 41:10–20.

Yip, Moira. 1988. "Template Morphology and the Direction of Association." *Natural Language and Linguistic Theory* 6:551–78.

Yoon, James Hye-Suk. 1986. "Reconciling Lexical Integrity with Affixation in Syntax." In Joyce McDonough and Bernadette Plunkett, eds., *Proceedings of NELS 17*, vol. 2, 663–84. GLSA, Department of Linguistics, University of Massachusetts, Amherst.

Zubizaretta, Maria Luisa. 1985. "The Relation between Morphophonology and Morphosyntax: The Case of Romance Causatives." *LI* 16:247–89.

Zwicky, Arnold M. 1977. "On Clitics." Reproduced by Indiana University Linguistics Club, Bloomington.

———. 1982. "An Expanded View of Morphology in the Syntax-Phonology Interface." Preprint for the 13th International Congress of Linguists, Tokyo.

———. 1984. "Heads." In A. Zwicky and R. Wallace, eds., *Papers on Morphology, Ohio State Working Papers in Linguistics no. 29*, 50–69. Columbus: Ohio State University.

———. 1985. "Clitics and Particles." *Language* 61:283–305.

Zwicky, Arnold M., and Joel A. Nevis. 1986. "Immediate Precedence in GPSG." *Ohio State Working Papers in Linguistics no. 32*, 133–38. Columbus: Department of Linguistics, Ohio State University.

Zwicky, Arnold M., and Geoffrey K. Pullum. 1983. "Cliticization vs. Inflection: English *n't*." *Language* 59:502–13.

Name Index

General Index

Accent, Tongan definitive, 120–24
Acquisition of language, 14, 42, 221
Actor, semantic, 15
Adjectival nouns, 41
Adjectives
  intensional, 95
  Sorbian personal, 159–61
Adpositions, 131, 227. *See also* Postpositions, Prepositions
  and case marking, 130
  incorporation of, 130
Adverbials
  dummy, 167–68
  scope of, 164
  sentence, 146, 181
  speech-act, 210
  spreading in Yiddish, 227
  temporal, 170
Affixes, 27. *See also* Prefixes, Suffixes
  agreement, 196
  clitics as phrasal affixes, 1
  postinflectional, 174
  verb-forming, 84
Agents, semantic, 210
Agreement, 159, 198–206
  Chichewa object, 136
  Danish, 196
  Huastic, 140–43
  of modifiers, 39
  morphology and syntax of, 39
  Spanish gender, 39–40
    verbal, 202–6
  subject-verb, 12–14, 196
Aktionsart, 143
Albanian inflection and pronominal clitics, 55–58
Ambiguity, 167, 222
Amharic clitic definite articles, 68–70
Anaphoric islands, 88–89

Antipassives, 228
Arabic possessives, 207
Archicategories, 22
Arguments
  predicate in, 177
  semantic, 11, 166, 194
  syntactic, 11
Articles, definite
  Amharic, 68
  Bulgarian, 58, 117
  Danish, 58, 115–17
  French, 61, 64, 73
  Greek, 66, 70
  Icelandic, 108, 113–15
  Italian, 66
  Macedonian, 58, 117–20
Aspect, 111, 124–26, 143, 168–70
Association lines
  crossing of, xi, 107
  double, 145
Assymetry of modular strength, 164
Atomicity of lexical items, 185
Augmentatives, 157
Australian languages. *See* Dyirbal, Walmadjari
Autosegmental Phonology, x, 26, 107
  autosegmental spreading in, 57
Auxiliary verbs, 127–29, 191
  English, 1–2, 48–50
  Walmadjari, 142–43

Bantu languages. *See* Chichewa, Kirundi
BAR, 23
Bar level in morphology, 28
Base component, 6–9
Binding theory, 195. *See also* Variables
Bracketing Erasure Principle, 55, 188
  paradoxes, 208
Breton verbal inflection, 199–202